Sun and Shado

Maud Howe Elliott

Alpha Editions

This edition published in 2024

ISBN : 9789364734448

Design and Setting By
Alpha Editions
www.alphaedis.com
Email - info@alphaedis.com

Contents

CHILD'S PLAY

ON *the silver sands of First Beach in the Island of Rhode Island, children were at play digging foundations, raising fortifications, laying out the parks and streets of a city. They worked long and hard; time was short, and the tide was coming in. Each wave, as it hissed and broke upon the beach, sent its thin line of foam a little nearer the brave outer wall of the town. Then came the inevitable inundation; the children shrieked with glee as the city wall crumbled, the church steeple toppled down, the courthouse collapsed. When nothing of the thriving sand city remained, save its trees and flowers,—floating bunches of red and green seaweed—the children, tired with much digging, sat down and looked across the water.*

"What is over there?" asked the youngest, pointing an uncertain finger to the East.

"That is the Atlantic Ocean," answered the eldest, "the nearest land is the coast of Spain."

"When I grow up I shall go there," said the youngest, "to see what Spain is like."

After many years the child sailed across the Atlantic from the New World to the Old, passed between the Pillars of Hercules, through the "southern entrance of the ocean," and landed on the Rock of Gibraltar. Sitting there by the lighthouse of Europa Point, and looking back across the waste of waters, the child had a vision of the city on the sands. This Rock, this last spur of Europe, how many sand cities has it seen washed away by the tides of time? The Calpe of the Phœnicians, the Jebel al Tarac of the Arabs, the Gibraltar of the Spaniards. Where Queen Adelaide's lighthouse now sends its ray of light out into the darkness, the famous shrine of the Virgen de Europa once stood. Here, once upon a time, Jupiter, in the shape of a milk-white bull, plunged into the sea with the lovely Europa on his back, and swam with her to Crete, where she became the mother of Minos, whose ruined palace has just been discovered in that wonderful island of Crete. The land, more steadfast than the sea, keeps in its breast some of the things men prize most. In the palace of Minos they found a small, finely modeled, gold figure of a man with a bull's head, cast in memory of the son of Jupiter and the lovely Europa.

As the stars pricked out from the blue, the child perceived they were the stars she knew at home, and that the constellation of Taurus was visible,—Taurus, the bull, still the animal of worship and of sacrifice in the Peninsula.

"When I have seen what Spain is like, I will tell the other children about it," said the child; then she took out the guidebook and opened the map.

I

THE THORN IN SPAIN'S SIDE

IF   you will look at the general map of Spain and Portugal, you will see that the outlines of the Peninsula suggest the head of a man—a broad, square head, with a high forehead and plenty of room for a large brain. The profile, lying sharply cut on the blue Atlantic, shows a crest of disordered hair, a slightly swelling forehead, a long, sensitive, aristocratic nose with a sharply cut nostril, firm lips set close together, a fine chin tapering to a small pointed beard, a slight fulness under the chin; the throat, set well back and surrounded by a blue collar—the Straits of Gibraltar—joins the head to the shoulders—the continent of Africa. The more you look at the face, the more certain you become that it is a familiar one, that it is the face of one you hold dear, till at last complete recognition flashes upon you; it is the face of Don Quixote de la Mancha! Look again; it is a face such as Velasquez painted, not once, but many times; it is the typical Spanish face, proud, high-bred, reserved.

So you need not land alone and unwelcomed upon the shore of fabled Hispagna, now looming dim and blue upon the horizon, now growing distinct and green. Two great spirits, Cervantes and Velasquez, come to meet you! Their hands are stretched out to you; if you so elect, they will walk with you in all your wanderings, and with their help you shall know Spain.

Gibraltar, a lion couchant, head on paws, fronts the sea. Cross the bay from Algeciras, the lion rears its head—a lion no longer—the pillar of the coast of Europe, blue at first, then purple; when you are close in its shadow you look up at a grim gray mountain towering above you. It greets you like an old friend. You have known it under many names; first as Calpe under its first master, Hercules, for that glorious old fellow, the first "Great African Traveler," was here. Wishing to show other travelers who should come after that the "inner seas," where it was safe to sail, ended here, he took up a mountain and tore it in two to make the bounds; half he set down in Africa, on the south, half in Europe, on the north. These are the Columns of Hercules; the African column is Abyle; the European, Calpe.

"*Ne plus ultra,*" said Hercules, as he wrapped his lion's skin about him and set sail for Libya to call on Atlas. Every time you write the sign for the dollar ($) you draw the Columns of Hercules and the scroll for his parting words, "*Ne plus ultra.*"

Carthage was here! The poor Carthaginians built a tower on Calpe, to watch for the dreaded Roman galleys sweeping down from Ostia, while in Rome's senate implacable Cato thundered his eternal *"Delenda est Carthago."* Of course the Romans were here,—it is impossible to escape them; wherever you travel in Europe or Africa you are always meeting those grave ghosts!

Tarik was here; he and his Berbers, sailing over from Morocco, landed on Calpe, and built a magnificent castle fortress to protect their retreat and keep open the way back to Africa. Moors and Berbers made a long stay in Europe; they held the Rock seven hundred years, until Moor and Mahomet were driven out by Ferdinand and Isabel,—a service Spain holds the Christian world has too soon forgotten. A pitiful flying remnant of the Moors of Granada took ship at Gibraltar and sailed back to Morocco, leaving behind them the imperishable Legacy of the Moor, taking with them the keys of their houses in that lost paradise, Granada. Since Tarik landed, the Rock has stood fourteen sieges, has passed from master to master, but this is still the Hill of Tarik (Jebel Tarik), though we pronounce it Gibraltar.

So, coming after Hercules, Carthage, Rome, Tarik, we are here! We landed at night. As we passed down the steamer's companionway to the tug, the *Kaiser* roared a hoarse farewell, her screw beat the "inner sea" to a white lather. From the upper deck a girl's handkerchief fluttered, a man's voice cried "Good luck!" Two thousand Italian steerage passengers, the menace and amusement of the voyage, chaffed and laughed at us from the lower deck. For nine days the steamer *Kaiser*, sailing on even keel, had been all our world; a creature-comfortable world, with only too much beef, beer, and skittles.

"There are no boats but the German—except a few of the English— fit to cross the Atlantic," a fat Hanoverian drummer said at dinner, that last evening on board; "Germans and English are the only sailors."

Don Jaime, the Andalusian, who sat opposite, looked at him.

"Claro," he assented, graciously, in Spanish, "but—do you happen to know how many Germans and English Columbus had with him on his caravel?"

The Hanoverian only grunted, like the pig he was.

The tug sheered away; we looked up from our dancing cockle-shell to the *Kaiser*, looming vast above us, shutting out the stars. The glare of her lights, the throb of her engines were still the all-important facts of the universe, until—a long finger of light stretched out from Tarik's Hill and touched us.

"You see?" said a voice in the dark beside us, "the searchlight! Gibraltar never sleeps."

The searchlight faded, the tender turned her nose to shore. The *Kaiser*, a little floating bit of Germany, was left behind; before us towered England, a mighty Rock hung from peak to base with chains of diamond lights. The tender drew alongside the Old Mole. At the gate a young English sergeant in a smart uniform looked us over.

"Are you a British subject, sir?" he said to J., the first man ashore. J. said he was.

"Pass in, sir," said the sergeant; then to me: "British subject, marm?"

"I am an American——" I began.

"One shilling, if you please, marm; after gunfire only subjects may enter Gibraltar without——"

"That is to say," I explained, "I am the wife of this gentleman; *you* may consider me a—a British sub——"

"Very good, marm, certainly," murmured the sergeant, consolingly; "pass in."

"So an American birthright is only worth one shilling?" J. jeered, and the international incident was closed, for the moment.

We slept at the Hotel Cecil, a comfortable house, with Spanish waiters and Hispano-Anglo fare. At breakfast we made the acquaintance of a pretty young officer, who wore his watch in a leather bracelet on his wrist. He laughed at our impatience to have done with tea and marmalade and be off to see the sights.

"Not much to see in Gib," he said, "a beastly place! There's the Trafalgar Cemetery, if you care for that sort of thing. See that old chap with the beard? If you want a guide he's the best. He's lying in wait for you, a real Rock Scorpion; don't let him sting you on the 'tips.' He's a native; must have come into the world before the law forbidding aliens to be born in Gibraltar."

We thought that law must be hard to enforce. He said it was, but that there was so little living room on the Rock "they" were very strict about it. All ladies, except the wives of British subjects, must cross over to the main land before the birth of their children. Spain, he said, liked the law, because in the old days it had sometimes happened that sons of Spaniards born on the Rock had refused to serve in the Spanish army, claiming to be British subjects.

We asked how long strangers might stay in Gibraltar. He said that generally speaking they might stay as long as they wished. The hotel proprietor would get us the necessary permit; it might be extended for ten days. The Governor, Sir George White (he who was in command in Ladysmith when the garrison was relieved), was very exact about such matters.

Again commending us to Old Scorp, our friend with the watch bracelet left us, and we went out "for to admire and to see." We avoided Old Scorp, a little gray creeping man with shabby European clothes, but he saluted us with the air of one who bides his time.

First we explored the North Town, crouching at the Rock's base. Waterport Street, the main artery of trade, lies at the lowest level, the town rising in a series of terraces two hundred feet above. Houses, churches, hospitals, barracks, stables, all built of a uniform gray limestone, seem to have been honeycombed out of the Rock. The names at the street corners have a bold British military flavor; Prince Edward's Ramp, Bomb House Lane, Devil's Gap Steps, Victualling House Lane, Ragged Staff Stairs. The shops are small and stuffy, with stale meagre wares; the high-sounding names over their doors, Moorish, Spanish, Jewish names, such as Alcantara, Barabiche, Vallerinos, Montegriffos, show in whose hands the trade of Gibraltar has fallen. There are many names beginning with Ben, such as Beneluz and Beneliel. I believe that all the "Bens" are of Moorish descent: I have known a good many such, their dark, impenetrable eyes, their skilful hands, the frequent touch of genius they show, are a part of the Moor's Legacy.

It was still early morning; the sky was a vault of blue fire, the air was keen with the salt and seaweed of the Mediterranean. The orange trees in the garden of the old Franciscan convent—now the Governor's house—were covered with fruit and blossoms; there was a sound of bugles, the tramp of a regiment in Commercial Square; the soft cracked bells of the old cathedral clanged the hour; from far away, where the gunners were at practice, came the deep boom of cannon. Color, life, movement all around us! This was no time to dream, to remember, to entertain ghosts; breathless we looked through the kaleidoscope to-day at the gay little pieces flickering with the pulse of time!

North Town has the most variegated population in Europe; to match it one must cross the Straits to Tangiers. A British officer passed on a small milk-white stallion; an Ethiopian, with gold earrings, and a beauty line gashed on either cheek; a pair of sharp-eyed Jewish children, books under arm, on their way to school; an Andalusian widow, draped like a Tanagra figurine with soft dusky veils hanging to her shoe; another officer of higher rank, a blond man with a face like a mask, who gave us one quick challenge of the eye as he went his way—and I was aware that I was a guest, while he was at home, a master in his own house. He was followed by two ladies, his British wife and daughter, all fresh and shining with soap and energy. Both were Saxons, with hair like spun gold and calm blue eyes; they wore London clothes, and drove an English cob in an Irish jaunting car. They were at home, too, and looked as if the earth belonged to them. There were many soldiers loafing in twos and threes, marching in files, walking singly— all with a jauntiness, a buoyancy, that no other mere mortal men possess. Some of them—oh, joy!—wore real uniforms with red coats; dull clod-colored khaki is good enough for war, in peace there is no excuse for it.

The dash of winter in the air that was as the elixir of life to the English, making their horses prance, their cheeks glow, their eyes sparkle, affected the other inhabitants differently; the Spaniards looked pale, the Moors ashen. We met Don Jaime, black sombrero pulled over the eyes, black capa thrown over the shoulder, toga-fashion, muffling mouth and chin and showing an amber plush lining. The Don uncovered with a noble gesture, but we did not stop to speak to him, he was in such evident terror of taking cold. There were frigid tears in the almond eyes of Mr. Pohoomull as he stood at the door of the Indo-Persian Bazaar inviting us to enter. Though he wore a lovely gray embroidered cashmere cap and a Persian lamb coat, his teeth chattered. We lingered somewhat, beguiled by his Benares trays, Burmese silver, Persian carpets, ivory elephants, and were only saved from bankruptcy by the vision of a figure in the street, more truly Oriental than anything in Mr. Pohoomull's shop. A tall, bronzed Moor in a green turban, a pink kaftan, yellow slippers, and a big hairy brown *sulham*, drawn over his head and falling to his knees, walked slowly down the middle of the road, driving before him with a rod as long as himself a flock of green and bronze turkeys. We followed to the Moorish market, where he entered into discussion with another Morisco in a white *sulham* and red morocco slippers, presumably touching the price of turkeys. As an excuse to linger near, we bought pistachio nuts in a fresh lettuce leaf, dates from the desert on their yellow stalks, golden apples of Hesperides—they called them tangerines—with dark, glossy leaves. The market was noisy with the bickering of poultry, pigeons, and netted quails in wicker baskets. In the English market on the other side of the way, we bought for half a *peseta* violets, roses, and splendid Tyrian purple bourganvillia. The flower sellers, a group of withered women sitting on the ground, looked like the Fates. The fish market was a picture. The fish of the Mediterranean seem brighter colored than other fish. Like wet jewels the red mullet, like silver the turbot, like many-colored enamels the big variegated conger eels the Romans liked so well. Gibraltar, which produces nothing, is splendidly victualled. The beef comes from Morocco, the vegetables from Spain, the fruit from every Mediterranean port. At the fruit stalls were bunches of Spanish grapes, long, purple, white, hanging thick overhead, a background for Barbary baskets filled with citrons, persimmons, cocoanuts, apples, and pears. In the foreground were heaps of black olives and smooth green melons, the latter a cross between watermelon and cantaloupe. The Spaniards know how to keep them fresh half the winter. The vegetable stalls were quite as handsome in their way, the color used skillfully in broad masses. Deep chrome gourds, violet eggplant, a long cane basket of vermilion tomatoes and gray-green artichokes; the beauty of color so enthralled us that we were not quick enough in making way for a majestic British matron, followed by a neat Spanish maid. The lady must have been at least a colonel's wife—if such go to market—for she looked through us, without seeing us, as if we had been so much glass. To make amends, the little servant gave us soft welcoming glances, but we felt abashed and went sadly away. As we left the market, we saw our young officer of the watch bracelet sniffing at the carcass of a mighty new-killed pig—then we knew that he was of the "commissariat."

Outside the market we met the turkey-herd again; he had sold no turkeys, but added a pair of white ones to his flock. As we stood admiring him, Patsy joined us, kodak in hand.

"I must snap that Moor," he said; "please stand before me. If he sees me he will be frightened and think I mean to do him a mischief." Patsy adjusted his camera; he was on the point of turning the button when a policeman interfered:

"Beg pardon, sir, it's against the rules to photograph the fortifications."

"But I wasn't," Patsy explained. "I was only taking a shot at that old boy with the turkeys."

The man pointed to the bastion behind the Moor; it would certainly have come within the kodak's focus. We tried to comfort Patsy by reminding him that Gibraltar was a fortress, that we were here on sufferance; but he was much chagrined and kept repeating that he was not a spy. At that moment of discomfiture we heard a voice, deep as an organ note, behind us, rumbling out the words:

"I am the book."

We turned and saw Old Scorp.

"I am the *Century*."

"Looks old enough to be," murmured Patsy.

"I am *Harper's Magazine*."

"Indeed? You scarcely look it," said J.

"Don't you see?" I cried, "he is the *guide*, he has been mentioned in *Harper* and the *Century*."

"Take him along!" begged Patsy. "He knows the ropes; he'll keep us from getting into any more scrapes."

Old Scorp had crawled in our wake all the morning; his time had come; he claimed us for his own. From that moment till we left the Rock, we were scarcely out of his company, except when asleep or at meals. When not busy guiding travelers, he acted as Moorish interpreter of the law court. A little gliding man, like a composite of all the peoples who have held the Rock, his clothes were English, his manners Spanish, his fanatical eyes were Berber, his energy, in spite of his age, ancient Roman, his keenness as to pounds, shillings, and pence was Phœnician, his manner of cracking a nut—where had I seen that action? In the monkey cage at the Zoo.

The original inhabitants of Gibraltar, a tribe of half-tame, tailless apes, still hold the steep west front of the Rock. They are descended from those apes of Tarshish sent to Solomon, together with peacocks, ivory, and gold, every three years. They live on the summit, where the sweet palmetto and the prickly pear grow. In summer, when man and monkey grill upon the arid Rock, the soldiers at the Signal Station save water for their poor relations, and look the other way when the simian troop goes on a raid to rob the Governor's fruit garden; they even keep a sort of parish register of monkey births and deaths. How these blue Barbary apes, the only African monkeys in Europe, ever found their way here, is a mystery, like the presence of the Basques in the Pyrenees.

"I wonder if they were here before the convulsion of nature that tore apart the coasts of Africa and Europe," Patsy ruminated.

Why not say, when Hercules tore them apart? It's so much prettier!

From the market-place we went to the parade-ground, a quadrangle surrounded by solid stone barracks, where a squad of the King's Own were drilling. Inside the barracks a military band played Sousa's "Stars and Stripes Forever." The King's Own were brisk, young, and fresh-looking newcomers, with the beef and beer of Old England still in their blood; they will not have such pretty complexions when they leave, after three summers on the Rock. The climate that we found delicious in December must be terrific in July. Scorp admitted that it was a trifle warm, though it suited him; we could fancy him basking on the Rock, as if he belonged in one of its crevices. At luncheon we asked Bracelet how he found the summer here.

From what he said, Gibraltar cannot be a nice place when the black levanter blows, the dark cloud cap settles on the summit, the clamminess comes into the air, and the stifling east wind takes the heart out of a man and sets his nerves jangling, till he feels like Prometheus chained to the burning Rock. They make out very well in the winter, Bracelet said, with the warships coming and going, people from home running down to the Hotel Maria Cristina over in Algeciras, and occasional shooting trips in the Atlas Mountains. Of course, the great institution is the Calpe Hunt.

"Fox hunting *here*?" Patsy interrupted.

"No, no, over there." Bracelet nodded towards the narrow ribbon of sand that ties the Rock to Spain. "In the old days, though, the place swarmed with foxes. Rockwood and Ranter, the first couple of hounds an old parson had out from England, gave 'em some rattling good runs up the face of the Rock."

More ghosts—the ghosts of the first two foxhounds whose names, Rockwood and Ranter, are a matter of history. Never was such a place for ghosts as Mons Calpe!

Patsy catechized Bracelet about the hunting half through luncheon; that was not fair. He asked more than his share of questions; when it comes to dogs, horses, or sport of any kind, men never are fair, they are so greedy. I had a hundred questions I wanted to ask, but I had to listen and pretend to be interested. From November, after the rains are over, till March, when the ground is too dry to carry the scent, they have two joyous runs a week. It's the only thing that makes life here possible. The ride to the meets is almost always along the Spanish beach; some of them are a goodish distance; Long Stables, for instance, is thirteen miles away, Almoraima is twelve. We could imagine the relief of a gallop in the salt air after being cooped up on the Rock. There is every sort of country,—thick woods, coverts, crags; only, Bracelet complained, no jumping, because there are no fences or hedges in this benighted land. Everybody hunts, of course. An old gentleman, a sort of Nestor of the chase, died as he had lived, following the hounds. He was drowned at Washerwoman's Ford the other day, on his way home from the meet. Quite a decent exit, wasn't it? To die in the saddle at the end of a day's hunting. He was a goodish age, too, turned seventy-six.

We had one disappointment: demanding to be taken to St. Michael's Cave, we learned that it was no longer shown. Scorp, who in his far-off youth had known it well, was easily led to talk of the mysterious cave. I was the only one of the party who had grace to listen. The others were welcome to monopolize Bracelet—young, handsome, full of delicious insularity; I preferred the little old gray man. There are many impetuous merry lads;

there is but one Rock Scorpion! There was something reptilian about the man. His language, full of Oriental allegory, moved sluggishly along, then broke into sudden bursts of antediluvian slang, and on every possible occasion stung us with the words, "You tip the hand."

"'*Metuendus acumine caude*,' Ovid says of the scorpion," Patsy quoted, "or, as one might say, Fearful with the sting of his tip!"

According to Old Scorp, the entrance to St. Michael's Cave is now one thousand feet above the sea, about two thirds up the face of the mountain. Once upon a time the sea was level with the cave. Had not he and his brother, when they were boys, found fossil shells there, and the remains of a sea beach outside? The entrance was low, he remembered, but inside it was big as the Mosque of Cordova. Its wonderful stalactite columns, fifty feet high, looked like yellow alabaster; there were pointed arches springing from column to column. Lighted up with blue fire, as he had once seen the cave, it was a sight that, man or boy, he had never seen equalled. Except for its being so dark, those who lived here had a fine commodious dwelling. Yes, men have lived, fought, and died in the great cave, and left their flint knives, their stone axes, and their bones to tell the tale. Women have lived and worked there; they left their necklaces, their anklets, their bone needles, their household pottery behind them. There have been feasts here, for amphoræ with traces of wine have been found. There were other caves—oh, many! sea caves and land caves; some "professors" say that the old name Calpe means caved mountain. Whether or not that is true, Scorp, of his own knowledge, assured us that the Rock is full of secret caverns. As if these were not enough, the English are always burrowing and tunnelling. They have dug three tunnels under the Rock; in one they found what is more precious than gold, good water. No, we might not see the tunnels, not even the last of the smaller caves—the secrets of the mountain are jealously guarded.

Listening to the old man's talk, we climbed a street of stairs cutting directly through a tangle of narrow alleys where Jews and other aliens live, to the upper level of North Town, where we found the Church of the Sacred Heart, its doors hospitably open. As it was the only door in Gibraltar, except the Cecil's, that had not been shut and barred against us, we went in. The smell of the incense, the red light of the candles, was pleasantly familiar; the statues of saints and Virgin greeted us like old friends.

"I haf a friend in Brooklyn, Unity States," said a voice beside us. "He send me weekly paper. I hope you know my friend—his name is———. Mebbe he spoke with you of Father Jims, of the Sacred Heart?"

Father Jims was young and soft-eyed, with a face such as Murillo painted in his "St. Joseph and the Holy Child." He was so sure we had come to find him out, with some message from his friend, that it went to our hearts to undeceive him. He said he meant shortly to go to Brooklyn; from what his friend wrote, *there* was a rare field for missionary work! Father Jims was a Catalan; his eyes burned with a zeal that augured well for his mission among the heathen of Brooklyn. He showed us the modest treasures of his church, and presented us with a picture of St. Bernard, the patron of Gibraltar. As we parted we gave him a little money for his poor; he took it with a radiant smile I shall not soon forget. Among all the tremendous impressions we brought away from Gibraltar, the smile of the little Spanish servant maid in the market-place, and the smile of the poor Catalan priest in the church, are the kindest, and will perhaps remain with us the longest.

Near the church is the fine new hospital; an inscription tells that Lord Napier, of Magdala, laid the foundation stone.

In Lord Napier's hospital there are women nurses. Teaching and nursing nuns are in charge of several charitable institutions, and in the post office reigns a postmistress; so, though Gibraltar is the most mannish, English-speaking place I know, there is plenty of civic and charitable work for women. It was strange to learn that the place is a colony and a port, as well as a fortress. On this tiny speck of earth you can find all the complex machinery of civil, military, and colonial existence, as neatly organized as life in an ant-hill. As to the port, it is now of consequence as a coaling station only. Prosaic enough, compared to the palmy days when it was the first smugglers' headquarters of the Mediterranean! Tobacco is still smuggled into Spain, where it is a government monopoly, and is, consequently, very bad and very dear. The smuggling is largely carried on by dogs. The poor innocents are taken out in a boat at night from Gibraltar; when near the Spanish coast, small water-tight casks filled with contraband tobacco are fastened on either side of them, they are put overboard and swim to land. They learn not to bark or make a noise, but to scramble silently ashore into the arms of their *contrabandista* partners, just as in the days of the Deerfield Massacre, babies in New England were taught not to cry on account of the Indians.

After luncheon we went to see the "Galleries." Our Scorp convoyed us; Gunner Wilkinson, a lean old war dog, received us and led the way into a dim passage, with sanded floor and whitewashed roof, tunnelled out of the bowels of the Rock. The narrow gallery ascends at an easy slope, now and again widening out into a small chamber, as a Roman catacomb expands into the chapel of Christian martyr or saint. Only here, in this aerial catacomb, instead of the statue of a saint, stands a great gun, its black nozzle poking through a loophole. The Gunner explained the working, patting the gun as one pats a favorite horse. At the lightest touch the monster swung smoothly on its swivel, and the loophole was free for us to look out at the magnificent view. Below us was Gibraltar Bay, the cork woods of Algeciras, and the blue line of Sierras beyond. We were in no hurry to leave the gallery, as we should probably never be here again. Gunner Wilkinson refused a shilling, but accepted a cigar; and finally understanding that we really were interested in his wonderful Cyclopean galleries, he unbent and gossiped about them in a friendly way.

During the "Great Siege," a non-commissioned officer, Sergeant Ince, heard the commandant, General Eliott, say that he would give a thousand dollars to be able to drop shells on the enemy from a certain point where the Rock's face was a sheer precipice. The practical genius of the plain soldier found out the way. If there was no place for the guns on the Rock, make a place for them in the Rock. So the famous Rock Batteries, at Ince's suggestion, were blasted out of the living cliffs. They had done great service in their day, but now, frankly, this cannon, that to me looked so deadly, was quite out of date. The real guns were mounted—elsewhere! Yes, La Vieja (the old dog) had a new set of teeth; she could bite now as well as bark. Beyond this the Gunner would say nothing of the modern defences, nor of those secret forbidden parts of "Gib" I longed to see. His talk was all of old wars, old heroes, of Ince, who rose from the ranks and was made an ensign of the Royal Garrison Battalion as a reward for his batteries. One day, when he was an aged man, riding to his work on an ancient nag, he met the Governor, the Duke of Kent, the father of "*the* Queen."

"That horse is too old for you, Mr. Ince," said the Duke.

"I like to ride easy, your Royal Highness," Ince answered meekly.

"Right," said the Duke, "but you deserve a better mount."

A few days later the Duke sent Ince a fiery young horse, far too spirited for the old overseer to manage. The next time the Duke met Ince he was riding his shambling nag. The Duke stopped and asked where the new horse was. Ince confessed that it was more than he could manage, and begged leave to send it back to the Duke's stable.

"No, no, Overseer, if you can't ride him, put him in your pocket," said the Duke handsomely. Ince took the hint and sold the horse for a good price.

Gunner Wilkinson talked of Nelson's visit and the banquet given him in St. George's Hall, the magnificent rock chamber at the end of the galleries, as if it had all happened last year, and first, last, and always he talked of the great siege.

A red flash, a puff of white smoke, a dull roar told that a yacht had just entered the harbor. As I looked through the narrow loophole, watching the sailors furl the sails, I glanced across the bay to the cork woods of Algeciras, and the lower foothills of the Sierras—and again I *remembered* the past. This is the thirteenth of April, 1783, the great day of the "Great Siege," that began on a September morning three years before, when Mrs. Skinner touched off the first gun of the defence to General Eliott's signal, "Britons strike home." This day, the allies believe, will see the obstinate garrison that has held out so long, against scurvy and starvation within, as well as the enemy's guns without, come to terms. The old General who has lived for more than a week on four ounces of rice per diem, just to prove how little a man need eat to live and fight, will hoist the white flag before evening gunfire. Down there in the bay lies the combined fleet of France and Spain, forty-seven "sail of the line"—real line of battleships, with white figureheads and wings and pleasant windowed balconies astern, and nice brass cannon shining through long rows of portholes. Alongside these three deckers and frigates are the strangest craft Gibraltar Bay has ever seen—ten famous unsubmergible, incombustible, floating batteries; uncouth monsters with bulging sides padded with wet sand, and hanging roofs covered with damp hides. Those Algeciras hills are crowded with spectators, come from all over Spain, to see the fall of Gibraltar. For eight hours the besiegers' five hundred guns roared and spat fire and shells, and the garrison's ninety and six answered with Boyd's deadly hot shot. The bay was a gallant sight at sunrise—who would have seen it at evening gunfire? Not the people who had come to watch the great victory; they melted away from the hills like summer snow, for the victory was to the "old dog!" The indestructible floating batteries were destroyed, the beautiful ships sunk or in flames, their sides blackened, their sails tattered. That day's fight cost the garrison something less than two hundred men, and the allies more than two thousand.

"Old Eliott stood there on the King's Bastion during the fight," the Gunner said. I wondered if he had shouted the slogun of his people in the debatable land. The Gunner asked what that might be. I gave him the old border cry of the Black Eliotts:

"My name is little Jock Eliott, and wha' daur meddle wi' me?"

Wilkinson, chuckling grimly, repeated it, surmised that "per'aps 'ee did," and gave this parting anecdote:

When, after peace was declared, the French commander, Duc de Crillon, visited Gibraltar, Eliott showed him Ince's galleries. De Crillon called the attention of his suite with these words:

"Notice, gentlemen, that these works are worthy of the Romans."

(Shade of Scipio Africanus! didst hear and wert appeased?)

While in the Gunner's company we heard much rolling of drums and sounding of "tuckets"; some military business was going on not far away. It was stirring to the pulses, and made us feel martial and bloodthirsty. We parted with the Gunner at evening gunfire; when we shook hands my bones crunched in his mighty grip, but I believe I did not flinch. We marched back to the hotel, keeping step to the march a military band was playing in the Alameda. That night, just as the floor of my room at the Cecil began to heave with the slow even roll of the *Kaiser*, a strain of sleepy lullaby music melted into my dream. I roused and looked at the watch. It was ten o'clock; the bugler at the barracks was playing "taps" on a silver bugle. It was all true! We were here, sleeping in the "Key to the Mediterranean!"

II

A SIBYL OF RONDA

DAWN in a garden of Andalusia…. To the south, across the Straits of Gibraltar, the faint purple outlines of the Atlas Mountains mark the mysterious coast of Africa. To the north, beyond the green *vega*, four ranges of clear cut Sierras Gazoulos rise, one behind the other, from gray, vaporous valleys of mist. The only sounds are the rhythmic breaking of waves on the beach; the short breathing of a herd of goats—black, tawny, and white, with coarse hair and fierce, yellow eyes, and the crisp crunch, crunch of their teeth cropping the roadside grass. The night flowers hang their heads and go to sleep, the day flowers lift their faces to the sun; the smell of heliotrope drenched in dew is an unforgetable thing. Breakfast is memorable, too; dates from Morocco, and rich Spanish coffee flavored with cinnamon, served under an arbor of Marechal Neil roses.

So began our first day in Spain, at a place the Romans called Portus Albus, and the Moors—they settled here soon after landing on Gibraltar, Jezirat-I-Kadra—"the green island." Can you derive the modern name of Algeciras from that? You must. Our old friend Tarik was here,—witness the great aqueduct he built, that still brings Algeciras his royal gift of water, always the legacy of Roman or of Moor.

To-day, Gibraltar is England's key to the Mediterranean; yesterday, Algeciras was the Moors' key to Spain. They held the Peninsula seven hundred years, think of it!—nearly twice as long as white men have held America; then it was wrenched from them, the door was locked against them. Less than three hundred years ago our ancestors landed on Plymouth Rock, but how should we, in New England, feel if the Indians, the Mexicans, or the Canadians rose up and drove us out of our stately cities, our green pastures, our fertile wheat fields? The Moors made a brave stand at Algeciras—it was their last ditch—and put up a good fight here. In the year 1344, the town was besieged by Alonzo XI of Castile, with the help of crusaders from every part of Christendom. The siege lasted twenty months. Chaucer, writing forty years later, describes a true knight as one who "had fought at Algecir," as we might say of one of Thermopylæ's Three Hundred or of Balaclava's Six Hundred. In 1760, four hundred years afterwards, the Spanish King, Charles III, rebuilt and fortified the place, "to be a hornet's nest against the English." For one hundred years Gibraltar and Algeciras— now deadly places, both of them bristling with guns, full of dynamite— have glowered at each other across the bay. The other day the English came again to Algeciras. Armed this time with British capital, they have built one of the hotels of the world here, and called it the Reina Maria Cristina, as a compliment to the Spanish Queen Mother.

"We did not expect to find such a fine hotel in Spain," I said to the capable English manageress.

"Ah, well! we hardly count this as Spain, you know!" she answered, with a fine insular contempt for all things "foreign."

"She's right!" cried Patsy. "*Por Dios*. Shall we never get out of England?" and willy-nilly he carried us off to lunch at Don Jaime's *fonda*, in the old part of the town.

The Don was waiting for us on a bench outside the inn door, smoking his inevitable cigarette, in the soft spring air. He looked a little bleary about the eyes, as if he had not had enough sleep.

"Don Jaime is up early to-day for our sake," Patsy explained; "as he goes to bed at four in the morning, he does not usually appear before two in the afternoon."

"The morning is a disease," said the Don. "I find it best not to go out until the day is well aired."

"Please observe," Patsy interrupted, "that this place has a proper odor of garlic; at last we are out of the smell of English roast beef!"

The Don sighed. "Nevertheless, I comfortably recall the roast beef we had at school in Stoneyhurst," he said; "it was rare, with plenty good, red gravy."

"That was all right in England; we're in Andalusia now. Let's begin with an *olla*, then a dish of rice, saffron, *pimientos*, and little birds,—and wine from that fattest wineskin. I counted ten of them outside in the road, leaning jovially together against the wall of the *fonda*."

When he got his wine from the "fattest wineskin"—it tasted a little of the "leather botelle"—Patsy raised his glass.

"We will drink," he cried, "to everything Spanish, *muchachas, ollas, dons, torrones*, and *fondas*, and confusion to all interlopers. Isn't this jolly little place better than the Maria Cristina? Isn't the company more friendly and far more diverting? See the notary and the doctor at the table near the door; at the next, the priest and the professor (they're both taking snuff); that fat, military man with the green gloves is a colonel of infantry. Those swell English officers you admired so much at the Reina Cristina simply own the hotel! We're admitted to the smoking and billiard rooms purely on sufferance. I like your inn best, Don Jaime."

"Ah, well," said the Don, "I like bath every morning, and all that luxushness when I stayed at the Reina, though it was much pain to put on cocktail coat every night for dinner."

"Treasure every gem of speech he lets fall," murmured Patsy, "they grow rarer—don't you notice?—as his English comes back to him."

"He's always been like that," said J., "it's because he learned English when he was young." "Some days he speaks as well as you or I, then again he talks a hodge podge no man can understand."

"What's the matter with the wine, Don?" cried Patsy. "You don't like it."

"Wine is not agreeable to my belly," said the Don. "I will take to keep you company, *un poco de ginebra, de campaña,* with much water."

"You must not expect ice," Patsy explained.

"You will not hanker for it," said the Don, taking a clay water bottle from the shelf behind him. "This *alcarraza* is—how you say? holey—no, porous, keeps water as cold as you might drink him, by evaporation." He poured out the water and put the *alcarraza* back. It had a rounded bottom and could not stand upright. The Romans used the same kind of vessel; you see them at Pompeii. They were made in this shape because they were used to pour libations of lustral water to Vesta, and would have been defiled if they had been set down on the ground.

By this time the fruit was put on the table. All the other guests had left the room except the priest and the professor, who were playing a game of dominoes. A large melon was placed before J. He looked at me as he cut it:

"You remember what I have always said? Till you come to Spain it is impossible to know what a melon can be."

"No earthly melon can taste as good as this one smells," said Patsy. "It is as if all the spices of Arabia had been let loose in this room!"

The servants had withdrawn, the clatter of the dishes had ceased. Some one opened a window; from the garden came the music of a guitar played by a master hand, a man's voice singing a song of Andalusia:

"Me han dicho que tu te casas,
y asi lo dice la gente,
todo sera en un dia
tu casamiento y mi muerte."

(They have told me thou art to wed, so people say; all shall be in one day, thy marriage and my death.)

Don Jaime's thimbleful of gin and his two cups of black coffee—he ate scarcely anything—had waked him up wonderfully. He smoked, with my permission, between the courses throughout lunch, flicking the ash from his cigarette with the phenomenally long nail of his little finger; his hands were white, handsome, and exquisitely kept. Lunch over and the serenade finished, Don Jaime settled his old black *sombrero* jauntily on the side of his head, buttoned up his threadbare coat—its darning was a work of art—and declared himself ready to show us the town.

"You would like to paint it red, wouldn't you?" said Patsy.

"White better is suited to that climate," said Don Jaime. *His* slang was current in the England of the sixties, and he took ours literally, but he laughed buoyantly because Patsy laughed.

Algeciras is a clean, pretty town, with neat, whitewashed houses, handsome iron gratings to doors and casements, and curious metal gargoyles and gutters painted green. Here and there from a window, or, in the more important houses, from a balcony like a small grated out of doors boudoir, leaned a handsome Algeciras girl, her dark, smooth hair beautifully dressed, with a bright flower worn over the middle of the forehead,—a pink rose, a white camelia, or one of the gorgeous red or yellow carnations one must come to Andalusia to see. We walked in the *alameda*, a well laid out promenade, with neat little gardens, each with a small pavilion on either side. We loitered in the city square, admired its beauties, and the handsome uniforms of the smart, well set up Spanish officers, drinking coffee and smoking cigarettes outside the more fashionable cafés.

"*Miré* (look)! this is the bull-fighters' café," said Don Jaime, as we turned into a side street, "and there is Bombito, the first matador in Spain. He has come down from Madrid for the bull-fight to-morrow."

An open door gave a glimpse of a tawdry interior with large mirrors, red plush seats, and atrocious decorations. At a table near the window sat the matador, a magnificently built man, with a frank, open face and a courageous eye. He was dressed in Andalusian costume,—a short, close-fitting coat like an Eton jacket, red sash, very tight trousers, wide-brimmed hat of hard gray felt. His hair, tied in a cue, was turned up under his hat; his full ruffled shirt was fastened by large diamonds; a superb cabuchon ruby burned on his finger. Around him sat a group of *aficionados*, the fancy, the young bloods of Algeciras. As we passed, Bombito, looking up, recognized Don Jaime. The matador smiled and nodded, and the *aficionados* turned to see the fortunate man to whom Bombito waved his hand.

"Spain at last, Spain of the songs I have sung, the pictures on fans and guava boxes I have collected," Patsy burbled joyously.

"*Quando los matadores matan en la corrida, van a la plaza bonitas con flores y abanicos.*" (When the matadors are killing in the bull ring, come the pretty girls with flowers and fans.)

Not far from the plaza, as we were passing a house of quality, with seraphic green gargoyles, Don Jaime halted and looked sharply across the way. A correct young man, in a rakish gray sombrero, stood at the opposite corner waiting, not loitering like us; it was evident that he was here with a purpose.

"Behold the *novio*!" said the Don; "I feared he dead or married."

Patsy asked who the gentleman with the varnished boots might be, who was gazing at an upper window with a white blind; he, apparently, did not see us. The Don explained that he was a *novio* (fiancé) *haciendo el oso* (doing the bear). He had heard it said that every afternoon, for five years, this faithful lover had stood outside the window of his beloved for exactly three hours!

"Is he mad?"

"Is love lunatics? Then must be vasty, crazy palaces by all Spain. He follow one antique custom, what we call '*cosas de España.*'"

Sunset found us far from the town on a lonely path skirting the coast. We looked through the ragged, blue cactus hedge at the beautiful view; watched the flame kindle and flash out from the lighthouse on Isla Verde; the ferry boat, *Elvira*, pass on her last trip from Gibraltar to Algeciras. A few steps further on the path brought us out upon a bold headland where, out of sight of the town, an old house sloughed and sagged on its foundations. A large fig tree grew on one side of the porch, a cork tree on the other; a tame lamb lifted its head from nibbling the grass and bleated a long "ba-a-a."

"Picturesque, isn't it?" said Patsy. His gaze, idly roving over the landscape, concentrated and grew intent as the door opened, and a girl in a red dress, with a yellow handkerchief over her head, came out of the old house. It was as if a rough oyster shell had opened and shown the perfect pearl it held.

"I say, don't you think it wicked to be so handsome?" groaned Patsy.

With a light, graceful step the girl walked to the edge of the cliff. A straggling path led down to the beach where an old, patched boat lay on its side. On a shelf of clean sand, below a tiny, ill-kept kitchen garden, lay an elderly man dressed in good black clothes—it was Sunday. The girl, evidently his daughter, called him to come in, the sun had gone down, he would catch cold. The old fellow obstinately refused to move; he was very comfortable where he was. Then, seeing us, he scrambled to his feet:

"Olá, olá! Engerlish, Engerlish!" he hailed us gleefully, waving an arm over his disreputable head. Two grave men of his own class, who passed at that moment, reproved him sternly, but he was in the incorrigibly merry stage and continued to wave and shout:

"Engerlish, Engerlish! How much? Very dear, goddam."

"This is my third visit to Spain," said J., "and that is the first drunken man I have seen even here."

"*Claro*," said Don Jaime, "we are not afflict with that vice of drunkenness."

A rusty brown water spaniel, lying near the old drunkard, rose, yawned, stretched itself fore and aft, and sniffed at Patsy's boots.

"Notice where the hair is worn off his back?" Patsy murmured, taking a burr out of the dog's long, flapping ear. "A strap has done that—a strap, I suspect, that fastens together two little water-tight kegs filled with tobacco from Gibraltar. Smuggler! Is the old fellow your partner? Where's the entrance to the smuggler's cave? Don, we've discovered a *contrabandista's* den!"

"May be!" laughed Don Jaime.

The spaniel lost interest in us and sat down to search for fleas. The girl had persuaded her father to come indoors. She supported him as he staggered towards the house.

"I'm off; it must mortify her to have us see him." Patsy strode ahead; we followed. Soon the fierce, prickly blades of the blue cactus hid the house from view.

"A pretty gel, not?" was the Don's comment.

"I wonder what her name is?" said Patsy. "Dolores, Pepita? It was worth the price of the journey just to see her face!" He was silent during the rest of the walk, keeping well ahead of us and singing snatches of an old song:

*"vous connaissez que j'ai por mie
une Andalouse a l'oeil lutin———"*

We left Algeciras before daylight for Ronda. If the Spaniard sleeps late at home, on his travels he must be an early bird,—the trains all seem to start between midnight and cockcrow. Don Jaime remained behind. Some night, he explained, when he felt particularly fit, he would omit going to bed; otherwise he must pass all his life in Algeciras; to get up in time for that hobgoblin train was not possible.

Across the bay we could make out the faint silhouette of Gibraltar against the ashen sky, a black lion asleep under the pallid day-star. The swift-coming dawn little by little transformed it to a gray lion dormant on an amethyst sea. Long after the great caved mountain was lost to sight, a distant growl shook the air.

"Morning gunfire at the Rock," said Patsy, "that's the last we shall hear of the British Lion for some time."

Sunrise came while we were in the heart of a dark forest. The hoary old trees had mighty, wide-spreading boughs, covered thick with small, gray-green leaves like the ilex; the trunks were old and frail—some of them mere hollow shells that might have housed a dryad or a satyr. They stood well apart from each other, the undergrowth and dead wood carefully trimmed away from their roots.

"See how well cared for the forest patriarchs are," said Patsy. "They must be kept alive as long as possible, like some old people, because they are the main support of the community."

Gold-tipped arrows of sunlight now began to pierce the thick green shadows of the forest, and striking the old trunks and the heavy lower branches brought out their wonderful tints.

"Look at those gorgeous rainbow trees! See the colors,—mother of pearl, carmine, violet, lavender,—what does it mean?" I cried.

It meant, I found, that this was the cork forest, and that the bark of the cork trees had lately been cut. Those rainbow colors soon fade, however, like the pink and white complexion of youth.

At the next station stood many cars laden with rough cork.

"The coarse, outer layers are used for fishing nets and life preservers. To even things up," Patsy explained, "they keep the fine, inner pinkish layers to bottle up those two great life destroyers, the drugs and liquors of the world."

The way now led over the Sierra Rondena, through the wildest, most beautiful part of Andalusia; past thickets of gum cistus, covered with glorious, golden-hearted, white blossoms; across green *vegas* enamelled with clumps of amber gorse; through waves of daisies, white and yellow, regiments of scarlet poppies marching through the pale green wheat, multitudes of cornflowers, morning glories, and ruby-headed alfalfa, king of all the handsome clover tribe. In this company of old friends a stranger flower stooped through the fields, half drooping, half mourning, a purple hood pulled over its head almost hiding the small blue bells hanging from the bending stalk. In that holiday crowd it looked like a hooded monk, a purple *penitente* at a carnival. I could never learn its true name, so we called it the Spanish Friar....

"Lift thine eyes, oh, lift thine eyes to the mountains, whence cometh help!" sang Patsy.

Intoxicated with the flower feast, the way had brought us within sight of the distant Sierras without our being aware. The mountains came to meet us, nearer, nearer; then, all at once, we were in their midst; the tall blue peaks came crowding all about us. As the engine panted "up, up" the mountain pass, the way crossed a flashing mountain torrent leaping down, down to the *vega* and the sea beyond; it looked more like a river of emeralds and snow than mere green water and white foam.

"Andalusia, once Vandalusia, named for the Vandals, who tarried here before their wild dash across the Alps down into Italy. Andalusia, 'ultima terræ' of the ancients, the uttermost parts of the earth, where good old Jonah longed to flee, small blame to him," Patsy maundered on, sleepily giving us bits of guidebook information.

"Andalusia, Vandalusia, Vandalusia, Andalusia." The wheels sang it like a lullaby. "Anda——"

"Ronda, Ronda!" cried the guard. We rubbed our eyes, snatched our belongings, tumbled out of the compartment to the platform, and almost into the arms of the Sibyl of Ronda, patiently waiting for us there, like Fate. She was a tiny old woman, draped like a Tanagra statuette, in veils of soft, rusty black: her face was like a damask rose that has withered on its stalk; the eyes alone, diamond bright, were young, full of fire. With a tremulous hand she offered J. a box of matches. An officious young man, with oiled hair and a green cravat, pushed her rudely aside. She was not to trouble the gentlefolk, responsibility for whose welfare in Ronda he assumed. Was he not the "offeecial" guide? Did he not speak English?

"We can speak English ourselves, and we don't want a guide," J. interposed. "We want a philosopher and friend. If we must have somebody to toot us about, I vote we take the Sibyl."

"What? Prefer an old thing like that to an active young man like me?" The official guide was incredulous!

"Isn't she a little old?" I ventured.

"Did you ever see handsomer wrinkles? They are perfectly classic," said J.

"And the twinkle in her eye!" Patsy supported him. "Wrinkles and twinkles against stall-fed guidebookery? The old girl for me. She's over eighty, she says; she was born in Ronda; has lived here all her life. She must know more about it than that Algerine pirate with the emerald tie. Past eighty, you said, didn't you?"

"*Ochanta dos; perro en Ronda los ombres a ochanta son pollones,*" the Sibyl answered. I am eighty-two, but in Ronda men of eighty are only chickens.

"I understand her Spanish!" cried Patsy. "That settles it; sealed to the Sibyl! I'll go bond she will let us in for something worth seeing." As usual, Patsy and J. had their way, and the active young man, angry and chapfallen, watched us with a sinister look, as we pottered slowly along beside the Sibyl. Our guides were mostly chosen for beauty, or charm. On the whole the plan worked well enough.

The Romans showed their usual colossal common sense in choosing the site of Arunda. Rome always was the model city they kept in mind. Three things, they rightly held, were necessary to a city; a not too distant view of mountains, to uplift the soul of the citizen; a fine climate to stimulate his body; a river for boys to swim and fish in, and for men to traffic by. When they found this high, fertile plain shut in by an amphitheatre of mountains, with one lone hill in the midst, surrounded and cut in halves by a rushing river, they built their city of Arunda on the cleft, river-girt rock we call Ronda. The Moors, who cleverly dovetailed their towns and their civilization into what Rome left, built their town of Ronda with the ruins of Arunda. We found remains of both Roman and Moorish walls. The modern town, built by the "Catholic Kings," Ferdinand and Isabel, is remarkable chiefly for the wonderful view from the *alameda*. You look down a sheer six hundred feet to the green *vega*, and the turbulent river Guadelevin fretting and fuming below. After roaring and raging through the Tajo, the deep chasm that divides Ronda, the river tumbles with a series of mad leaps and bounds to the plain beyond. Cutting a few antics with eddies and whirlpools, Guadelevin finally gets himself in hand, and goes soberly to work; turns the wheels of the old Moorish mills, makes flour for Ronda, as the Moors taught him to do; lends his strength to a new labor, for, marvel of marvels, old Moorish Ronda is lighted by electricity. In summer, when the river shrinks to a mere thread, its waning power is carefully husbanded and the water is led by pipes to do its work. Water, always water, alpha and omega of civilization! No town that could not be well supplied with water from the snowy Sierras or from some mountain lake was ever founded by Roman or Moor. Their wisdom is clearer now than ever before. What city prospers, lacking the Siamese twins of successful manufacture, water power, and electricity?

A flock of evil-looking birds hovered over a lonely thicket of tamarisks, close by the foot of the wall.

"From there," said the Sibyl, pointing to the tamarisks, "they throw the dead horses over the walls, after the bull-fights. The vultures soon pick their bones!" Grrrr! The ugly word spoiled the lovely view.

The Sibyl lived in the old, Moorish part of the city, that is called the Ciudad. She led us through the steep, narrow streets, pointing out the show houses. Here lived the grim Moorish king, Almoneted. He drank his wine from the skulls of enemies whose heads he had cut off, made into goblets, and inlaid with splendid jewels. Patsy, in his rococo Spanish, wondered if Almoneted had hoped to inherit the courage that once flashed from the sockets he stopped with emerald and ruby. The Sibyl twinkled all over at his suggestion.

"*Claro,*" she said, "it was doubtless his idea."

She showed us the Mina, an underground staircase of three hundred and sixty-five steps, one for every day in the year, like the churches in old Rome, leading down to the river. It was built so that, in case of siege, Ronda should not be cut off from water. Moorish caution! The Romans of Arunda apparently never contemplated such a possibility. The houses of the Ciudad are oriental in character, with blank, whitewashed walls, and rare, grated windows; they are all built to look as much alike as possible, in order to avoid attracting attention. The doors are the only distinguishing feature; all of them are massive, and built for defence; some are of walnut, some of oak, iron barred, iron bound, studded with bronze bosses or brass ornaments. Oh, redoubtable doors of old Ronda! What stores of wealth, what moons of beauty did you guard for the jealous Moors that made you?

The Sibyl understood all Patsy meant but could not say. The moment their eyes met, flash, flash, a secret code was established between them. Thanks to her, one of those mysterious doors was opened to us, and we saw the interior of one of those old Moorish houses, whose key, perhaps, is treasured by some Moor of Morocco to-day, for when they were driven back to Africa, the Moors took the keys of their houses in Andalusia and Granada with them, against the day they should return and reclaim their lost paradise. These keys have been handed down from generation to generation; some of them hang to-day in the Moorish houses of Tangiers and Tetuan.

When we were tired with much sightseeing, the Sibyl hospitably took us home to rest. In the patio of her house we found enchanting Moorish columns with slender shafts, and capitals that must have been copied from the Corinthian capitals the Romans used so much in Spain, only these are lighter and less formal, and have more feeling of the lovely form of the curling acanthus leaf. The patio, a survival of the Roman atrium, is an open court in the middle of the house, surrounded by a roofed corridor, where, during the warm weather, the life of an Andalusian family centres. In the Sibyl's patio stood an old Moorish well with an Arabic inscription. I cast longing eyes at it.

"Whatever you see," said J., "admire nothing that can be carried off by the modern Vandals, who have looted Italy and are looting Spain. If you do, she'll sell it."

"The old Vandals were a decent lot in comparison," Patsy agreed. "History has maligned them. If they did 'lift' a little property now and again, they, at least, left the owners the privilege of enjoying a virtuous indignation! These modern buyers, spoilers, barbarians, buy the victim's consent, add ignominy to spoiliation!"

A pair of goldfinches gossipped about their housekeeping in a wattle cage hung near the old Moorish well. A lemon tree in a glazed earthenware pot (it had one green lemon) and some gorgeous double carnations, variegated dark red and yellow, planted in a petroleum can, stood close to the well where they could be easily watered. As she passed, the Sibyl pinched off a dead leaf with a touch that was a caress,—these were her growing things, this was her pleasaunce.

In the living-room, which was the kitchen, too, was a quaint, carved stone fireplace. On the balcony outside was a gilt iron grill, surmounted by a battered pomegranate "final," sure some day to find its way into a "collection." The house was clean, in spite of the horde of children it sheltered, the Sibyl's great-grandchildren, for whose sake she sells matches at Ronda station.

The mother sat on a low stool rocking a wooden cradle with her foot; her hands were busy shelling *garbanzoz*, chickpeas, for the *olla*. Twin infants, lusty as Romulus and Remus, slept in the cradle; a pair of babes a size larger played with each other's toes in a long, bath-shaped, wicker basket; a girl of five pretended to help her mother with the *garbanzoz*. As we entered, the mother rose, welcomed us with grave ceremony, offered us food and drink and assured us that this house and everything it contained was ours: "*Esta muy a la disposicion de Vmd.*" It is very much at your disposal, the pretty old phrase goes.

Her face was plain beside the Sibyl's, time had etched every line *there* with an artist's fine care, but she had the grace, the reserve, the proud bearing of the Andaluz that poets have praised before, and since, De Musset, whose Andaluz lived in Barcelona, and was a Catalan, after all. As the youngsters were very near of an age, when the mother offered to give us everything in sight I asked if she could spare a baby? She looked almost pretty as she unbent, smiled, patted the biggest, and answered, with a twinkle like the old woman's, that there were none too many—indeed, that there were four more at school.

"Nine children, what a fine large family!" The Sibyl shrugged her shoulders, rolled up her eyes, and lifted a withered hand to heaven in protest.

"Granny doesn't think it much of a family; she had seven boys and seven girls."

"It is true," the Sibyl nodded, and stroked her lean flanks with tremulous hands; "this," she looked at her grandchild as if she expected great things of her, "is the seventh daughter of my seventh daughter."

When, our visit over, we rose to take leave, spokesman Patsy produced the phrase from his vocabulary that he had been conning:

"*Muchas memorias. Adios.*"

The Andaluz put this aside as too final. "*Hasta luego,*" she said, with her slow, sweet smile,—"Till we meet again."

"*Vamos!*" said the Sibyl, and showed the way to the door.

As we left the house of many children, we met a cavalcade of gay young people riding out of town. The men rode horses, the girls mules or donkeys. The woman's saddle was curiously made with crisscross arms and a back like an armchair. They were evidently well to do farmer folk; all wore good clothes and were well mounted. Several of them had ruddy, northern complexions. The Sibyl laid this to the excellent climate,—"In Ronda, we do not know when it is summer," she said. The last of the cavalcade to pass was a large, gray mule with as pretty a couple as you might see, seated on his broad back. We felt sure they were bride and groom. The man, a handsome fellow, full of the lust of life, sat very straight in saddle; the slim girl on the pillion behind, her arm about his waist, was full of bridal coquetries. She wore red stockings, a rose behind her ear, a lace-trimmed petticoat. An old, yellowish, time-worn guitar was slung over her shoulders by a cherry ribbon. As they rode past us, both young people smiled and nodded to the Sibyl.

"Your friends?" Patsy asked.

"My relatives." Proud that we should see them, and that they should see us, her face kindled; so did Patsy's. We all walked on through the tortuous Moorish *calle* with a lighter step, a braver heart for that chance meeting. It seemed as if we had caught some reflection of the hope, health, and love shining in their young faces.

"I play the guitar myself, after a fashion, not Spanish fashion, alack!" said Patsy. "Shade of Espinal! I won't leave Ronda till I have had a lesson. He lived here, Espinal, who gave the fifth string, perfected the guitar, made it what it is—what it can be in a Spaniard's hands."

A tall, arrogant-looking priest, with head held high, passed at this moment and challenged us with the eye, as the British officer had challenged us at Gibraltar. It seemed that he was master here, as that other had been master on the Rock.

"If I were a priest of Ronda I should hold up my head," said Patsy, "just because Espinal was a priest. He did other things worth doing beside giving us the fifth string: invented the decima, wrote a book, Marcus de Obregan, that's read to-day, three hundred years after; translated Horace— a pleasant task—lived to be eight years older than the Sibyl, died at ninety, still in the ring, still fighting. I like Ronda; let's buy a house and settle here!"

"Almoneted's house for choice," said J., and they began alloting quarters forthwith. The window with the north light should be the studio, the room on the courtyard far from noise, the library. In every town we visited, and they approved of, they made plans for passing the rest of our lives there.

The convent chapel smelt of lavender. The sunlight pouring through the rose window over the high altar was so strong that you saw tiny motes floating in the sunbeams. They could not have been dust, for the chapel was immaculate, a temple of purity from the worn marble flags under foot to the swinging silver lamps overhead, all freshly trimmed like the lamps of the wise virgins. The Virgin's lace handkerchief was a triumph of clear starching. She was dressed in black and wore only a few of her jewels—the Sibyl said—because it was Lent; we should see her at Easter! The Virgin's velvet dress was in the style of the sixteenth century; she wore a hoop, a ruff, and a long pointed bodice.

The Sibyl was not devout. She took the holy water to cross herself, mechanically, and made the most indifferent little duck for a courtesy as she passed before the altar. She looked with a cold eye on dear San Antonio di Padua, though he must be popular in Ronda, from the number of candles burning before him. Her indifference was in marked contrast to the piety of two freshly powdered young ladies, who were coming out of the chapel as we entered. They were of the great world; their combs and shoes were unquestionably from Paris.

"But the eyes, the eyes are Andalusian, and the torrents of black hair piled and puffed under those blessed black mantillas!" murmured Patsy, as they passed, smelling sweet of heliotrope and rice powder. The taller had a rosary of gold and pearls in her left hand, a fan in the right; the pearls slipped through her fingers, her lips moved; she was evidently "telling her beads." As they passed the statue of Santa Teresa, both knelt and crossed themselves with extraordinary reverence.

"Remember what Don Jaime said," Patsy reminded us; "that the common people of Spain take their religion very easily; everybody did when he was young, till the Queen Mother made it fashionable to be *devote*, when she came to Spain, bringing back the Jesuits and all the rest of them in her train. As a boy, the Don never remembers having seen a monk or a nun."

In spite of her "indifference," the Sibyl had held stanchly to her proposal that we should visit the convent where she had learned to sew and to embroider. Mass was just over, the priest had left the altar, the sacristan was snuffing out the candles. We had a glimpse of black veiled figures passing slowly behind the altar from one unseen chamber to another; they were followed by slighter, more lightly moving figures in white that flitted ethereally where the others walked solidly. Two by two they passed behind the altar with a noiseless step. When the last one had vanished, the priest and the sacristan disappeared into the sacristy, and we were left alone, with San Antonio and the other saints.

One end of the chapel was shut off by two heavy iron gratings, one behind the other. On the other side of the grill was a close-latticed screen, through which we could see a heavy, black curtain; the movement of the folds showed that we were being watched by some one on the other side of the triple barrier. After a short delay a novice slipped quietly into the chapel, a sprite of a girl with bright eyes and rosy cheeks, dressed in white serge and crisp linen. She asked us for "alms for the Holy Sacrament." Patsy produced our offering. The little novice's eyes opened roundly as her small red hand closed on the coin; she courtesied, so prettily, and flitted away as lightly as she came. As she passed the grill, she breathed some word of necromancy—it sounded like "blankichisserando." Then, silently, the black curtain was withdrawn; we saw a stout red porteress with a bunch of huge keys in her hand, a key turned grudgingly in a rusty lock, a hinge squeaked, the lattice parted, the convent walls flew back! We had a glimpse of veiled figures flying helter skelter; then through the grim, double iron grating we looked into the *sanctum sanctorum* of the nuns. A long, lonely room with rows of uncomfortably narrow, high-backed benches and narrow tables, over which hung some good crystal chandeliers filled with wax candles. Though it shone with neatness, it was the most cheerless living-room imaginable. In the middle, close to the grating, stood a tall, graceful woman, who looked like a Vestal of ancient Rome. Her taper, aristocratic hands were folded in a clasp that suggested strength rather than meekness; her small head, finely set upon the shoulders, was held high and proudly.

"The Abbess wishes to speak with you," whispered the Sibyl.

"How long," asked the Abbess—her voice like a far away chime of silver bells,—"how long do you remain in Ronda?"

I said our stay was short, no one had told us how much there was to see in Ronda.

"There is but one Ronda in the world," she said. The bells sounded nearer. The Sibyl nodded agreement. "It is the truth," she murmured.

"You are of Ronda?" I made out to ask.

The Abbess shook her head, and answered with a splendid pride, "*Soy hija di Granada*" (I am a daughter of Granada), as if that were the proudest title in the world. There was more bronze than silver in the bells now.

"What is the work you do in the convent?"

"We pray for the entire world." Her voice all silver again. Then, as an after-thought and of far less consequence:

"We have a school of needlework. Our embroidery is not unknown outside of Ronda; it has been heard of even outside of Spain." I felt abashed that I had not heard of it.

"You will, perhaps, return to Ronda for the fair in May? Many strangers are here then. Should you come back we shall always be glad to see you at the convent."

We felt that we were dismissed. I thanked the Abbess as best I could, in my halting Spanish, for her courtesy. She smiled a cold, holy smile; her last words were a benediction:

"*Vayan Vds. con Dios!*"

I had a glimpse of the little novice standing on tiptoe looking at Patsy over the Abbess's shoulder, with round, bright eyes, then the black curtains drew noiselessly together, the stout red porteress shut the wooden lattice with a loud clang, and turned the protesting key in the lock. The cold beauty of the Abbess, the fresh comeliness of the novice, were hidden behind the triple barrier: curtain, lattice, and cruel iron bars in double rank. No outstretched hand from within that grating could ever touch another hand reaching to meet it from the other side.

"We shall come back to Ronda for the fair," said Patsy, cheerfully, as he took leave of the Sibyl at the station. "If not this year, another year. The Abbess has invited us: mind that you are here to meet us at the train!"

The Sibyl smiled, a brave, old, withered smile, and waved her tiny, wrinkled hand:

"*Hasta otra vista!*"

She would do her best to keep the tryst!

III

THE WHITE VEIL

CONCEPCION   sitting in the patio under a golden shower of yellow Bankshire roses! That was our first impression of Seville. Pemberton, tall and lean, stood beside her, nervously twirling his stick. We hurried down to the courtyard; introductions followed.

"*Mes amigos, Concepcion.* She doesn't speak a word of English—all the better for your Spanish. She is Sevilliana born. We will do our best between us to show you the town in—how many days or hours do you mean to stay?"

"Weeks or months, rather; you don't know what you are letting yourself in for," warned J.

"The longer the better. Concepcion is sometimes busy with the children, housekeeping, or millinery. I never have anything to do."

Concepcion welcomed us with soft eyes, a gracious flurry of civilities, glanced at her watch, and looked meaningly at Pemberton.

"Yes," he said, "it's time to start. The

OUR LADY OF O., SEVILLE.

ceremony of Rending the White Veil, the first act of the drama, begins at ten o'clock."

It was the Wednesday of Holy Week. We had timed our arrival in Seville with an eye to that service. Had it not been for Concepcion, we might have missed it, after all. It was wonderful enough to sit in the patio with the paired Moorish columns, the green and blue *azulejos*, listening to the fountain, and the green love-birds in their gilded cage, looking at Concepcion, her little feet tucked under her chair, her fan gently agitated, her mantilla almost as black as her curls.

Outside, in the Plaza del Pacifico, the sun lay hot on the tawny earth; among the glossy green leaves of the orange trees, golden fruit and waxen blossom hung side by side. The air was sweet with the smell of them. A little boy took off his jacket and fluttered it like a *muleta* (the matador's red cloak) in his companion's face. In a moment the two boys were hard at it— playing at bull-fighting. We lingered to watch them.

"Seville is even better than I remembered," said Patsy. "I must have been here before (I knew that he had not); I seem to have known it all my life. What a lot of our friends, dead and alive, came from here! The

Emperor Trajan was a Sevilliano, so were Don Juan and Velasquez, so is Villegas. Figaro, brass basin, white apron, and all, met us at the gate last night when we arrived, and ran beside the carriage, pointing out the black arrows at the corners showing the way."

Was Rossini ever in Seville? Not that it signifies; he divined it all, if he did not see it. His creatures, Figaro, Rosina, Don Bartolo, are of the glorious company of its ghosts.

Seville is a siren city. The river Guadalquiver throws an arm about her; genius, when it may, follows suit and embraces the darling of Andalusia.

"I'll show you Figaro's barber shop some day," said Pemberton over his shoulder. "It's near my place. Yes, I'm a householder. You know the proverb? 'Whom God loves, he gives a house in Seville.'"

"Find us one, and we'll settle here, too!" Patsy exclaimed.

"We will talk about that later," said Pemberton. "Now, I am taking you to the cathedral. Before you see it, I ask you to consider the immortal resolution passed by its founders before the first stone was laid. 'Let us build,' they resolved, 'a monument that shall make posterity declare that we were mad.' That was a good bluff, wasn't it?"

"The only thing about posterity that you can bank on," Patsy sagely put in, "is that it won't say what is expected of it!"

"*Claro!* Posterity, you and I and Concepcion here, say those men were the sanest of their time. They, their architects, and their artists support this city to-day. I don't know how the taxes could get paid without the money you travelers bring. The cathedral is the thing that draws you, and the pageants and *fiestas*—they have all grown up out of it, are part and parcel of it. The 'monument' of those 'madmen' is the Heart of Seville. I wish we had a few such lunatics at home. *They* only thought about building the house of God. We waste ourselves in inventing ingenious devices for heating and lighting the churches of men, and let slip the great opportunity!"

We were walking, while Pemberton poured out his vehement torrent of talk, through a narrow, twisting *calle*, innocent of sidewalks, between tall Morisco houses with openwork gates, catching tantalizing glimpses of patios where roses riot, fountains sing, cedars whisper. If there be jealous iron-bound doors in gracious Seville, like those of grim, old Moorish Ronda, they stand hospitably ajar. As we turned a corner, Pemberton stopped us with a gesture:

"Look," he said, "the Giralda!"

Across a plaza where fringed palms rustle, at the end of a *calle* still in faint lilac shadow, stood a tall square tower of tenderest rose color. The Giralda, once the minaret of old Abu Yacob's mosque, dominates Seville as the Giglio of Giotto dominates Florence, by its imperial right of beauty. The bronze Victory on the summit turned lightly with the breeze; her Roman helmet, her standard, and the olive branch in her hand sharply etched against the fiery blue sky. In the belfry the old green bells—all Christians baptized—San Miquel, el Cantor, Santa Maria, la Gorda, swung to and fro, calling the people to prayer as their predecessor, the muezzin, once called them.

"It is very late," murmured Concepcion. She spoke slowly, distinctly; I understood her then and after. My Spanish was "coming back to me:" at sixteen I could chatter like a magpie in West Indian Castilian. We hurried on, losing the Giralda to find it again standing like a tall sentinel beside the cathedral. This was our first meeting with Gothic architecture in Spain. The pure lines of pointed window and door, the airy, flying buttresses, the graceful parapet crowning the roof rose stately above us, solemn and inspiring, a very gospel carven in warm gray stone.

"The cathedral is the Heart of Seville," said Pemberton, "it is a unique thing. No church in Christendom, no Greek temple or Buddhist shrine can compare with it. Not because it is the largest Gothic cathedral and the third largest church in the world, but because it has breath, because it is alive."

An aged beggar, clean and respectable, lifted the heavy leathern curtain that hung over the door. "*Una limosna por el amor de Dios,*" he whispered. Concepcion dropped a *perro chico* (literally a small dog, a copper coin worth one cent) into his trembling old hand.

"*Dios se lo paga a V.,*" said the beggar, a neat, self-respecting mendicant whose voice lacked the whine of Italy. God himself will pay it to you!

In the rich, dusky spaces of the nave, near the *puerta mayor*, a marble slab is let into the pavement. Carved upon the slab are the familiar device of the three brave caravels and the proud motto, "*á Castilla y á Leon, mundo nuebo dié Colon.*"

"This is the tomb of that good son, Ferdinand Columbus," said Pemberton. A cord tightened round my heart. "That's a link with the past that holds, isn't it?"

From that moment it seemed as if we all caught fire from Pemberton, saw through his eyes, felt with his intensity of feeling. The sweeping aisles, the steadfast columns, the soaring arches of that cathedral seemed elemental things, like their prototypes, the forest lanes, the giants of the primeval wood. We could almost feel the spring of pine needles underfoot, smell the resin, see the sunlight striking through the tops of tall pines swaying together, arching the forest path.

The *coro* the distinguishing feature of Spanish cathedrals—it is like a chapel set down in the middle of a church—interferes less with the impression of the whole building at Seville than in any other cathedral we saw. In the outer aisles, which are free of the *coro*, you have an uninterrupted view of the entire length of the building, and can realize its sublime proportions, get a sense of the harmony of the whole; the ease with which the vast columns uphold the roof, and divide the whole space into its proper parts. In itself, the *coro* is like an exquisitely wrought gem in a chaste and simple setting. It is shut off from the nave on the side of the *puerta mayor*, by a marble façade containing fine bas-reliefs, and a painting of the Virgin by Francesco Pacheco, father-in-law and teacher of Velasquez. On the side towards the *capilla mayor* and the high altar, the *coro* is isolated by a magnificent wrought-iron screen where, high up in groups of threes, hang the golden mass bells. Around the interior of the *coro* runs a double row of choir stalls, marvels of wood carving, in part grotesque, where the carver's fancy ran riot and reproduced the faces of the men, beasts, and devils that had haunted his childish dreams.

SEVILLE CATHEDRAL.

Those goblin, demon heads are carved low down, where the hand rests, the knees push. They are worn away, polished smooth by the rubbing of the palms and the calves of generations of monks. Safe above, where the uplifted eye strikes, are the heavenly visions,—angels, saints, prophets, the Virgin in glory, fresh as the day old Nufro Sanchez carved them. In the middle of the *coro* stands the tall *facistol* holding the yellow vellum music books open at the page where the monkish illuminators painted their most beautiful miniatures.

"There's Villegas's picture," J. whispered, as we passed the *coro*, "the old choirmaster holding up his baton, scolding the choristers. I know every inch of this church; there's not a corner he has not painted."

"And how he has painted it!" sighed Pemberton; "as a man paints the portrait of his mother. How you feel the artists, dead and alive, who have worked here; that's part of the fascination of the place."

"Put the camp chairs there," said Concepcion. She had found us the perfect position, between the *coro* and the *capilla mayor*. "Did he tell you that screen is gilded with the first gold that came from the Americas?"

The ship that brought that first gold must have been the size of the Mayflower, from the amount of "first gold" it is supposed to have brought to Spain.

There was no crowd, only a few women dressed like Concepcion, all in black; some poor bodies, a sprinkling of tourists, and one brown Franciscan. The sunlight pouring through the painted window of the Assumption stained the nearest columns blood-red, sapphire, emerald. In the *coro*, sombre and rich, the crimson and scarlet cloaks of the old canons, sitting slumbrous in the stalls, glowed like jewels in the dusk. Grouped in couples about the *facistol* were the choir boys, their black-letter scores held between them. The high altar of the *capilla mayor* was covered by a thick, White Veil, that hung from the groined roof to the floor. Two by two the tonsured acolytes in long purple gowns, with tassels of gold and violet, prepared for the service, dressed the pulpits, laid ready the missals. The three officiating priests appeared, each preceded by a pair of altar boys in scarlet and ivory, carrying silver candlesticks twice as tall as they. The priest at the middle pulpit was a big, powerful man, with a fine resonant voice. His intoning of the gospel was masterly; Concepcion said the finest in Seville, if not in Spain. The old priest with the delicate, spiritual face, like a wax mask with jewel eyes, and the high treble voice, must have been as good at intoning in his day. The little boys who held the candles close for his old eyes to see, leaned towards him with a pleasant, human tenderness. It was easy to see there was love in their service.

"*Et posuit eum in monumento*," the old priest quavered out the last words of the story, as it is told by Luke; the three celebrants left the altar with much ceremony of book and bell and kiss ecclesiastical, and took their stand before the white veiled altar; the purple acolytes swung their gold censers till we saw the glowing coals; the smoke of frankincense and spice rose up in clouds. There came a moment of strained silence. The only sound was the clinking of the censer chains. The air between priests and people was thick and blue with incense.

Brrrrrrrrrrm, brrrrrrrrrrrm! The silence was shattered by a loud clap of thunder, another and another, as if a fierce tempest had sprung up outside. While the thunder rolled and echoed through the aisles, the White Veil was rent from top to bottom, fell to the ground, and disappeared as if by magic. In its place hung the Black Veil. Before this stood in studied attitudes the big priest, the old priest, and a little priest. The brown Franciscan kneeling by the great tenabrium had thrown back his head in ecstasy.

"Look," whispered Pemberton, "the Saint Anthony of Murillo; I will show you the picture in the baptistry; it's the one the figure of Anthony was cut out from and sent to New York. They have put the piece back, but the 'joining' shows."

We came out of the cathedral into the light and perfume of the Court of Oranges, sat down upon a sun-warmed marble bench, and looked up at the pigeons flitting about the Giralda. A little cloud floated before the face of the sun, a shadow fell upon the fountain.

"That fountain where the women are gossiping is the old Moorish *midhâ*, where the musselmen washed before prayer, as I have seen them do in Turkey. Women weren't allowed in the Court of Oranges then," mused Pemberton. "Where we sit, the temples of Astarte and of Salambo once stood. It's curious how you catch the echoes of the older religions in these ceremonies of Holy Week. Some of the rites were practiced before Rome was. The mosque, the Moors who worshipped there, seem things of yesterday, in comparison."

"Almost of to-day, that cry, that man are more than half Arab."

"*Agua, agua fresca!*" The cry twanged of the Orient. The water seller, lean and brown, with impenetrable black velvet eyes, turned into the courtyard. He was dressed all in white, with

ENTRANCE TO COURT OF ORANGES, SEVILLE.

odd, hemp-soled shoes,—a grave man who offered water from his clean cup, then passed on his way, his cry growing faint, fainter, till it was drowned in the clangor of *el Cantor*, the great, green, bronze bell of the Giralda.

The afternoon of Holy Wednesday found us in the Plaza de la Constitucion. Before the florid façade of the Casa de Ayutamiento a grand stand had been built. In the center was a dais hung with crimson velvet, garlanded with flowers. Under a gold embroidered canopy stood three gilded thrones.

"For the King, the Queen Mother, and the Infanta Maria Teresa," Concepcion explained. Opposite, across the plaza, Pemberton pointed out the Audienza, a handsome Renaissance building, over whose door were the arms of Charles V, the Pillars of Hercules with the old motto borrowed from the old hero, *ne plus ultra*. A marble column shows where the public executions once took place. The plaza, scene of tournaments, bull-fights, and carnival fêtes, was crowded by those who could afford the best seats for the processions of penitence, the famous pageants of Holy Week. The audience assembled in twos and threes, the dark, full-bosomed Andalusian women, with fan and mantilla, the men in uniform or afternoon dress. In a neighboring box sat a young girl with a lovely oval face, masses of wavy black hair, and eyes like cool, brown agates.

"That is Luz," said Pemberton, "called the prettiest girl in Seville." He looked at Concepcion as he said it.

"There is a woman who is as beautiful," I said, truthfully, and knew that Pemberton was my friend for life.

Luz had many visitors (the seats in her box were never empty), they came and went like moths about a candle. One remained, a monk in a brown habit, the Franciscan of the cathedral. In spite of his rope girdle, his bare sandaled feet, he had once belonged to that world of fashion where Luz rules, and where he was still at home.

A fanfare of trumpets rang out above the babble and the laughter. Fans were closed, flirtations broken off. Luz turned in her seat; all eyes were fixed on the corner where the Calle de Serpientes turns into the plaza. Down the narrow street, out into the full light of the square, rode a troop of resplendent cavalry,—white Andalusian horses with delicate, high-stepping feet, men who sat straight in the saddle, in spite of rich trappings and gorgeous uniforms. The *penitentes* followed, sombre, masked men in long, purple velvet gowns, the train folded over the arm, showing violet silk stockings and silver-buckled shoes. From their tall, pointed caps hung down the antefaces covering the entire head, falling low upon the breast: through the eyeholes one caught the flash of dark eyes. In their gloved hands they carried silver staffs of office ten feet high. Behind walked the *Nazerenos*. The foremost carried a large cross; the others, standards of the order, or flaming torches that smoked and flickered as they walked. Before the *penitentes* passed in front of the grand stand, they spread out their trains that trailed behind them on the ground. In the midst of these maskers strode a band of Roman centurions,—helmets, cuirasses, spears, and standards with the familiar S P Q R glancing in the sun. The music to which they marched had a melancholy refrain, a sort of insistant grieving that knocked at the heart.

"The funeral march of Eslava; you will know it well before Easter," said Pemberton.

"*Ai, ai!*" A great sigh breathed by a thousand people as the first *paso* came in sight,—a huge float moving, as if miraculously, down the Street of Serpents out into the plaza. On a base of wrought silver, at the height of a man's shoulder, stood a life-sized statue of the Virgin.

"*Nuestra Señora de la Vittoria*," murmured Concepcion.

The statue, of painted wood, was sumptuously dressed. The front of her robe was of costly lace; over this fell from the shoulders a train of black velvet, two yards long, heavily embroidered in gold arabesques. The hair was real. On the head sparkled a stupendous diamond crown. Slowly, slowly the float drew near, wrapped in a cloud of incense from the censers of the *penitentes*. A rain of flowers fell from window and balcony; the velvet and gold baldequin over the Virgin's head was almost hidden by lilies and roses. At her feet were flaunting daffodils in silver vases, and row on row of blazing candles at various heights. She was covered from throat to waist with superb jewels, strings of pearls, diamonds, and sapphires. Her wrists were laden with bracelets, in her hand she carried a lace pocket handkerchief. As she entered the plaza a tremendous peal shook the soft air; the vast green bells of the Giralda seemed to fling themselves like live creatures towards Mary. The glitter of the gewgaws, the glow of the candles lighted up the face, showed the tears (pearls of great price) on the cheeks, the beauty and tenderness of the expression.

"A masterpiece by the sculptor, Montañes, the friend of Velasquez," said Pemberton. In spite of all the frippery of the dress you feel the hand of the master sculptor in the painted statue. The

THE SCULPTOR MARTINEZ
MONTANES.
Velasquez

PORTRAIT OF THE
ARTIST'S SON
Greco

loving, tender face, the feminine outstretched arms divinely express the eternal womanly.

"Miré, Miré, Vd! el Rey y la Reina!" whispered Concepcion. She had not been too much engrossed to see the young King and his mother take their places. The *paso* turned slowly as if on a pivot till the queen celestial faced the queen terrestrial. The King uncovered and saluted, the Queen Mother, Cristina Maria, courtesied,—so they stood facing each other for a single heart-beat, then the King left the dais, walked down into the plaza, and took his place at the head of those masked men.

"Don Alfonzo is the Elder Brother of the Confraternity of the Cigar Makers," whispered Concepcion. "See, he escorts their patron, our Lady of Victory, through the plaza."

To the mournful grieving of Eslava's dirge, the Virgin of the cigar makers, escorted by the King, disappeared on the way to her station in the cathedral.

"Te dea major eris!" murmured Pemberton, "so they carried Salambo through Seville. I hope you admired the dress; it was new this year, a present from the ladies of Seville. It cost one hundred and fifty thousand *pesetas*; I know because I helped pay for it. You saw there were bread riots last week, not fifty miles from here? It's the old spirit of Seville, the spirit that built the cathedral during the hundred years when Spain was pouring out blood and money like water in defence of the faith. We can always get what we really want in Seville, and most other places!"

During the long waits between the acts of the drama of the Passion, the little dramas of every-day life went on all around us. In the boxes the young people looked into each other's eyes, the *duennas* manœuvred, encouraged the eligible, frowned on the ineligible. A slim young officer in a cloak slipped a note into Luz's hand as he passed her box, and only the Franciscan saw it. In the crowd below, the flirt of an orange skirt challenged beauty in the grand stand.

"Imperio, the dancing girl," said Pemberton. "She's come home for the fêtes. That old fellow, her father, is the crack matador tailor; he makes all Bombito's toggery."

"Miré," whispered Concepcion, "The Lord dressed in a handsome tunic of cloth of silver, embroidered in gold."

The entry into Jerusalem, a realistic float, was passing. It represented the Master mounted on an ass, Peter, John, and Sant Iago kneeling before him. This was followed by a large *paso*, illustrating the Betrayal in the Garden. Peter, sword in hand, Judas—he was always dressed in yellow, the color of treachery—the Roman soldiers as well as the Christ, are all the work of Montañes. It is said that Montañes while he was at work on this, often got up at night to look at it, and was once overheard to say, "How could I have done anything so beautiful?" In spite of the Master's ruby velvet robe and the tawdry gilt rays behind his head, the thing took hold of one, the picture "bit" into the memory plate and will not easily be erased. There was a moment of silence as the scenes of the Passion were presented in these wonderful vivid pictures, but as soon as each paso swung by the grand stand, the laughter and flirtation began again. The tragic *paso* of the Crucifixion was escorted by a brotherhood of boy *penitentes* followed by a band of child musicians. Directly behind the cross marched a tiny drummer in uniform, beating a big drum. If he was not a dwarf, he could not have been more than four years old.

"What a funny little boy!" murmured Concepcion, wiping the tears of laughter from her eyes. The supreme scene of the Crucifixion, the figures all by Roldan, the sculptor who spares no grim detail of pain, was followed by stifled laughter. The merriment struck an awful anti-climax.

"Remember," Pemberton explained, "you are seeing this thing for the first time; these people have seen it all their lives; familiarity breeds, not contempt, but a certain callousness. The young women are so strictly guarded, you must not blame them if they 'make eyes' a little. This is one of their few chances to see and be seen."

"Do you make as much of Christmas as of Holy Week?" I asked Concepcion, to turn the conversation. "Which is the greater *fiesta*?"

"There are three great *fiestas* of the Church," she answered, "but Christmas is, undoubtedly, the greatest. There is a saying, 'Who does not fast on the vigil of Christmas is either a Turk or a dog.' This is true for people of our religion, for at midnight the Niño Jesus was born. I do not know how it is with you, for we are Catholics and you are Christians."

"In what does the difference lie?"

"In the manner of baptism. You are baptized all over in a great vat with water only; we, with water, oil, and salt that is put in the mouth. There are also other ceremonies,—there is the godmother who holds the candle."

"What are the Christmas services like?"

"Ah, you must return, if only to see the dancing of the *seises* in the cathedral. I am told this can be seen only at Seville. The *seises* are boys, who wear curious dresses and long blond curls. It is an ancient custom,—my husband says, in memory of the Israelites dancing before the ark, but I think differently."

"At one time there was an effort to break up the dance of the *seises*," Pemberton interrupted. "Some busybody complained to the Pope that it was a heathenish thing. The result of the meddling was a papal bull ordering that the dancing should stop when the dresses were worn out. That was long and long ago; the dresses have not worn out yet. They are renewed a piece at a time, one year a sleeve, another year a cap, so the day has never come when they are completely outworn. Our *seises* still dance at Christmas, Corpus Christi, and the feast of the Conception—that's my wife's *fiesta*, you know."

"The Christmas ceremonies in the villages are also interesting," said Concepcion. "I once saw a procession when the Niño Jesus was carried through the streets. It was a very large image, the size of a big baby. It had a beautiful head, and was nicely swaddled. One Christmas as they were carrying him on his procession (this was years and years ago), there was a quarrel in the crowd and one man stabbed another. The Niño Jesus grew pale and turned his head on one side, so that he might not see that dreadful sight. He has remained in that attitude ever since. I myself have seen the Niño. Yes, it was a wonderful happening. It is a much venerated image and has always remained in the care of the good Franciscan monks."

Concepcion saw that I was interested, that Pemberton was busy explaining things to the others, and, out of the immense goodness of her heart, she went on to speak to me of religious matters.

"I have always heard it said," she began, "that there are seven religions."

"I, too, have heard it, indeed, my pastor has written a book on the subject;[1] can you tell me their names?"

"Not all of them. There are Catholics, Christians, and those who worship Mahomet. There are the Israelites,—they have the strangest religion! They worship a calf's head. In their church they put on the queerest garments, gather round a great calf's head in the middle, and sing such a curious hymn, 'Wow, Wow!' It sounds like that. It would make you laugh, only they will not let you into the synagogue, and if you do just manage to peep in, they drive you out."

I told her of the wailing of the Jews outside the wall of Jerusalem, hoping to rouse some sympathy for them, but Concepcion could feel none.

"Though," she acknowledged, "our Lord *was* an Israelite. He did not become a Catholic till he was thirty-three years old, when He had Himself baptized by San Juan Battisto. Before that He occupied Himself with preaching His religion."

I asked Concepcion which of the saints was her especial patron.

"The blessed saints are all very good," she answered, "but I myself do not put much dependence on them. I place all my hopes on the Virgin."

As Concepcion talked, the sun went down; long shadows fell across the plaza. The pale rose-colored Giralda glowed a deeper pink in the sunset, and then faded. The new moon came up in the faint lavender sky and hung, a golden scimitar, the evening star beside it, over the tower. In the minaret where the muezzin once cried his shrill "*Allah il Allah*," San Miquel and el Cantor, rocked and pealed, saluting each float as it passed.

"See, the crescent and the star over the Giralda," said Pemberton; "the cross gleams red on the cathedral. Mary reigns in Mahomet's place, and her robe is worked in the arabesques of the Moors."

Walking home, we came upon a *paso* at rest in a side street. The velvet hangings that fall from the base to the ground were parted. We caught a glimpse of the hidden motive power, twenty-five or thirty men, with quaint, padded turbans on their heads, the ends hanging down and covering the shoulder. The water seller in his white garments was in attendance. He filled and refilled his glass, passing it to the thirsty bearers, who drank, and mopped their faces silently. The masked *penitentes* stood at ease, fanning themselves, the *Nazerenos* trimmed their torches.

"*Vamos!*" The leader struck the ground with his silver staff; the velvet hangings fell in place (the embossed pattern was so contrived that the air holes were invisible), and the heavy *paso* moved steadily down the *calle* on the heads and shoulders of those hidden men.

In the processions of Holy Thursday and Good Friday afternoons, the mysteries of the Passion were represented again and again with endless variations. The *pasos* seemed to grow more splendid, the dresses and accessories more lavish. The brotherhoods, called *hermandads* or *cofradias*, have charge of the floats, called *pasos* or *andas*, the statues, and all the paraphernalia of the pageants. There is a certain rivalry between them; some excel in one particular, some in another. One of the treasures I remember was a huge and very beautiful crucifix of tortoise shell and silver. The dresses of *penitentes* and *Nazerenos* were never alike; some were in white with blue masks, some in black and silver. They all followed the same plan, the head and face were so disguised that it was impossible to recognize the man in the penitent's dress. The *Hermandad* of *Nuestro Padre Jesus de la Passion*, founded in the sixteenth century, is the oldest brotherhood. In its early days the *Hermanos de Sangue* scourged themselves as they walked barefoot through the streets. Those who carried the torches were distinguished from the flagellants by the title *Hermanos de Luz.*

"Brothers of light," Pemberton translated it. "Who would not be glad to deserve such a title? To be a true 'Brother of light!'"

IV

THE BLACK VEIL

Tres jueves hay en el año	Three Thursdays in the year
que relumbran mas que el sol;	Shine brighter than the sun;
Corpus Christi, Jueves Santo,	Corpus Christi, Holy Thursday,
y el dia de la Ascencion.	And the day of the Ascension.

"Hark, Pan pipes!" said J., "don't you hear that lovely thin music of the shepherd's flute?"

"Here in Seville? Is it possible?"

"Why not? All things are possible when you are living half in the tenth century, half in the twentieth!"

The sylvan melody, shrilling louder, pierced the city's drone. At our gate the piper paused and played his little tune again. He was a tall young man with a bold eye and a gay lilt of the head. His blue apron was tucked under his jacket, he wore a red rose behind his ear. There was something free and debonair about him that spoke the youth of the world; his music stirred the blood. I could have followed him and his pipe through the streets without a thought of the business of the day.

"A wandering knife grinder from La Mancha," said J., pulling out his sketchbook. "Find some scissors or something for him to sharpen. Can't you keep him busy a moment, while I try to draw him?"

He would not stay; you cannot deceive a Manchegan. He saw at a glance there was "nothing doing" for him in our patio; sounded his flute and went lightly on his way, his wheel at his back. If knives were to grind, he was ready to grind them even on a *fiesta grande* like Holy Thursday.

Before his music was out of earshot, Concepcion appeared at the gate, a pink japonica in her hair, her fan the same color, a shade darker. Behind her, like a tall, thin shadow, came Pemberton.

"Another fan? Do you never carry the same twice?"

"Oh, yes, she has to, poor child," said Pemberton. "She possesses only fifty-five fans; Luz, I hear, owns three hundred and fifty. You're feeling fit, I hope? We have a long day before us. We go first to San Lorenzo to see the monument,—sepulchre you call it in Italy. Concepcion says we shall be in time to see the arrival of the royal party. They must go on foot like the rest of us to-day; not a bell may ring, not a wheel turn in all Seville, this week, from Wednesday night till Saturday noon."

Only the wheel of the Brother of Light, the wandering knife grinder of La Mancha!

The Plaza San Lorenzo was filled with people, the trees with small boys; a mannerly crowd with no hoodlums; indeed, I think the genus does not exist in Spain. Soon the word was passed: "They are coming." The throng shifted, a way was made for the king's halberdiers, fierce men with twisted moustachios and bronzed skins, the very flower of the army. Their duty is to guard, day and night, the person of the King. The civil governor, Lopez Balesteros, followed with his aides, and the Alcalde of Seville, a bulky, puffing man. His gown and his fat made it hard for him to keep the pace of those tough, quick-marching swashbucklers. Last, surrounded by his major domos of the week and his gentlemen of the chamber, the King, long of leg, slender of body, with the heavy, underhung jaw, the slovenly nether lip of the Hapsburgs, a boyish dignity, and a frank smile all his own. He wore a smart uniform with a white plumed helmet.

PORTRAIT OF PHILIP II. *Coello*

"Don Alfonzo has as many incarnations as Jupiter," said Pemberton. "To-day he is a major general of cavalry. Notice that gold chain and tell me, if you can, what it is."

The chain, wide and flat, with elaborately wrought links, was flung over the King's shoulders. From it hung a little gold animal uncomfortably tied by the middle; its head and legs all flopping down in a dreadful way, like a horse being hoisted on board ship.

"By the great horn spoon!" cried Patsy; "it's the grand order of the Golden Fleece! I would rather own that than be King of Spain."

The golden toy hung on the young King's breast just as it hangs in Alonzo Coello's portrait of Philip II. Beside the King walked his mother— she looks a bigot worthy of Philip's house—and his sister, the Infanta Maria Teresa, enough like him, in spite of her white mantilla, to be his twin.

Sanchez Lozano, Elder Brother of the Parish Confraternity, José Ponce, the archpriest, and half a dozen other bigwigs met the royalties at the door of San Lorenzo. The bigwigs made oration, long and loud, the King took off his helmet and mopped his crimson face. It was a cruelly hot day for the season.

"They work the boy hard," said Pemberton. "He was at the cathedral at half past nine, this morning, and led the procession to deposit the Host in the monument. Next he went to the church of San Salvador; this is his third sepulchre. They have walked him all over the place; warm work in that thick uniform. If every Spaniard earned his salt as honestly as Don Alfonzo, Spain would not be where she is to-day."

Pemberton heard afterwards, from one of the Brothers, what passed in the church while we waited in the plaza. The King, after praying by the sepulchre, a flower-decked, candle-lighted space before the altar, and admiring the *pasos* of the Virgin of Solitude and the Christ of Great Power, talked with the elder Brother, asked if he too, walked masked in the procession of penitence. Sanchez Lozano said that he did, and reminded Don Alfonzo that Isabel II, the King's grandmother, and Ferdinand VII, his great grandfather, had been members of this Brotherhood. The King and the Infanta, without more ado, took the oath and signed the articles of the Brotherhood.

"Of course it had all been cut, dried, and smoked beforehand," Pemberton added. "Royalty does not often have an opportunity to enjoy the unforeseen!"

When they came out of church, the King had faded to a healthy pink; we no longer feared apoplexy for him. The gorgeous, sweating company crossed the plaza, the crowd cheered, the ladies in the balconies clapped hands and waved 'kerchiefs.

"Come," said Pemberton, "to see beauty, follow in a monarch's wake. We shall find the handsomest women of Seville inside the church."

A dozen ladies, their flushed, excited faces reflecting the royal smile, clustered about the sad Virgin. A señorita, in black gauze with pink camelias in her hair and bodice, tapped a silver money tray with a copper coin:

"Did they desire to purchase a photograph of our Lady?" She spoke to me, she looked at Patsy.

A nun in a coarse habit passed; the rough woolen of her gown caught in the hem of the young lady's silk dress, and showed a pair of little feet in flesh-colored silk stockings and satin shoes.

"At the feet of the young lady," said Patsy, "I desire greatly to purchase a photograph. Will she do me the divine favor of choosing?"

"I kiss the hand of the horseman. It appears this large one is the most good; it is, as well, the more dear."

The slight lisp, the smell of jasmines, the turn of wrist, as the pink fan opened and shut, were all familiar. Where—when—had we seen her? Patsy knew: it was Luz of the agate eyes!

I forget what day it was that Pemberton and I stayed at the cathedral after mass to hear the Archbishop's sermon, but this seems a good time to tell about it. The Archbishop was a refined, silvery old ascetic, who looked like Cardinal Newman. He preached as the students of the Theatre Français talk, as if speech were first a fine art, second an expression of thought. Pausing now and then from exhaustion, he poured out an eloquent appeal to love the Mother of God. After service the Archbishop was escorted to the episcopal palace near the cathedral, by a sacristan, carrying a silver mace, another with a tall, double cross, and six haughty young priests in new purple silk gowns.

"Do you notice," asked Pemberton, "the difference between the Italian and the Spanish priests? The Italian looks at you sidelong, when you are not looking; sizes up your feeling about him and his church. Your Spaniard is a bird of a different feather; he doesn't give a maravedi what you think of him. You are on trial, not he. The only question is, are you what you should be? That he is, there can be no peradventure."

We joined the crowd of women and beggars following the Archbishop in his fine violet robe, scarlet moire skull-cap, and amethyst cross. A wild-eyed woman with a bruised face threw herself at his feet, holding up a despairing hand as if in appeal. Tired and feeble, the old man paused patiently, and said some words of fatherly comfort. She kissed the great sapphire on his transparent old hand and drew back weeping, as if ashamed.

"The heart of man changeth not," said Pemberton. "In the days of the Inquisition there were priests tender-hearted as the Archbishop. He could not send a cat to torture or the stake. That big priest, with the brutal jaw, the one who limps, looks cruel as Torquemada; he would condemn a man to la Parra (the dungeon in the Bishop's Palace over there) as quick as winking—if he could!"

The shadow on the sun-dial over the palace door pointed to twelve. We followed the women into the handsome courtyard, hung with blue and striped hangings, and watched the Archbishop totter feebly up the fine marble stair. At the door he turned and gave the episcopal blessing, two fingers raised, and went indoors with his escort. He was followed by people bearing gifts of fruit and cakes. Four strong men carried up a large tray of yellow frosted pyramids stuck all over with candied cherries.

"Red and yellow, the Spanish colors," said Pemberton. "I hope Torquemada and the others stay to luncheon and eat up those pyramids; they would not be good for the Archbishop."

On Holy Thursday afternoon, the ceremony of the Washing of Feet was celebrated in the cathedral. The King, it was said, would take the first rôle; the Archbishop, however, officiated in his place. On a platform before the high altar stood the benches for the apostles. The twelve poor old men who impersonated them came toddling in, each carrying a clean, fringed towel over his shoulder. They took the shoe and stocking from the right foot. One old fellow, Concepcion's friend, the beggar at the cathedral door, was so infirm that he could scarcely untie his shoe. He persisted bravely, though, and to him Torquemada, who assisted the Archbishop, first presented the silver basin. The pauper placed his foot in it, Torquemada poured water from a silver flagon; the old Archbishop, kneeling, kissed the beggar's foot.

"Isn't it a pleasant ceremony?" said Pemberton. "Poor old chaps, no wonder they look so proud. To-day they have dined with the Archbishop in his palace, and those fine new clothes are their very own for keeps."

The service was followed by the singing of the *tenebrae*. It was growing dark in the cathedral; all the light and color were concentrated in the *coro*, glowing like a live jewel in the centre of the shadowy church. An aged crone, a battered derelict on life's stream, drifted by, touching here and there at altar and at shrine, as at so many friendly ports. She came to anchor before our Lady of Good Counsel, and took out her rosary. At every *pater noster* she kissed her beads. Those pathetic, mumbling old lips must have had sore need of something to kiss. She pressed them over and over again on the cold glass that covered a little chromo of Our Lady of Good Counsel, set conveniently low in the wall, for the kisses of the forlorn old lips that missed perhaps the warm cheeks of child or grandchild. Outside the *coro*, below the black veil that hung before the altar, stood the vast bronze *tenebrium*, with its fifteen great candles. An acolyte with a long torch kindled the candles, and the first lamentation rang through the cathedral. One by one, as each pitiful lament commemorating the suffering and death of Christ trailed into silence, a candle was extinguished, till the fourteen symbolical of the apostles were all put out. It grew darker and darker; at last only the taper at the top remained alight in memory of Christ, the unquenchable light of the world.

Later that evening we returned to the cathedral for the miserere. The Calle de Sierpes was filled with a holiday crowd. In the balconies outside the cafés, at the street corners, were groups of young and old, little children, graybeards, and grandams; during Holy Week it seemed that nobody in Seville went to bed.

"*El Liberal!*" A newsboy offered the sheet, wet from the press.

"*Agua, agua fresca!*" The grave water seller followed close on his heels.

"*Dos por uno perro chico*," cried a correct old man, with beautifully curled silver hair and beard, selling shoe laces. A woman who looked like a caryatid, with a basket of royal purple flags on her head, bought a pair of laces. A young girl with a dimple, carrying her boots in one hand and two large dried codfish in the other, accidentally jostled me. The caryatid, evidently her mother, cried, "*Cuidada!*" rather sharply.

"*Dispense V.,*" said the dimple, blushing and distressed at the mischance.

"*Manos blancas no ofendan*" (white hands never hurt), said Pemberton.

"What good manners these people have!" I said, as we passed on, leaving the girl still under the shadow of the caryatid's displeasure.

"The finest manners in the world," Pemberton agreed.

In the cathedral flickering torches shone on a vast congregation met to hear Eslava's miserere: matadors, gypsies, nuns, babies, beggars, beauties of court and theatre. Every girl in a mantilla looked a heroine, every lad with a straight back, a hero, in that witchery of light and shadow. From our places neither orchestra nor musicians were in sight, only solemn columns, long aisles, and twinkling lamps before pictured Nativity and Pietá. Two votive candles were burning before Santa Teresa, showing the wax ex-votos of little hands, legs, and feet, hanging from long braids of hair around the shrine. Near the *puerta mayor* a blaze of glory shone from the white and gold monument over the tomb of Ferdinand Columbus, where the Host had been that morning deposited to remain till the first mass on Saturday morning, surrounded by kneeling monks.

"I fancy," said Pemberton, "that here, in the cathedral where he was chapel master, Eslava planned his miserere,—caught, while he sat dreaming at the organ, the divine harmonies it repeats."

The twin organs called and answered each other, the deep notes thrilled and thundered through the aisles. The clear boy voices scaled the heights of song; the mellow altos held the middle ground, the deep basses welded voices, organs, instruments, into a full glorious harmony that swept the soul. The miserere over, one by one the great *pasos* of the afternoon's procession, taking on a new and awful beauty in the dim cathedral, swung slowly down the aisle, halting at the monument on the way to their several stations.

"This seems to link Columbus with the *fiestas*," said Pemberton, "and makes me feel that I, too, have some part in them,—he is so much more ours than theirs!"

As we came down the steps of the cathedral, we passed the knife grinder of La Mancha. He had taken off his apron, and left his pipe and wheel at home. As he strolled along under the burning stars, he hummed a snatch of the music we had just heard, and hummed it correctly.

"Rich and poor, vagrant and King, there is room for us all in the Heart of Seville," sighed Pemberton.

Good Friday

That night the King slept in the old palace of the Alcazar. Did he sleep? In the gardens the nightingales were singing to split their throats; palms and orange trees rustled, fountains whispered of things that might well keep a lover awake. Here in the old palace of the Moorish kings lived the beautiful Maria del Padilla, beloved of Pedro the Cruel. Here died the royal Moor, Abu Said, murdered by his host, Don Pedro, for his jewels. The rarest, the great spinel ruby, Pedro gave to Edward, the Black Prince. Henry V wore it in his helmet at Agincourt,—to-day it glows in the front of England's royal crown. England, always England! How often, for good or evil, the fates of the reigning houses of Spain and England have intertwined!

"Ena," sang the nightingales; "Ena," rippled the fountain,—for the King was a lover. If he slept that night it must have been to dream of the yellow hair and the blue eyes of the English princess who, one happy day, shall wander with him through the mazes, gather the roses of that matchless garden of the Alcazar.

There was serious business for Don Alfonzo that Good Friday morning. As he came down to the patio (passing the splendid chamber where Maria de Padilla bathed, and where Don Pedro's courtiers showed their gallantry by drinking the water of her bath), the drums and fifes of his halberdiers sounded the royal march. Lopez Ballesteros, the Governor, was waiting; with him, Garcia Pierto, Minister of Grace and Justice. Preceded by the halberdiers, followed by the Court, they all set off together for the cathedral. The way was lined by soldiers with furled flags. In the *capilla mayor* a throne had been placed for the King; here he sat with his grandees and generals (one of them called Pacheco, a descendant, perhaps, of the old painter, writer, and familiar of the Inquisition, who taught Velasquez), and listened to the singing of the Passion. The great Crucifix of Montañes was then uncovered, and the royal party moved to the *coro*, where the King performed the act of adoration, and made his offering of an ounce of gold.

At the act of adoration, Don Alfonzo was confronted by his Minister of Justice, carrying a basketful of parchment scrolls, each tied with a black ribbon.

"Señor," said the Minister, "do you pardon the condemned felons whose names are written here?"

"I pardon them, that God may pardon me," answered the King. One by one he untied the black ribbons and retied the scrolls with white silk cord.

The wild woman with the bruised face the Archbishop had comforted that day in the street, had forced herself as near the front as the guard allowed. She peered between two halberdiers, watching the ceremony with desperate eyes. Was the name she loved among the fourteen names of felons condemned to death, written on those white decrees of pardon?

"Did you ever," asked Pemberton, "see a ceremony so touching, so human, in the dead cathedrals of England, or even in St. Peter's?"

PORTRAIT OF VELASQUEZ, BY PORTRAIT OF THE ARTIST'S
HIMSELF. WIFE. *Velasquez*

We left by the Door of the Lizard, passing under the big stuffed crocodile that gives the name.

"See that horrid beast!" said Concepcion. "A present from the Sultan of Turkey to Alonzo el Savio, whose daughter he wished to marry. I think our Don Alfonzo will take nicer presents when he starts for England to-morrow."

I asked if the people were pleased with the proposed marriage.

"Mad about it," said Pemberton. "The Princess Ena will have a warm welcome; may she bring as good luck as Elenor Plantagenet brought, when she came to marry Alfonzo III of Castille. Their daughter Berenguela (she was a rare one), joined Leon and Castille, and practically laid the foundation of United Spain. Look for the woman, you know, and you will find her at the bottom of most things practical!"

On the borderland of sleep that night, I was overtaken and called back to earth by the wail of Eslava's dirge. I sprang up and ran to the balcony to watch the passing of a midnight procession. It was very late, the air was chill, the stars pale, the *calle* deserted, save for the *penitentes* and *Nazerenos* (*hidalgos* all) in white gowns, black antefaces, and scapularies. On the first *paso* stood the Virgin of Solitude, who, by rule of the order, may only be absent from the church of San Lorenzo for the two hours after midnight on Good Friday. The second *paso* represented Calvary. The body of the Christ nailed to the cross shone pale and ghastly in the torchlight; the footsteps of the masked men sounded like muffled drums in the funeral march. Before the Christ walked a female penitent representing Santa

Veronica: her hair fell over her shoulders in a dark flood. She carried in extended hands the handkerchief, whereon, the legend says, the Master dried his face on his way through the Street of Sorrows, leaving the impress of His features on the linen. A second penitent followed the cross, a young woman all in white, who personified Mary Magdalen, carrying a box of ointment. There was something familiar about this Magdalen. As she passed, a rose fell from a balcony, catching in her curls. She looked up; could it be Concepcion, walking so painfully with bare feet over the rough cobbles?

Sabbado de Gloria

"*Vayan Vds. con Dios*," said the beggar at the cathedral door, lifting the heavy leather curtain for us.

The black veil still hung before the altar, the bells had not yet spoken. Life seemed at a standstill. There was no present, only the momentous past, in the Heart of Seville that bright Saturday of Glory. In the *coro* a pair of stooping, weedy old men—twin brothers—with ancient bassoons under their arms, several violins, flutes, and bass viols, added their music to the voices of the choir. There was an acute sense of waiting, of holding the breath in anticipation of some great event. Concepcion was very silent. There were dark rings under her dovelike eyes. In a moment all was changed. The bells of the Giralda burst out in sudden clamor. Thunder once again rolled through the cathedral, the black veil parted and fell to the ground, revealing the *retablo* of Dancart. In this wonderful altar-piece the sculptor has carved in larchwood the story of the life whose last hours on earth Seville has been living over again during the last three days! It is all here, told once again in faithful, loving art. Instead of wandering from chapel to shrine to read it pictured in marble, wood, color, miniature, and fine needlework,—an Annunciation here, a Nativity there, it is all here in the *retablo* illustrated by a series of marvellous wood carvings. Concepcion studied them with me, pointing out her favorite panels.

"Behold the blessed Saint Anne, the grandmother of God, San José, husband of Nuestra Señora. These be Peter and Paul,—two of our saints."

"They are saints of us all," Pemberton interrupted, "Christians as well as Catholics. Peter and Paul pray for us all!"

Concepcion was glad of that. "You asked," she said, confidentially to me, "something of the blessed saints. At the convent where I was educated, they have a great reverence for San José. Last year the nuns were in much need of a house in the country where they might go in summer. So they tied a little house around the neck of the statue of San José. Well, what do you think? Last August a lady died and left the convent her country house.

Would you believe it? The house is exactly like the little house the sisters tied about San José's neck. The other day, being in great need of a pig, they tied a small pig about the saint's neck. That prayer has not been answered, but the sisters are sure that they will have their pig before the month of Mary is over."

"Prophecies sometimes fulfill themselves," said Pemberton. "What Concepcion tells you is perfectly true; I know the house; it is just possible some one in the convent knew it, too. Do not say so to Concepcion. If she had not 'taken up' with me, she might, some day, have been the prioress of that convent."

Domingo de la Resurrecion

There was little sleep in Seville the night of Sabbado de Gloria! The streets were crowded, the music and the laughter only stopping when the Easter bells began to ring. Under our windows three boys squatted on the ground playing at cards and rattling dice. They were "flush of cash"; *perro chicos* and *grandes* clinked as they changed hands.

"*Cacahuete!*" cried the peanut man. The largest cardplayer bought a double handful of nuts, dividing them fairly with the other two.

"*Eá! los altramuzes!*" The seller of lupins, a peasant in a brown capa, stopped at the hail. After some haggling, the second sized boy laid in a stock of the large green lupin beans the people eat at all odd times of day and night. The *chicos* munched their lupins, spat, and munched again, their game of *brisca* going cheerfully on, not without some discussion. The smallest lad, he who wore a working blouse and a blue cap, won heavily. At the end of the hand he scooped the coppers into his pocket, scrambled to his feet and strolled jauntily away singing:

"*En los sopas y amores los primeros son los mejores*" (with soups and with loves, the first are the best).

"*Vengo sofocado!*" (I suffocate with rage) cried the big boy who had lost most. "*Maldita sia tu estampa!*" (accursed be thy beastly portrait).

Was he mean enough to draw out of the game when he was winning? The winner crossed the street, loitered outside a sweets shop opposite, flattened his snub nose against the pane, and gazed at the goodies. At last he entered the shop, reappearing with a paper bag full of sweets of Jijona, cakes of almond paste and honey. The cakes were shared equally, the big boy shuffled the cards, the little one "shook" for deal, and the interrupted game of *brisca* began again.

Let into the wall of the corner house was a shrine with a lamp before it. The light fell on the face of a pretty girl behind the iron bars of the lower window. She was talking eagerly with a soldier standing outside in the street, a lover, plucking the hen turkey, as the saying goes.

Easter morning we went to the cathedral by the sacristy, filled with kneeling women in black mantillas. A long line of penitents waited outside each confessional: as we came in, Torquemada slipped into the one nearest the door. At the altar rail knelt a row of communicants. An old priest and a young server walked up and down the ever recruited line, administering the communion. The server carried a lighted candle, the priest a gold chalice with the wafer. At each communicant they stopped, the priest took a wafer from the ciborium, made the sign of the cross, and placed it in the mouth of the person before him.

"See how quiet all this is," said Pemberton; "and this is the real thing! Now for the cathedral, the stage of the church, the last act of the drama. Nowhere in the world can you see so splendid a mass as you will see to-day."

Archpriests and priests were glorious in priceless embroidered vestments. Boys and acolytes must have been chosen for their beauty. The little fellows were like cherubs; the elder lads, like angels. The boys stood in groups of three, the candles burned in threes; the *retablo* was lighted by trios of candles,—the mystic number was repeated at every point. On the lower altar steps stood the scarlet and ivory altar boys, each holding a mighty silver candlestick, so tall that the base of the candle stood at the height of the shoulder, and the winged silver angel supporting the taper rose far above the head. From every spire of the great *retablo* sprang a crucifix, the highest towering up in to the dim roof. Under this crucifix was a painted, wooden group of Virgin and Child. Directly below, in a straight line, one behind the other, stood the three celebrants in their Easter splendor. At one side blazed the vast paschal candle.

"It is of the most fine wax," Concepcion whispered, "and of the weight of twelve kilos."

At the moment of the elevation, two stiff, gawky tourists, Germans, I think, stood by, guidebook in hand, staring at the ceremony with no pretence of being anything but spectators.

The Archbishop held up the wafer in his transparent old hands; thick clouds of incense rose; at every tinkle of the golden mass bells, Concepcion, kneeling beside me, crouched lower. A young deacon in a white robe motioned the outlanders to kneel. They paid no attention; he approached and whispered what he had said in pantomime; again they refused. Then, like a young archangel, he drove them from the place with his silver staff. They shrugged stiff, protesting shoulders, and moved on.

Mass over, a procession formed. Two cherubs walking backwards, held open the illuminated missal for the Archbishop to read the prayers; followed Torquemada and the other priests, the old canons from the *coro*, the choristers, their long goffered white sleeves folded over their arms, their black letter scores held between them, singing as they walked, to the bassoon accompaniment of those two old weedy brothers. Near a gigantic, faded fresco of Saint Christopher, the ferryman with the Niño Jesus on his arm, they stopped beside the tomb of Columbus, a brand new bronze monument in the aisle that makes the right arm of the cross—a place of high honor. Here the first prayer was recited. We waited by the tomb, watched the procession with the glittering cross, the lights, the incense, the booming bassoons, move slowly down the aisle, stopping at one and another of the chapels.

"As a work of art that monument is simply impossible," said Pemberton; "humanly, it means something. You catch the idea? Those four kings in armor stand for Castille, Leon, Arragon, and Granada. In that sarcophagus they bear on their shoulders lies what is left of the dust of Columbus."

A vision of life's morning came back to me! The cathedral at Santo Domingo City on Easter day; my father, my mother, and myself standing by the place in the worn brick pavements that then covered the dust of the Great Admiral. There had been a mass, with incense and candles, and splendid priests, that Easter in Hispaniola, and we had watched, in the plaza before the cathedral, Judas burned in effigy!

"Columbus was born to wander!" said Pemberton. "Even his poor bones have no rest. From Valladolid, where he died, they were taken to Seville; from Seville to Santo Domingo; from Santo Domingo to Havana; from there,—read the inscription, that tells the story.

"Quando la ingrata America se emancipe de la madre España, Sevilla obtuvo el deposito de los restos de Colon y su ayutamiente eligio este monumento."

"The sculptor was a poor artist and a good Spaniard," said Pemberton. "In spite of the thing's being so baroque, taken with the inscription, and the date, 1901, it is moving; it expresses the pride and humiliation of this brave people who won the new world only to lose it. I tell my friends here that the loss of Cuba and the Philippines was the dawn of a renaissance, the beginning of a new Spain. It was cutting back the vine that had gone to wood. Now the sap runs, there is new life, fresh growth. Knockdown blows are what men and nations need to get up their muscle. He said it,—your father: 'Obstacles are things to be overcome!'"

The pigeons fluttered in and out of the Giralda, careless of the great bells swinging to and fro, and the shadow of their wings wove a new pattern on the face of the roseate tower.

"Christ is risen!" The bells rang out the triumphant pean. A shadow larger than that cast by a dove's wing passed over the face of the Giralda.

"Take Concepcion home with you," said Pemberton, quickly, in English; "she did not see it. Do not, if you can help it, tell her." He led the way to a side street, made some excuse to his wife,

THE GIRALDA, SEVILLE.

and left us. We took Concepcion home; an hour later Pemberton joined us.

"There was nothing to do; of course she was quite dead. One leaps to certain death from the top of the Giralda. You remember that woman with the bruised face who spoke to the Archbishop? It was she; *his* name, you see, was not written on one of those decrees of pardon!"

Later in the afternoon, Concepcion appeared, a black chenille dotted mantilla of the old style over her head, a white *manton de mantilla* worked with purple grapes, draped, Andaluz fashion, over her shoulders.

"Are you ready?" she cried. Her eyes flashed, her cool, olive cheeks were flushed. She smiled more than usual, for the mere pleasure, it seemed, of showing teeth that were as matched pearls on a string.

"Are you ready?" she repeated. "*Tengo mucha prisa*" (I am in a great hurry).

"Ready—for what,—where are we going?"

"*A los torros, los torros* (to the bulls)! Did he not tell you? My husband has taken seats for us all *a la sombre*" (in the shade).

So this week of vigil, penitence, and prayer was all a preparation for the Easter bull-fight!

"I have seen Bombito, the matador, ride by on his way to the *corrida*," said Concepcion, "it is time, *vamonos a la calle!*"

There was a disappointment in store for Concepcion; she was met at the entrance with the announcement, "No bull-fight to-day on account of the picadors' strike."

V

SEVILLE FAIR

THE   Guadalquiver was a swollen, tawny flood, whirling dead leaves and dry branches down to the sea.

"Look," said Pemberton, "the river has piled enough firewood against the piers of Triana bridge to keep a thrifty family a month." A small boat, sculled by an old fisherman with gold earrings and a blue jersey, crept slowly towards the largest pile of brushwood at the middle pier. "I'm glad Isidro comes in for that bit of luck; he is a good sort, brings us fish every fast day, and doesn't know I have a *bula de cruzada* and may eat meat o' Fridays. We shall see him at the house soon; when the river is at the flood we sometimes get shad,—an advantage of living in Seville."

As he roped the driftwood to the stern, the old fellow sang in a high, quavering voice a popular *copla*:

"Antiquamente eran dulces todas las aguas del mar;
se baño mi amor en ellas y se volvieron salas."

(Once on a time all the waters of the sea were sweet;
My love bathed in them and they turned salt.)

Other women are praised as sweet, the Andaluz as salt! Andalusian salt is the supreme quality, wit, sparkle, humor, grace combined.

A white yacht, a fine lady of the sea, lay alongside the river bank near the Paseo de las Delicias. Sailors were busy polishing brass that shone before, scrubbing decks already clean as starched damask. A blond viking sitting aft, mending a sail, sang a stave that told where he and the yacht *Peerless* hailed from.

"I wish I was in Baltimore, O, O, O, O,
A dancing on the sanded floor a long time ago!"

By the Torre del Oro, the *Buenaventura*, from Malaga, a rusty freight steamer, was taking on cargo. The stevedores, like busy brown ants, trotted to and fro, stooping under bales of cotton from the Isla Mayor in the delta. The mole smelt tarry and sea-faring; looked prosperous, bustling, alive. Watching sailors, stevedores, longshoremen, we tried to visualize our emotions, but alas, the set pieces of sentimental fireworks, prepared beforehand, wouldn't go off! We reminded ourselves that here, in this port of Seville, the Tribunal of the Indies, the whole trade of the Americas once centred. From the shadow of that old Moorish tower of gold, the Spanish galleons sailed for the new world, carrying the yeast and ferment of young adventurous blood, bringing back—a poor exchange—the ingots of the Incas. Alas! No ghost, not even of Columbus sailing up the Guadalquiver that Palm Sunday of his triumph, could materialize in that vital atmosphere of oozing kegs, fish-nets, and oakum. A swart gypsy dropped a line into the river, a crane flapped across the sky, a fish leaped, flashing silver in the sun; the wonderbook of life was still to read; history and its ghosts must wait for old age and winter fireside.

It had rained for three days and nights, to the discomfort of flocks, herds, dealers, breeders, gypsies, and *compradores*. From Ronda and Utrera in the south, from Huelva in the west, from Aguilar, Lerida, from all over Andalusia, the animals were being driven in for the *Feria*, the great animal fair that follows the *fiestas* of Holy Week.

The thrifty ones, early on the ground, were already settled in the city of tents and cottages, that had sprung up on the Prado de San Sebastian. The laggards fared badly; the downpour had made the roads worse than ever. The inns were crowded, for even those who usually slept, cooked, and ate in their covered carts struggled to get under shelter while that torrential rain lasted. Then, just in time to save the situation, the sun came out.

From the quay we drove along the bank of the Guadalquiver, through orange groves washed clean and smelling of rain, and olive groves where the little, silvery leaves were still dark with the wetting. From a rise in the sodden road we saw the entire horizon, felt the sky like a fiery blue cup overhead; at the edge, where it rested on the earth, there was warm, colorless light; in the middle, deep cobalt. It was impossible, early as it was, to look at the sun; there was not a fleck of cloud anywhere. Though the earth was drying as quickly as sun and soft air could contrive, the middle of the road was still a lake of mud.

"*Arré, arré!* dog of a horse!" the sounds of blows and curses shattered the crystal silence. A brave, blind horse again and again made a mighty effort, stretching its lean neck and straining its poor body to pull a *carreta* out of the muddy rut where the wheels stuck fast. His master encouraged him by striking him over the head; his companion, a starved dog, by snapping at his heels. Pemberton's hand tightened nervously on his whip, as if he would have liked to lay it about the man's ears: Patsy was over the wheel like a flash, and out in the muddy road.

"What a pity, my friend, your wife and children must get out to lighten the load," he said; "it is the only way; I have had great experience in such matters. You help them, while I——" he had the bridle in his hand, and was petting the panting horse as he talked. A gaunt woman suckling an infant sat in the back of the *carreta*; a little girl leaned against one knee, at the other crouched a boy shaking with fever; a raven drooped in a battered cage, near a big drum half hidden by a heap of spangled and velvet rags; a pair of castanets and a tambourine lay in the girl's lap. By these poor possessions, their tools of trade, we knew them for what they were.

"Mountebanks, on their way to the fair," said Pemberton; "poor things, one can hardly hope they will add much to the gaiety of nations!"

"See you later," said Patsy, waving his free hand to us. We drove on and left him haranguing, hectoring, but helping, always helping, that forlorn family of *feriantes* (fairgoers).

After those three last days of Holy Week, when from one end of Seville to the other we never met wagon, carriage, or beast of burden, it came like a surprise to find the streets crowded with all sorts of interesting vehicles. The heavy traffic is carried in big, picturesque carts drawn by bulls, oxen, donkeys, and mules. The cattle are magnificent, especially the bulls, who answer easily to the goad. The backs of these draft animals are shaven in patterns, the work of gypsy *esquiladores*. In the cold weather a blanket covers the shaven part, its limits outlined by a neatly cut border. A monogram, a coat-of-arms, even a sentence describing the owner's virtues, is sometimes shaven on the rump. The yoke is bound to the horns of the cattle, as you see it in the old Greek vase pictures; the beasts pull with the head, all the weight and strain coming on the neck. This has a fine pictorial effect, but is far harder on the creatures than yoking at the shoulders.

An ox cart, with a cruel load of stone, drawn by two patient, cream-colored bulls, lumbered along on archaic solid wheels that shrieked for axle grease. The bulls, strong, beautiful, worthy to draw the car of Dionysius, moved their heads restlessly from side to side. As the cart jounced over a loose cobble, their poor noses trembled with pain. A street porter stood waiting till the cart had passed to cross the road. He carried a heavy load on his back, secured by a strap fastened round the forehead; he trembled, too, and seemed, like the bulls, to be working at great disadvantage.

Pemberton shook his whip at the bulls. "Cowards," he cried, "failures, outcasts of the ring; too timid or too kind to fight,—unworthy the short, merry life of the fighting bull, good for nothing but work!"

A blue cart with ochre stripes creaked by, behind a tandem of four mules led by a white donkey, all jingling with little bells, the harnesses gay with red tags, tassels, and brass nailheads.

"*Firmé, firmé macho!*" The muleteer, a jolly young chap with a proper "going to the fair" look to match his team, cracked his long whip over their heads. A dog tied to the bridle of a tiny donkey, almost hidden by his load of cabbages, cleverly piloted the ass through the crowd; the owner, a stalwart woman laden with vegetables, followed at a distance.

"And some people say animals can't reason!" Pemberton exclaimed. "That dog has got more sense than many men I know. The woman is Costanza, Isidro's wife, who brings us our vegetables every day; that boy tagging behind is Concepcion's godson."

We were now close to the Feria, and the way was crowded with *feriantes* and cattle.

There was a sense of joyous life in the air. Everybody was in holiday humor, as if the sun had dried all tears, driven away blues and vapors, if such exist in golden Seville.

"During the three days of the *Feria*," Pemberton explained, "Seville is deserted; life centres here, in the Prado San Sebastian; trade, business, society are bodily transported from city to fair ground. It's really a democratic festival; a great annual outing for all classes. The morning is the time to see the business end; the evening, the social. We'll begin with the market, where the animals are bought and sold."

At the mule mart business was brisk, handsome carriage mules as well as pack mules changing hands at good prices. To know what a carnation or a mule can be, you must go to Spain, where both grow larger and handsomer than anywhere else. There is a legend of a mule belonging to the first Don Carlos, over fifteen hands high. Theoretically, the mule has the privilege of drawing the royal carriages. Though Don Alfonzo prefers an automobile, the little children of the late Princess of the Asturias take their airing every day behind a spanking four-in-hand of swift, black mules.

Up and down the middle of the Prado San Sebastian rode the jockeys, showing off their horses. A tall, black stallion, with red nostrils, curvetted past. The man on his back—he rode like a centaur, man and beast seeming one piece—had a familiar look; where had we seen that ruddy face, those handsome legs, that striped blanket before? The fretting stallion jostled a white horse ridden by a weather-beaten old trader.

"*Perdone Vd. amigo mio!*" said the young *chalan*, lifting his gray felt sombrero. Then we recognized the Sibyl's friend, the bridegroom of Ronda.

"*No es nada amigo*," answered the man on the white, as politely; the exhibition of good manners was as fine as the horsemanship.

"I will give you twelve thousand *reales* for the black," said a gentleman in a cloak, to the man from Ronda.

"*Caballero*, if I could only afford to make you a gift! Try him, he has the perfect *paso Castellano!*"

"Twelve thousand, not a *real* more."

"*Antes muerto que cansado!*" (He'd die sooner than tire.)

"Twelve thousand, not another maravedi." The bargain was finally struck, *chalan* and *caballero* going off together to bind it.

"The pace of these Andalusian horses," Pemberton pointed out, "is easy as a rocking-chair; there is nothing like it. It comes from their galloping with the fore feet and trotting with the hind. Arabian blood? Ah! there is the mystery of the Cordova breed. Where did they get it? De Soto took out a lot of the stock to America; they ran wild on the western plains: our bronchos are their descendants. Though the build has changed, you recognize the family traits in the American mustang."

The white, a beautiful fiery creature, with floss-silk mane hanging to his knees, a tail that would have swept the ground had it not been knotted up, Patsy was convinced must be an Arabian.

"He looks it," Pemberton "allowed." "The Arab horse, unfortunately, is not what it once was; it has been spoiled—by what, do you think? The Mauser rifle! In the old days a Bedouin's safety depended on his horse's speed; to outride his enemy and the reach of his enemy's spear was his prime need. Then it was a matter of life and death to keep up the breed. The old order changeth, even in the desert. Now, the Bedouins are armed with rifles; no horse can travel as fast as a rifle bullet flies; the Bedouin grows careless, his horse deteriorates. In England, where they're all mad, there's one man mad, or sane enough, to put his heart and his money into trying to save the noble race from extinction, the sort of a thing only a poet like Wilfred Blunt would try to do."

"*Tres, ocho, todos*," from behind a gypsy tent came the staccato cry of the *morra* players. Two men faced each other, throwing out the hand with a quick movement, each crying at the same moment his guess of the total number of fingers shown; a dangerous old game, ending, too often, in a fight.

There was great animation in the pig market; the prices were the highest in years; the demand for sucking pigs was larger than the supply. A magnificent old Mother Grunt, with a litter of black piglets snuggling about her, wore the blue ribbon of the prize winner round her fat neck. The owner, a well-dressed young farmer, stood beside the likely family.

"May I have a photograph of the pig?" I asked.

"The honor is great," said the farmer, "but the photographer lives far from here, and to-morrow I put the earth between us."

"How foolish thou art!" explained a shrewd old farmer, carrying a white lamb in his arms. "It is the little black box of the stranger lady that makes the picture." They all struck attitudes, the kodak snapped, I set the film for the next shot; the farmer wished to look into the kodak where he thought he could see the photograph of the prize pig. The matter was explained to him, and the offer made to send him a photograph when the film should be developed. J. handed him his pencil and note-book, and asked him to write his name and address.

"*Ojalá*, if I only knew how to write!" he sighed. "It is greatly to be lamented. I should value a portrait of my sow; she is without peradventure the finest I have raised. I shall not meet her again, for I have sold her to a *labrador* of Jimena."

"Tell me your name; I will write it in this book, where it will not be forgotten."

"I call myself Basilio, name of baptism, Miquel; name of father——"

"That is not necessary; from what town?"

"Pueblo of birth, Escacena del Campo, Provincia de Huelva."

Finding us interested in live stock, Miquel showed his other animals, and led the way to the roped-in corral, where a bunch of his sheep stood hanging their patient heads, as if shy to find themselves so much admired. The merinos were superb, with fine, silvery fleeces; the horns of the old wether might have inspired the Ionic order! The mere rumor of such splendid creatures would account for the cruise of the Argonauts. As handsome in their way were the small, brown sheep, with black faces and adorable, close-curled, black horns. While Miquel and J. exchanged views on sheep, a seedy, shabby gentleman in shiny clothes and a frayed shirt joined us. He took off his hat with a flourish, and made me a deep bow.

"Missis, I am Renaldo Lopez, ex-ofeecial de marina," he said, in a bass voice, deep as a lion's. "I offré my service to accompany and visit monuments; gib Spanish lessons (spik vero Castellano, no Andalusian) in pupils resident or in professor home, prices moderates." He recited the words as if repeating a lesson. I thanked him, accepted his card, and turned back to handsome Miquel, who was explaining to J. that besides raising the best wool in the province, he was not behind the rest of the world in the matter of wheat; he would dare say his was the best grown within a hundred leagues. If we passed near Escacena del Campo we must stop at his farm. He could show us the sister of the prize pig, whose photograph we *would* remember to send? The poor, shabby-genteel ex-ofeecial de marina, could not believe that Miquel, grower of the best wheat, raiser of the fattest pigs and the finest sheep in the province was more interesting to us than he was! Though he could not read or write, Miquel could carry on civilization's two great basic industries—provide for the clothing and the feeding of man, and do it well! The professor of Castilian clung to us until an appointment was made for a lesson, then he departed, and we wandered off to the refreshment stands.

A group of handsome girls were gathered round a huge cauldron outside a neat booth, from which floated a delicious odor of fried cakes.

"Who's hungry?"

"Everybody!"

"Soledad!" A tall girl in a clean, print dress, a scarlet shawl pinned across her shoulders, a geranium in her coarse black hair, answered Pemberton's call.

"Serve *buñuelos* for all."

I asked Pemberton why he had used the second person instead of the third, in speaking to Soledad—what a name! It means solitude.

"It is the custom. The poorest Spaniard addresses the richest gypsy as 'thou,' on the ground that the Gitano is the inferior race. These people are *buñoleras;* they travel all over Spain from fair to fair, frying these *buñuelos*, a sort of sublimated fritter, their specialty. No one else has the art. I know this family; the women are a good sort; the men,—lazy rascals! Last summer they stole two of my sheep; lassooed them, lifted them clean out of the fold. I traced them to their camp. What do you suppose I found? Instead of my white sheep, two black sheep; they had the stuff all ready, and clapped the creatures in; by the time I got there they were already dyed."

An elderly woman, vigorous, bronzed, with the bold, unwinking eyes of the Romany, stood beside the cauldron making mysterious passes with a long spoon. Soledad waited by her side with a hot dish, and in a twinkling a pile of golden bubbles was before us, light, dry, exquisite as only fritters fried in pure olive oil can be.

"Fried air, with a trifle of pastry around it,

BULL-FIGHTERS. SPANISH GIPSIES.

is not exactly filling at the price," said Pemberton; "let us try some of those *bocas de la isla*, another specialty of the *Feria*." The *bocas* are a sort of shell fish of peculiar shape, tasting rather like a shrimp. Soledad, watching us cautiously taste them, said to reassure us:

"But—they are the most exquisite—what a flavor! They are the claws of lobsters that have been torn off and thrown back into the sea, where they turn into *bocas*!"

"Cocoanuts, dates, *torrones* of Alicante!" a bright-eyed Levantine, smelling trade, hurried up to us. We bought a handful of large dark Tetuan dates, a green cocoanut, a long thin bottle of attar of roses, and—a *torrone*— a paste of blended honey and almonds, that should be reserved for saints, since none others can be good enough to deserve it!

Luncheon over, we took leave of Soledad, and made our way to one of the humbler streets of the *Feria* in search of side shows. There was a choice of attractions, all of them decent. In one tent we saw a tame gorilla and a fat woman; in another a troupe of trained fleas shown off by an Italian. An air from Rigoletto, played by an orchestrion with drums, horns and cymbals drew a crowd of rustics. From a large tent came the twang of a guitar, the crack of castanets. A group of saucy gypsy lasses laid violent hands upon us Gorgios, whose palms, whether or no, they were bound to read.

"Brazen hussies," said Pemberton good-naturedly, buying them off; "a cut below those others, but virtuous,—who doubts it may get a knife thrust in the back!"

Outside the last and poorest amusement tent, we found Patsy's mountebanks. An old carpet was spread on the ground before the tent door; the woman in a spangled, maroon velvet robe, a gilt filet in her faded hair, beat the big drum. The raven, with the aid of the little girl and a pack of cards, was ready to tell fortunes. The man in pink tights balanced cleverly on a rolling ball: the boy stood with outstretched arms, first on the father's shoulders, and then climbed dizzily to his head. The turn ended in a clever somersault.

"*Ollé, ollé!*" the crowd encouraged.

"*Que te hace trabajar?*" cried the mountebank, the clown's strident voice is the same the world over, "*Que te hace trabajar?*" (What makes you work?)

"*El hambre!*" (hunger), answered the pinched child.

"*Tiene razon!*" (he is right), laughed Miquel, the farmer. The crowd applauded; a few coppers rattled in the girl's tambourine.

We came upon Patsy, lost since morning, outside a booth of primitive farming tools. The sickles, the rakes, the spades, shaped properly like spades in a pack of cards, even the hoes, had a certain rustic beauty that woke the Adam in every boy that passed, and made his fingers itch to handle them. Patsy balanced a mighty scythe knowingly, as one who has known the trick of mowing.

"That is just what I want for my picture of 'Time and the Woman,'" said J.; he looked with longing at the scythe.

"Of course, it is the very thing," said Patsy; "it has a lot of character. It doesn't look as if it had been turned out by a machine with a thousand others. Listen to this bell!" He tinkled the clapper of a beaten-copper sheep bell. "What a silver note! One wouldn't mind being wakened by this, when the cows go to pasture at daylight!"

"These juggets," Pemberton led the way to a booth where coarse glazed pottery was displayed, "are nice in color, aren't they?"

"The green and yellow bowls are just the thing to put about the Cornish place for the birds to drink and take their baths from," said Patsy. "Let us have a lot sent home with the scythe and the bell. How you feel the Moorish influence in the design,—you can't get away from *that*, can you? You might as well try to subtract the Norman from the English, as to subtract the Moor from the Spaniard; you come across him every moment, in the manners, in the language—all the words beginning with *al* are Moorish; in the dress,—the mantilla is the survival of the *yashmak*; in the sense of color and design, that flat, blue dish is a thing of beauty and absolutely Moorish in spirit."

"I can't enthuse about it any more than I could about the Alhambra, the Alcazar, or anything else that recalls the presence of those brutes in Spain," interrupted a small, keen-eyed man who had been listening to the talk.

Patsy was the first to recover his speech.

"That is a new point of view and very interesting," he said. "Does all Oriental art affect you so, or only Moorish?"

The little gentleman answered with another question: "You are Protestants?"

We could not deny the fact. The stranger sighed impatiently "Ah well, that explains many things! No traveler who is not a Catholic can understand or appreciate Spain."

"You can enjoy a lot you don't understand." Patsy stood to his guns.

"You miss the history, lose the background of the tapestry," the stranger went on testily. "I am tired of this fool talk about Moorish art; the Mosque of Cordova spoiled by being turned into a Christian church, and all the rest of it. Rubbish! I say it was a good thing to do!" His eyes shone, his cheeks burned, he held up a hand enforcing attention. "Listen to what I tell you,—Hell is not too hot, nor eternity too long to punish the sins of the Moors against the Christians of Spain."

"Do you know where you are standing?" Pemberton struck the earth with his heel as he said it. "This is the old *quemadero*, the burning-ground of the Inquisition. On this spot two thousand persons, many of them Moors, were tortured and burned alive in one year. Is there any circle in your Inferno for the Grand Inquisitors?"

"What is the use of remembering such disagreeable things? They are much better forgotten!" cried the stranger, irritably. "I took you for persons of more sense!" and he went off in a huff.

"I wish he had liked us better, I liked him so much," murmured Patsy. "It's the first rule of travel, isn't it?—talk with people you would not be likely to know at home, and learn their creeds."

"The second rule," said Pemberton, "is, visit different epochs as well as different countries. I have visited in the Middle Ages, the Dark Ages, the Ages of Stone and of Iron; only the Golden Age I have not found. Seville comes nearest to it! Follow the old trade routes, go where the bagmen go, make friends with traders and drummers. The gods of Greece came into Rome in the chapman's pack. Avoid, on your life, the smug hotels, the tourist tickets that make the great pleasure route of the world so comfortable, so safe, so dull. Take the checker and chance of travel. There is as much adventure left in the world as is good for a man, if he will take a risk or two!"

"The third rule is, buy no thing; spend all your money on impressions; they will be good as new when mementos are lost, stolen, or in the dust bin!"

"The fourth rule," said J., "is go slow. Yesterday three hundred tourists saw Seville in four hours. They were driven all over the place in batches, each man and woman of them tagged with the card of the hotel where they were billeted to dine. The *Liberal* said this morning that it was better to be four hundred years behind the world than to be in such a hurry. I am not sure the *Liberal* is not right."

That afternoon, Concepcion called for us in a smart two-seated cart drawn by fawn-colored mules with silken ears, varnished hoofs, and jingling bells. It was "up to her," Pemberton said, to show us the social end of the *Feria*.

"*Estoy vestida de maya!*" she cried gleefully; "does it please them?"

"How well dressed she is, a preciosity!" Patsy's vocabulary was growing. To be *vestida de maya* means to wear the lovely old Andalusian costume, still good form for *Feria* and bull-fights. Concepcion wore a yellow crape *manton de Manilla* (the fringe was ten inches long) embroidered with butterflies and roses; a white, blond lace mantilla, gold satin skirt with overdress of black net and chenille dots, lace mittens and tiny gold shoes. She carried the sort of fan collectors outside of Spain keep in a glass case,—the sticks of delicately carved mother-of-pearl; the painting, charming, eighteenth century miniature work. The artist had represented the two serious affairs in woman's life: religion,—illustrated by a scene from sacred history, Jerusalem with David standing before Saul; and love-making,—illustrated by an Arcadian vale, where a patched and powdered shepherdess and a silk-stockinged shepherd looked fondly at each other.

Concepcion took us first to the Parque Maria Luisa, once royal property; now a people's pleasure ground, more garden than park, with thickets of camelias, white, red, and pink, and wildernesses of roses climbing over rustic arbors, hiding dead trees, or blooming sedately in well-trimmed beds. We would have lingered in this paradise among the palms and orange trees—from an ilex grove the long, trilling cadence of a nightingale gave warning that the evening service of song was beginning—but Concepcion objected that there was nobody there, and gave the order: "To Las Delicias."

Four lines of carriages moved at a foot pace up and down the wide *paseo*. Groups of horsemen, officers and civilians picked their way through the throng. The promenades on either side were crowded with pedestrians. The defile of beauty was dazzling; the *señoritas* were all smiles and animation, using their eyes to deadly purpose; in Andalusia flirtation is not a lost, even a decadent art. Patsy, wounded on every side, groaned aloud, "I wish I was a Turk, I wish I was the Sultan of Turkey!"

"In his heart, every man is a Turk!"

"Starts so,—some learn that the best of all is to come home from a flower show, and find the single rose in the flower-pot on the window-sill, sweeter than all the rest."

So they gossiped in the carriage, while the mouse-colored mules fretted at the slow pace!

The west end, the fashionable quarter of the toy city of the *Feria*, has neat toy streets, dainty *casetas* like dolls' houses, cafés, and clubs. From Conception's account, it would seem that the Alcalde had merely waved his wand, and from the bare ground of the old *quemadero* the fairy city had sprung complete.

"You hire your *caseta* for the week," Pemberton explained, "and send out what furniture you need from your town house." As it grew dark, garlands of many-colored lights festooned the way; firefly lamps twinkled among the shrubbery, lanterns like great, illuminated fruits bloomed out from the dark trees; it seemed that we were wandering in Aladdin's palace. Between the Moorish arches of the Circole de Labradores we caught a glimpse of a pretty ball-room, where a crowd of waltzers swayed to the music of the Thousand and One Nights. Outside a private *caseta* painted like a Japanese tea house, Patsy halted and stood immovable, till, as one by one the crowd moved on, we edged our way to the front. The *caseta* was open to the street. Across a tiny verandah we saw the charming interior. An elderly, bald gentleman sat at a piano playing the letter air from La Perichole. In a corner a group of ladies talked together; a little girl in white came and hung over the piano, watching the musician's fingers.

A tall young officer with a roving blue eye and gold hair lying in crisp little curls on an ivory forehead, stood leaning against the wall, talking with a small, dark youth with a hawk nose, and black, impenetrable eyes where the fire smouldered but did not flash.

"That good-looking boy is Martin O'Shea," said Pemberton; "Irish— need you ask? The family has been settled here a hundred, perhaps three hundred years; his eye has not lost the Celtic light, or his tongue the edge. The other is Benamiel, Moorish descent, of course; they're both dangling after a certain girl, a friend of Concepcion's. Oh! that is part of the fascination of this wonderful, aloof, old Spain; you can trace the races here so clearly; somehow the strains don't seem to have become so blurred, so mixed, as in most parts of Europe."

The two young men cast impatient looks at a curtained door at the back. "*Pronto*," the signal came from the inner room. The music changed to a throbbing *seguidilla*, the curtain trembled, and out tripped two pretty girls *vestida de maya*.

"Do you see who it is?" whispered Patsy.

The taller was Luz, the other could only be her sister. Their castanets clicked, almost as naturally as fingers snap, as they took the first pose of the dance. One foot advanced, the other behind supporting the weight of the body; the right arm raised, the left extended, just as you see it in the dancing faun of Herculaneum. O'Shea took down a guitar from the peg where it hung, and swept the chords with that curious ringing touch of the Spaniard; Benamiel marked time by beating with his feet, clapping with his hands. The dance began. It was very graceful, above all very expressive, that was the great quality; it seemed the natural, spontaneous expression of those two lovely young creatures' joy in life, of their super-abundant vitality, of the young blood coursing through their veins. Though every posture, each bold advance and timid retreat was old as Egypt, the dance had all the beautiful freshness of a primitive art.

"*Viva la gracia!*" The cry came from a man in the crowd, Miquel, the farmer of Huelva.

"Good work for amateurs," said Pemberton, "but wait till you've seen the Imperio, then you will have an idea of what Spanish dancing is!"

"Why," Patsy asked, "doesn't that other girl dance?"

"Just because she is not a girl; she was married two years ago. It would not be good form; she has had her turn, now she must take a back seat and give the others a chance. Thank God we're still at that stage of social development." The young woman, a small *morena* (brunette) with a skin like a creamy magnolia blossom just beginning to turn brown, was very little older, and quite as pretty as the twin dancing stars; her foot tapped the floor, while her sisters danced and she sat talking with the elders.

"I think this could not happen outside of Spain, the most democratic of all countries," Pemberton went on. "Here every man is equal, not merely in the law's eye, but—what's far more important—in his own eyes, and proves it by allowing no other man to show better manners than he. These girls, the fine flower of Seville, may safely take their part, add their beauty and their grace as the crowning attraction of the *Feria*, because the man in the street will be as polite to them as the gentleman in the drawing-room."

"*Bendita sea la madre que ti pario,*" blessed be the mother that bore thee. It was Miquel's parting compliment to the señoritas, as he made his way out of the crowd. In the *caseta* visitors came and went; Luz was surrounded by admirers. An old man servant handed a tray with *agraz*, a drink made of pounded unripe grapes, clarified sugar and water, and *bolardos*, little sugar cakes to dissolve in this nectar of Andalusia. The *seguidilla* was followed by a *sevilliana*. When the buoyant feet seemed tired O'Shea sang *copla* after *copla*: the last he might have learned from his mother. It is at least as old as he:

"*Dos besos tengo en el alma*	Two kisses I have in my soul
que no se apartan de mi;	That will not part from me;
el ultimo de mi madre,	The last my mother gave me,
y el primero que te di."	And the first that I gave thee.

VI

A HOUSE IN SEVILLE

RODRIGO   , Pemberton's son, a grave child with eyes of brown fire, met us at the gate of the patio; by his side stood a white lamb, with a wreath of yellow primroses round its neck.

"You recognize the fleece of Huelva?" said Pemberton, "this is one of Miquel's flock; every child must have its pet lamb at Easter, you know." He opened the ancient iron gate,—the bars were lilies, tenderly wrought as if of a more precious metal,—and we passed through the *Zaguan* (vestibule) into the patio paved with marble, surrounded on all four sides by a corridor like a cloister. Behind the Moorish columns, graceful as palm trees, were walls lined with *azulejos*, blue, green, yellow glazed tiles of fascinating design, bewildering color. In the middle of the patio a jet of water leapt from an urn, danced in the sun, broke into a shower of living diamonds, fell laughing to a marble basin.

"In summer we practically live in this patio, that long bamboo chair is my favorite place. I lie there and read, or puzzle out the designs on those tiles,—they're over a hundred,—and listen to the fountain and the birds. What more does a man want in hot weather? Take care, Rodrigo, don't drown him!"

The child was trying to make the lamb drink; the gold fish darted from side to side in fright as its pink nose ruffled the water.

"We're still living up-stairs; by Corpus Christi we shall have *embajado*, as they say here. That means, moved down-stairs. It's the universal custom—the poorest house in Seville has two stories, the upper for cold weather, the lower for hot; you can't fancy the difference in the climate. When moving day comes, the awning is drawn over the patio, we bring all the furniture from the upper to the lower rooms—exactly the same size and shape, so everything fits—hang pictures and mirrors in the corridor; put the piano here, the plants from the terrace there between the columns. We'll have a look at the summer quarters, if you like; it may give you some idea of how we live in Seville in hot weather."

We followed him through large, dark rooms, high-ceiled and airy; caught glimpses of a mighty marble bath in a cool green chamber, of a kitchen where they cook with charcoal, and finally halted in a place mysterious as an alchemist's laboratory. There were cauldrons of beaten copper, measures for wet and dry, an antique balance with brass weights, strange glass vessels, a press, an old still. As we stood admiring a huge marble mortar, Concepcion came into the laboratory. She wore a short white dress and apron, and, on her chatelaine, a bunch of big keys.

"Always on time!" Pemberton exclaimed. "At half past nine every morning Concepcion unlocks the *despensa*, and gives out whatever is needed for the day."

"The grapes for the *agraz* are pounded in that mortar," said Concepcion, who saw I was interested in the strange vessels, "and those big stone rollers are used for crushing and grinding the chocolate."

"Do you remember how good the smell of chocolate is, when they are making you a cup at home?" said Pemberton. "Imagine what it must be to have the whole house filled with it! Ah! the making of the chocolate is an important event. Rodrigo and I are always impatient for it to begin."

"When the time has come to make the chocolate," Concepcion went on, "the cacao is bought. It comes in great sacks,—the best from the Havana, cinnamon from Ceylon—being sure it is the most fresh—sugar the finest, and supreme vanilla. When all is ready, we call the *chocolateros*, two good men, who make the chocolate under my direction, according to a family recipe. When it all is finished, it is poured out into those large troughs to cool. Then it is cut in squares; each large square is just big enough to make a cup of chocolate for grown-up people; and the little squares to make the children's chocolate. When hard, it is put away on these shelves; as the cupboard is airy it keeps itself for a year." When she learned that some housekeepers bought their chocolate ready made, Concepcion was scandalized. "It will be mixed with flour of chestnuts, or other inferior things; there is no chocolate like the Andalusian!" she declared.

In the *despensa*, a cool, stone grotto, hams, sausages, dried herbs, onions, and scarlet peppers hung from the roof; a dozen bloated goatskins leant against the wall.

"The oil," Pemberton explained, "was brought in from the farm on mule-back this morning. When it settles, we shall draw it off in those *amphoræ*," he pointed to a row of two-handled, red clay jars. "Those *tarros* are full of pork,—we killed a hundred pigs last November. The best of the meat is sent in town to us, the rest is kept at the farm for our work people; we feed our laborers in Andalusia, you know, and feed them well."

Concepcion told us that she herself always gave out the day's provisions; this was important, else disastrous things might happen. She stood by and saw cook take the pork from the *tarro*, where it was packed in the "butter of pig," or the game from the smaller barrels. These lower ones were full of the partridges Pemberton shot last season; some days he got a dozen, some days twenty. Those that were not eaten or given away were slightly boiled and packed in the butter of pig. They would keep six months if great care were used in taking them out, and only the wooden spoon touched the pig butter. If, as had happened, a careless servant puts in her hand to take out a partridge or a bit of pork, the whole *tarro* is lost; nothing can save it from going bad. The same is true of olives, put up in those tall *tinajas*. Once a human hand,—a metal spoon is almost as bad,—is dipped into that home-made pickle of vinegar, water, lemon, salt, and laurel leaves, the whole *tinaja* is ruined.

"These nice comfortable-looking round jars are made especially to hold Manchegan cheeses," said Pemberton. "They're like Parmesan, only better, made of sheep and goats' milk mixed. Once a year they bring them from La Mancha to sell; we always lay in a large stock; packed in those jars, with enough oil poured in to cover them, they keep indefinitely. Here is the cook. The momentous council of the day is about to open. Come, I'll show you the rest of the house, while Concepcion gives the orders. We'll have a look at the roses first."

Behind the patio was a second court, with orange and lemon trees; at one end grew an ancient cedar with hollow trunk and strange roots, like splay feet, that gripped the earth. A whiff of orange blossoms, the tinkle of a guitar, the voice of an unseen singer chanting a low wailing *malageña* greeted us as we entered. The walls were a living glory of roses; the yellow Bankshires hung in starry bunches; the white rose vines flung out floating banners of green, thick sprinkled with rose snow. A golden pheasant strutted and preened itself in the sun; from an aviary came the chatter of a happy family of birds.

"*Hijo de mi alma*," Pemberton said to Rodrigo, "you may not take the lamb up-stairs; stay with him till we come down."

Rodrigo, nothing disappointed, drew out a little cart, and seating himself in it turned the wheels so that the cart slid along the stone path in the middle of the garden, the lamb trotting beside; back and forth, back and forth, we heard the rattling of those wheels (I can hear them still) as the lonely boy and the lamb played together.

"Did you ever see a game of football?" Patsy asked the child. Rodrigo had only seen pictures of football, but he had seen *pelota*, and he could hit the bull's-eye with his arrow three times out of five.

"Rodrigo is a Spaniard; he is going into the army," Pemberton said, as he led the way up-stairs to the winter quarters. "My grandmother was a

Spaniard; my parents called themselves 'cosmopolitans'; some other people called them disgruntled Americans. I'm a man without a country,—one of that kind is enough in a family!"

He flared up with sudden passion. To make a diversion J. complimented him on the winter parlor, a bare, comfortable room with a few good pictures, the necessary furniture and a refreshing absence of junk.

"No little tables of jointed silver fish and jade idols here?" he said. "We're still half Orientals in Seville; we don't suffer from the dreadful 'too much' that is stifling you in America!"

The winter kitchen, all white marble and tiles, had a gas range, the most modern thing in the house, and deal tables scrubbed with soap and sand till you saw the grain of the wood. Something was said about the exquisite neatness of the house.

"Andalusians," Pemberton assured us, "are remarkably clean people. Did you notice our *calle*? You don't often see a street so well kept. Each householder is obliged to take care of the part before his house; competition is a good principle in street cleaning."

The upper corridor, giving access to the winter rooms, was shut in with glass; it led to the *azotea*, a terrace that overhung the court of roses. The flowers here had more sun and air than in the patio; the carnations were as big as coffee cups, the damask roses as large as saucers. A second flight of stairs led up to the winter bed and dressing-rooms.

"These mattresses are of carded wool," said Pemberton; "the blankets,—feel how light and soft they are,—were made at the farm, spun and woven by an old woman, the last survivor of my grandmother's servants. These sheepskins are spread under the mattresses for warmth, for tiled floors are cold. The fleece is of three years' growth; see, it is as fine as silk."

Laundry, drying-room, and terrace for bleaching and airing, were at the top of the house. The keen smell of good gum camphor met us on the stair; it came from a brass-bound cedar chest, standing open on the terrace. A dozen of Concepcion's feather fans dangled from a line.

"Now that you've seen the house in Seville God has given me," said Pemberton, "look at the view; it's the best thing about it!"

Below us lay the city with its narrow *calles*, sunny plazas, shining houses. In every patio, on every terrace and roof garden were flowers and caged birds. The air was musical with bells, song, laughter. Outside the old Roman city walls, spread the green Andalusian *vega*, with the yellow river, gleaming, where the sun touched it, like clouded amber. In the distance the *vega* was shut in by a circle of blue Sierras; snow lay on the shoulders of the hills, at whose feet the fruit trees were in blossom.

"Can anybody ever be sad in Seville?" cried Patsy. "Do people ever die or grow old here? Are there such things as tears?"

"There is a young lady down-stairs who must have shed a quart of tears since yesterday," said Pemberton. "Come and help Concepcion comfort her." He led the way down to the drawing-room. Sitting beside Concepcion, whose hand she had been holding, was a pretty girl, wearing a dress much too large for her.

"*Mi amiga*, Señorita Trinidad Fulano," Concepcion introduced her friend, who tried to look as if she had not been crying. Our hostess then bustled out of the room, and returned, followed by a neat maid with a tray of preserved sweet potatoes, some *huevos dulces*, a sort of sweetmeat made of sugar and yolk of egg, a delicate decanter, and a straw basket containing twelve long thin glasses no bigger round than a walking stick.

"A *caña* of manzanilla," said Pemberton, pouring out a clear amber liquid. "It is light for Spanish wine, no headache in it." Patsy, Concepcion and Trinidad were already chattering together like three magpies at the other end of the room. In the solemn silence that accompanied the tasting of the manzanilla, Concepcion's voice rang clear.

"For a woman to call herself beautiful, she must possess the nine essentials of beauty. Three things must she have that be black,—the hair, the eyes, the lashes; three that be red,—the lips, the palms, the cheeks; three that be white,—the hands, the neck, and the teeth."

Trinidad nodded. "*Claro*," she said, "she has expressed it divinely."

"Trinidad could hardly say less," Pemberton observed, "seeing that she herself possesses the nine indispensables. That is a Moorish proverb, though Concepcion learned it from the nuns, like the saying that the *sal a morena* wastes in a minute would last a blonde a week and a half. It is a good thing you came in to-day; Trinidad is cheering up already. She has been tremendously harried—had a visit from an angry parent this morning, and a visit from a despairing lover last night. He stood in the *calle* outside her window, talking with her till past twelve o'clock. You see she's *en deposito* with Concepcion."

At this moment Concepcion glided across the room—she moved with that peculiar poetry of motion of the Spanish woman—and joined us.

"Trinidad is very distinguished, no?" This was always her highest praise. "And intelligent, and instructed; *Ave Maria Purissima!* she can speak three idioms."

"You don't understand what being *en deposito* means," Pemberton went on, ignoring the interruption. "Having lately come of age, that is eighteen in Andalusia, Trinidad made application to a magistrate by means of an official document written and signed by herself stating that she wished to marry José Maria Benamiel; that her parents, with no sufficient reason, forbade the marriage; that——"

"*Pobrecitos!*" broke in Concepcion; "they have been making love these four years. He is a youth the most well-bred, the most distinguished——"

"Yesterday," Pemberton continued, "the magistrate called on Trinidad's father——"

"He came in a carriage," Concepcion reminded him.

"And after a heated interview, took Trinidad away from her father's house and brought her to ours. Here she will stay *en deposito* for three months. During this time, Concepcion is responsible for her. Trinidad is free to see Benamiel, always in the presence of some responsible third person, and her parents are free to visit her. They——"

"They are people the most egotistical, the most *interested!*" Concepcion burst out. "Can you imagine? they denied her clothes, *por Dios!* it is the truth: that is my dress she is wearing! who ever heard of so great a shame? Not one handkerchief allowed those hard-hearted ones their daughter to take away from their accursed house!"

"It is true, they all lost their tempers," said Pemberton lightly, "and behaved foolishly. I fancy we shall see a portmanteau before night; between ourselves, Trinidad might very well have kept on the dress she came away in yesterday. It is not a bad system, the *deposito*; it gives time for both love and anger to cool off. The girl is out of coercion here; she has a chance to make up her mind whether or no Benamiel is really the man for her. At the end of the three months, if she still wants him, she may marry him without her parents' consent."

"Do you think she will?"

"Pretty safe to. The old people will give in; there is nothing really against Benamiel, only they preferred O'Shea! Small blame to them. O'Shea did not know that Trinidad and Benamiel had already settled things between them. When he found it out he went back to Cordova, where he is stationed, and, Trinidad says, wanted to give to Benamiel a bracelet he had bought for her. Nice boy, O'Shea. Why is it that the nice girls always take the wrong—well, there's no use opening that chapter, if you must be going—it is time for your Spanish lesson—we'll tackle it some other time when we have the night before us!"

Don Renaldo, the ex-ofeecial de marina, was waiting to give Patsy and me our lessons in *vero Castellano*. His method was simple; he talked, while we listened. He began by explaining his rusty mourning suit, as he drew off his worn old leather gloves. "It is the thirtieth anniversary of the death of my father," he spoke slowly, so that we might follow him. "All the masses celebrated to-day in the church of San Sebastian will be applied to the repose of his soul." Patsy said he would like to hear one of the memorial masses, but it was already too late, they were all over.

"He was the most kind of fathers, the most benevolent of men, his benevolence was the cause of all his misfortunes in this world! To oblige a friend he signed his name to a note, understanding that it was a mere form. With those two strokes of the pen he signed away his fortune."

"He did not have a benevolent friend!" Patsy ejaculated.

"*Hombré!* He was a *caballero*, a gentleman of distinction—but—it is the truth, of business he was as ignorant as *mi pobre papa*! The catastrophe that ruined both, killed my papa; his friend died soon after of shame. Then Tio Jorge, my rich uncle, took me and brought me up as if I were his heir. Every year we went to Paris together; we lived with great elegance on the Rue de Rivoli; we had a box at the opera; I had my own carriage; my clothes came from Poole; at that time I was very elegant, and not, people said, bad looking. I am old now, but then!" He sighed and rolled up his eyes at the recollection of his elegant youth.

"You're not old, you're in the prime of life," said Patsy. Though Don Renaldo was not even elderly, he had given up the fight, went shabby and unshaven, with buttons missing from his frayed shirt.

"Suddenly Tio Jorge had a stroke of apoplexy,—I was at Monte Carlo at the time. I hurried to his bedside and took all care of him till he died. It was very sad, but it was my duty to see everything done as he would have wished. His funeral was the most luxurious ever seen in Valladolid. He was followed to the grave by the aristocracy, civil and military authorities, and whole communities of monks and nuns. There was a multitude of carriages, and to every coachman I gave a *propina* of fifty *pesetas*. After the funeral the will was opened. Well, what do you think he left me?"

"That depends upon whether or not you were the only heir," Patsy answered soothingly.

"He left me nothing! Money, palace, horses, plate, jewels, everything went to found a home for the widows and daughters of navy officers! the preference always to be given to the handsomest ones. The will was published; there followed ridicule the most painful from half the papers of Europe, from the Argentine, from all over the world. They called Tio Jorge a modern Don Juan Tenorio!"

"The old hunks deserved something worse than to be laughed at. I hope he's getting it now," murmured Patsy.

"May be—but that was not true; he was not an immoral man. He believed that beautiful ladies had greater difficulties to contend with than others."

"He might have left you a life interest," said Patsy; "the beautiful ladies could wait." While Don Renaldo did not allow himself to criticise Tio Jorge, our sympathy was as balm to him.

"I gave up my home, I gave up Paris—where I was too well known. I had frequented the best society. I came to Seville where I have no friends, where many travelers come;" he dropped into English. "I offré my service to accompany and visit monuments, gib lessons, recommend the hotels!"

"Everybody is bothered about money one way or the other;" Patsy tried to encourage him; "as long as you live, you either have got to earn the money you spend, or spend money that other people have earned. Brace up, *Amigo*! Think how much more fun it is to earn your own money than to spend money some other fellow has had the fun of earning!"

Don Renaldo looked steadily at him, groping for his meaning. "At first I envied people who have money," he confessed; "now I envy those who have work that they enjoy." He took up a book Patsy had told him was written by a friend of ours. "Your friend must be a very rich man."

"He just makes the two ends meet without lapping!"

"How could he afford to print this book? The binding is elegant, paper, print and engravings, superior; it must have cost a great deal!"

"So the publishers say."

"*Ojalá!* If I could only write."

Poor, pathetic soul, if he could only do any useful thing. A fortune had been spent on his education. He could ride and shoot straight, he could dance, and fence, and play every game under the sun, but his life investment yielded a small, precarious income. His only dividend-bearing stock, all that stood between him and starvation, was a passable knowledge of the French and English languages, part of the accomplishments of his elegant youth.

The lesson over, Don Renaldo gone, Patsy summed up his case. "A spent shot!" he said, "a poor thing, as capable of taking care of himself as a year old baby; more coals to Tio Jorge!"

One happy day, when we had almost given up hope of ever seeing him again, Don Jaime strolled jauntily into the patio, his sombrero gallantly cocked on one side, his worn coat carefully brushed, his trousers newly creased, a bunch of violets in his buttonhole. He was greeted with shrieks and screams of joy. Black coffee and *un poco de ginevra de campagna* (his only vices) were immediately ordered for him.

"I arrive only at middle night yesterday," he said, when accused of desertion. "I have made a loose, my brother-in-law, he is daid." Patsy asked if it was the husband of his sister who had died.

"Ah, no! brother to my woman. Me, my father, my grandfather were all unique childs; I have no sister—only a half a sister, Candalaria,—no brother, no honkle, no haunt; I am a widow and a horphan." We expressed sympathy for his loss. The Don assured us that his brother-in-law's death was a release.

"Poor man! he was secluded in—how you say? an insanitorium these long years. When he was daid, he had himself embaumed and transported to Cadiz, where is the pantheon of himself and his wife."

"We were just starting to drive to Italica," said J. "You'll go with us, Don? Where's your *capa*? You'll need it; it's cold this afternoon."

"Ah, no! I am warm inside, since I drinked the *ginevra*," he patted his stomach. "Ah well, it is heatier in Sevillia than in Cadiz, where I goed to escort the catafalque of my brother."

After that J. and Patsy took the Don away from me, and all that afternoon they kept him to themselves. I followed in another carriage with Pemberton. Bursts of riotous laughter came to us from their cab, as they passed us on the Alameda of Hercules. At the foot of that pleasant, shady mall, our coachman drew up under a pair of tall, gray granite columns.

"The old columns are from a Roman temple," said Pemberton. "These guardians of the town," he pointed to the battered old statue that stood on either column, "are Hercules the founder, and Julius Cæsar the second founder of Seville. Oh, yes! Hercules was here; he stopped and rested by the river, and founded Seville that time he wandered through the Peninsula, driving the lowing herds of Geyron before him."

We had crossed the tawny Guadalquiver, and were driving through Triano, the potters' suburb, named for the Emperor Trajan. An open doorway gave us a glimpse of a man working a wheel with his feet, and holding a newly moulded clay vase in his hands against the swiftly turning wheel.

"They still make the *azulejos*, and the pottery in Seville, as they did in the days of the Moors—how do I know? In the days of the Romans! Remember, when you come to build your house, that the tiles of Triano are the best, cheapest, and handsomest in the world; that Seville is a port; and that they can be shipped to you at a fair price. Shall we stop at the factory and see them? The place supplies the whole of Spain with crockery. Patsy would fall in love with the big garden pots, and the pretty jugs."

The most interesting thing we saw in the factory was the potter himself. Behind the splendid showrooms, where the fine majolicas and the common wares of the common people are displayed, in a dark, dank little corner, sat a man, half his body out of sight, working the potter's wheel. He sat on the edge of a square hole in the floor; his legs were hidden, but his feet were busy turning, turning the wheel. He was old and poor. His red hands had been in the wet clay who knows how many hours—how many days? He was spiritless and sad in face and bearing, but oh! the skill of those poor red hands! The shapeless lump of soft wet clay was thumped first upon the revolving stand, then as if by magic, though we saw it with our eyes, it took shape, grew lovely and alive under those hands that looked so sodden, and yet could turn that gray mud into shapes of beauty. A cup for a dying man's broth, a vase for a bride's rose, a basin to bathe a new-born child: as each was finished he held it up for a moment for us to see, then laid it down beside him with the others. I put a coin in the red, clayey hand. He gave a little mechanical nod, a word of thanks, and went back to his work. He earns less than an unskilled child would earn at home. It is doubtful if he can read or write. He works from dawn to dark—the sight of him gave me great pangs of homesickness! Pemberton could tell me of no movement to help this man to a freer life, to a day whose working hours do not absorb every heartbeat of power. There is only charity! Bread for the hungry, salve for the sick, almshouse for the worked-out human beast of burden. Oh! that I could help him to pass through the Gate of Hope into the Hospitable Land, where every one has his chance, where the ranks are always open.

Triano was already behind us, and we were out upon the Aracena road that runs to the north. Tramp, tramp, tramp, the sound of marching men came towards us out of a cloud of dust. A little farther on we passed a regiment of small brown soldiers; mere boys, most of them. They all wore sandals; some had stockings, some were without. They must have been on fatiguing work, they looked so tired and footsore. In the fields, a band of peasants were cutting the ruby alfalfa; the air was fragrant with the honey-sweet smell of it. The harsh whetting of scythes, the soft swish of sickles through the clover, the song of the leader of the mowers, an oldish man with a red handkerchief tied round his head, marked the time for the march of those weary soldiers,

Adiós padre, y adiós madre,	Goodbye father and mother;
adiós iglesia del pueblo,	Goodbye church of the village.
que voy á servir al rey	I must go and serve the king
los ochos años que lo debo.	For the eight years that I owe him.

One of the last of the soldiers, a superb blond man towering above the others, repeated the refrain of the mower's song:

"I must go and serve the king for the eight years that I owe him!"

"Nothing has changed since Strabo praised this pleasant valley," said Pemberton. "We still use sickles, and we still take the young men from the work of the fields, and turn them into soldiers, food for gunpowder."

Coming mysteriously towards us, down the straight white road, were half a dozen little moving heaps of newly cut clover. We could not see, until they were upon us, the legs of the tiny donkey trotting along under each fragrant load.

"In Greece," said Pemberton, "when they want to say a man is a clever, long-headed chap, they call him an ass. Of all asses, the Spanish is the wisest. The peasants work them hard, abuse them a little, but they love them and treat them like members of the family; that is why they are so intelligent."

We were passing through gray olive groves, between fields of emerald wheat: golden butterflies hovered about the wild lavender growing by the wayside. Here and there, peeping from orchard and ploughed field, were bits of ruins, all that is left of the once splendid forum, the temples and palaces of the old Roman city of Italica. At the guardian's hut, where we stopped to inquire the way to the circus, we saw a few poor antiquities, some Roman lamps and fragments of sculpture. The guardian was absent, and we looked in vain for a trace of the fine Roman mosaic pavement discovered a hundred years ago, of which we had heard.

A poor monk, Fray José Moscoso, built a wall round it, hoping to preserve the precious thing, but Soult's French soldiers destroyed it by turning the enclosure into a goat pen. There is an engraving of this mosaic in the Biblioteca Columbina at Seville. When the archæologists come to

Spain,—or rather when the Spanish archæologists carry their work farther,—there will be a rich treasure trove. Very little scientific excavation has been undertaken yet. The soil, so rich in archæological as well as in mineral and agricultural wealth, has hardly been scratched. That is one of the interesting things about Spain,—it has still so much to do. With all its wonderful, romantic past, it is still a young country, with a great future before it. The Spaniards have been so busy keeping the East out of the West, fighting the battles of other nations, keeping those wretched Bourbons on the thrones of Italy where they were not wanted, opening up the New World and making Spanish America, that they have neglected Spain. That was yesterday. To-day all is changed. Spain has pulled on the seven-league boots of the giant Progress, and is striding manfully ahead, making up for lost time.

It is easy enough to turn one's back upon the great army of ghosts at Seville in Fair time, when life is at the flood and the pulses leap with the thrill of it; in Sevilla Vieja, the old Roman city of Italica, it can't be done. Here are none but ghosts, and one old gabaloonzy man who acts, in the absence of the true guardian, as our guide; he is a shepherd and his sheep crop the grass that grows over Italica. He stopped his knitting to pick a wild orchid rooted into the crumbling arch of the old Roman amphitheatre.

"*Miré*," he said; "this is the bee flower. Can you see the bee?"

His needles clicked again, the only sound in the great circus save the noise of the sheep cropping the grass of the arena. In and out of the crimson alfalfa and the wild thyme, buzzed the wild bees gathering honey. They made a soft humming, at first confused, then growing clearer and clearer, till the faint hints of meaning in their song seemed to grow into words:

"Scipio Africanus founded me," sang the bees, speaking for Italica, "as a refuge for his veterans after the great war with Carthage."

Out of the shadowy archway leading to the wild beast dens, a stronger shadow fell on the grass. Here, in the city his love and care established for the old soldiers who followed him to victory and immortal glory, I saw magnanimous Scipio, and at his side, a fainter pair, Allutius the Celtiberian prince, with the fair woman both men loved, and whom the Roman, when he learned that she was affianced to Allutius, renounced, refusing all ransom, and asking as his only recompense the friendship of Allutius for the Republic. It was not stranger than all the rest that the shade of the bride looked like Trinidad.

"Three Emperors I gave to Rome,—Trajan, Hadrian, Theodosius!" ran the song of the bees, speaking for Italica forsaken.

Trajan—the good emperor of whom Rome still gossips and has so little harm to say? Why, it was only the other day that standing by your tomb in the Eternal City, in your forum, in the shadow of the great column that bears the record of your triumphs, I heard the old story, told and retold by poet, painter and sculptor; how clear it echoes through the ages! As you rode forth to battle, a poor widow stood at your bridle and would not let you pass, crying out for justice for her son, whom your soldiers had ridden down and killed, innocent of ill. You stopped on your triumphant way and gave that justice the poor woman cried out for, then rode on to victory. Five centuries after your death, in the time of Pope Gregory the Great, your skull was found, with the tongue still alive, so the great Gregory was able to hold parley with you.

"Trajan! Trajan! Where art thou?" cried Gregory.

"In hell," answered the Emperor.

"Why art thou in hell?"

"Because I was not baptized!"

At hearing this the grief of Gregory was so great that he went into the old church of St. Peter, and wept for Trajan in hell. And the tears of Pope Gregory fell down into hell, and quenched the flames of Trajan's torment.

I tell the tale as it was told to me by Giacomo Boni, at the foot of Trajan's column in the city of Rome. The spirit of Trajan has laid hold of Boni, even as it laid hold of the great Gregory, and he, too, arises to demand for Trajan the Just the tribute of our love.

When the others came back, I told Pemberton what had happened in the old circus, while they had been hunting for the forum of Ubs Italica.

"You'll find us dull company after such!" he laughed. "Visits from Scipio Africanus and Trajan are more exciting than one's neighbors, and much more easily returned."

"The trouble is such friendships are so one-sided!" Patsy objected. "What can I do for Marcus Aurelius? The greatest Spaniard of them all. He has done so much for me. His 'Meditations' made me think for the first time in my life."

"Haven't you learned yet that you can never return a real benefit to the person who conferred it? You can only hand it on, pay the debt to the first needy person you meet. Are we not all debtors to Greeks and Barbarians? All we can ever do for the dead is to keep their names from dying; and, what is so much more important, keep alive the flame that was in them, kindle other souls as they kindled yours. The fire Prometheus stole from heaven never goes out; it is carried from soul to soul as one torch is kindled from another, till the whole earth shall be lighted and no dark places left. The shame of shames is to have received that fire, and let the flame of it go out in you!"

A peasant man and woman, evidently strangers, strayed into the arena, and stood staring at the moss-covered stones. The man, a decent fellow with a pleasant smile and no teeth, greeted the knitting shepherd.

"This perhaps is the ruin of some great palace?" he said.

"It is the bull-ring," the shepherd corrected, "they say there was a city here once; you can see where the streets were; there are also bits of old churches and houses."

"*Valgame Dios!*" exclaimed the stranger, "perhaps this was an important town, before it was ruined a hundred years ago or more!"

"*No se sabé*," said the shepherd indifferently. He called his dog, who began to herd the sheep, running round and round them in a circle and barking furiously. The sun was westering; it lacked but an hour of setting; we were five miles from our dinner, and reluctantly we turned our backs on Italica, the buried city, with its twice ten hundred years, and drove back to Seville.

"It is a pestilential trait,—this pulling down old cities to build new;" said Pemberton, as we drove through the wretched village of Santiponce. "They pulled down Italica to get building material for Seville. Only the other day, hardly more than a hundred years ago, they took some of the stone of the old circus to make the road to Badajos. Men build cities as birds build nests; not many birds are satisfied with last year's nests, not many men with other men's cities."

"Have you heard," called Patsy from the other carriage, as with derisive hoots they passed us on the old Roman road, "Don Jaime goes with us to Cordova."

"As you please," said the Don; "or take ship and make a little crusade in the Mediterranean,—to Morocco, if you will."

The next day we left Seville, stopping on the way to the station for a last look at the cathedral. We entered by way of the Court of Oranges, paused beneath the orange trees laden with fruit and blossoms, and drew long breaths of the delicious fragrance. Here Concepcion and Trinidad joined us. Both wore the mantilla, still *de rigeur* for early mass. Concepcion had a yellow rose in her curls to match her fan. Trinidad carried a bunch of white rosebuds; she was wearing her own dress to-day; it showed the curves of beauty better than that loose frock of Concepcion's! Both young women looked fresh as roses with the night dew still on them, and smelt pleasantly of orange-flower water. As we stood gossiping by the old fountain, a pretty altar boy in white and scarlet finery came towards us, swinging a gold censer to keep the coals alight. As he passed he looked at Trinidad, and seemed to swing the censer towards her: for a moment we saw her in a cloud of blue incense smoke.

We made the tour of the cathedral, and took leave of Murillo's Guardian Angel and his San Antonio. A shaft of sunlight carried the stain of the painted glass, ruby, topaz, emerald, to the columns under the round window of the Assumption. The golden mass bells tinkled; they were saying mass in the

ST. JOSEPH AND THE INFANT JESUS. THE GUARDIAN ANGEL.
Murillo   *Murillo*

chapel royal before the silver altar where Saint Ferdinand is buried. Alive, he was King Ferdinand III; dead, he became a saint, because with his own hands he had carried fagots to burn heretics. A sound of hammers echoed through the great cathedral.

"The *fiestas* are over," said Pemberton; "they are taking down the monument over the tomb of Ferdinand Columbus."

As we passed out through the Puerta del Lagarte under the great crocodile, the twin organs thundered, the choir sang a deep "Amen," the bells in the Giralda clanged a parting peal.

"Heavens!" murmured Patsy, as from the train window we looked back at the darling of Andalusia, lying in the fold of Guadalquiver's arm, "what a beautiful world this is!" He blinked as he said it, as if there were tears in his eyes.

"Quien no ha vista Sevilla,
no ha vista maravilla."

VII

CORDOVA

Other towns may be better to live in. None are better to be born in than Cordova.—EL
GRAN CAPITAN

"The old Roman engineer who built Cordova Bridge did a good piece
of work," said Patsy. "See, those are his foundations; they are solid still,—it
is a good bridge yet! The arches are paltry, modern things beside them; they
were put up centuries later by a Moor called As-Sahn. It does not seem fair
that his name should be remembered, and the Roman's forgotten."

The Roman's work is not forgotten, and will not be, while Cordova
Bridge stands, and while the city arms remain a bridge on water. The weeds
push between the great stones, a lovely enamel of orange lichen covers the
staunch old piers, around which the amber Guadalquiver laps and
murmurs. The white highroad follows the river south to Seville; the way
north is barred by a range of purple Sierras.

Not even in Italica is the mark of Rome stronger

THE MOSQUE, CORDOVA.

THE MOSQUE, CORDOVA.

than in Cordova; the old bridge, the names of the streets, the memories of the famous Roman citizens who were born here, bring imperial Rome to mind at every moment. The Romans came to Cordova as conquerors carrying the eagles through Spain; they made the city the capital of Hispania Ulterior, and called it the Patrician Colony because so many of the Romans who settled here and married the graceful, dark-eyed Cordovese women were of patrician descent. The Roman rule, harsh at first, grew gentler, for while Rome ruled, Christianity came to Cordova, and pagan slavery softened to a milder form of vassalage.

"A man can do one of two things with his life," Patsy philosophized, "Build it all up into a monument to his own memory, or lay it down in paving stones—or a bridge—for other people to walk over. Which is the best worth while? As if one could choose!" He dropped a stone into the water, and watched the circles spread into larger and larger rings.

We had arrived at Cordova too late to see the Mosque, and had come directly from the station to the bridge to watch the thin current of life and traffic pulsing in and out of the dead alive old town. There is no place like a bridge for gathering impressions of a strange city.

"Hé hé, Macho!" an old muleteer with gold earrings threw a stone at the brown mule, leader of his team, just in time to prevent his running into a donkey that was crossing the bridge in the other direction, laden with paniers full of terra cotta jars. Before the mule train had disappeared, we heard a great clatter and rattling of loose screws and rivets, as an old chaise came lumbering along the white highroad from the direction of Seville, and stopped at the bridge gate. The custom-house officer, dozing on his bench, woke up, and asked the usual tiresome question.

"Have their Graces anything to declare?"

The gentleman Grace, apparently deaf, behaved as if he had neither seen nor heard the officer, and had only stopped to flick a horsefly from his fat white mare. The lady Grace shook her silver curls.

"No, nothing to declare," she said.

Strapped to the back of the chaise was a cylindrical, horsehair trunk, studded with brass nails.

"What might this contain?" The officer touched the trunk.

"Only our garments; we have been spending a week at the hacienda."

"Open it, please. How is this, a ham?"

"Our own. The tax was paid when the pig was killed; twelve *pesetas*. It was far too much."

"That is another matter. You must pay the tax on provisions brought into the city as well." The officer weighed the ham, and began to make a calculation with pencil and note-book. "There is also to be added the fine for not having declared the ham."

The lady's eyes snapped angrily, as she gave the officer a piece of her mind. "You are a miserable loafer! It is to pay salaries to such lazy fellows as you that honest people are robbed of their honest money!"

It was growing late. By the time the ham was settled for, the vivid blue of the western sky had turned soft apple-green. We climbed a crazy stair to the window of the gate, to avoid a drove of cattle driven across the bridge by a *vaquero* in a brown *capote*. The comfortable smell of kine came in at the window. On the other side of the Guadalquiver, in the golden haze of dust kicked up by those silly, helter-skeltering cows, lay Cordova. Before us rose the great Mosque; in the centre the towering masonry of the Christian Cathedral stood out in bold outline against the distant Sierra. The sun set quietly in the quiet sky; a few minutes after, the whole heaven was aflame with the glorious crimson after-glow; the river ran red; the whole earth shone with the reflection. The sunset was like the death of some great and unsuspected saint, some humble man, the glory of whose life is only known when he has gone and the whole world is filled with the light of the soul that has just passed from it.

"The moon will soon be up," said Patsy. "Let us wait for it. We are not likely to see sunset and moonrise from Cordova bridge again."

The custom-house officer made room for us on his wooden bench. As we sat watching the swallows flit back and forth over the river, Patsy told us stories about the great men who had lived at Cordova, and we all made believe we saw them cross the old bridge. A tall military man with a clanking sword passed through the gate.

"There goes Marcellus, the Tribune who conquered Cordova for Rome; our friend the engineer must have come here soon after him; isn't it a pity we can't find his name, when such silly ones are remembered?"

"He built a good bridge; does it matter whether he was called Caius or Cassius?"

"Why, yes, it matters to me," Patsy persisted. "There was another Marcellus who came to Cordova later, in Julius Cæsar's time. How talent runs in families! Cæsar sent him to rebuild the town after he had half destroyed it for taking Pompey's side in that old quarrel we boys used to fight over again at school. The Senecas came from here, too; there is a square named for them. You remember the story about Seneca's wife? When Nero sent word that Seneca must die, both he and his wife opened the veins in their arms. Seneca, who was much older than his wife, died first, whereupon Madam's women bound up her veins, and she lived several years after. There was talent in that family, too; the father was a writer, and Lucan, the poet, was either a cousin or nephew. Hullo! Look at the folds of that old beggar's capa; doesn't it look like a toga? Now remember that cantankerous face of Seneca's in the bust at the Naples Museum, and if you can't see Nero's tutor pottering over that old bridge you've no imagination!"

The swallows had all gone to their nests; the soft, fumbling flight of a pair of small bats wove a pattern against the fading sky.

"That portly gentleman on the white mule might well be Hosius, one time Bishop of Cordova. You never heard of him, perhaps, but you must have heard of the Nicene Creed," Patsy went on. It was evident that we had to listen to all he knew about Cordova.

"The next time you hear that creed repeated, remember Hosius, Bishop here in Cordova for sixty-three years; he presided at the Council of Nicea when the creed was made. That was after he had failed in the task

Constantine set him of persuading Arius to give up the Unitarian heresy. Think how often he must have ambled over this old bridge."

It always has been hard to persuade people to give up the Unitarian heresy! Whenever I hear the Nicene creed, I shall think of Bishop Hosius whom, that night of nights, we saw ride across the old Roman bridge at Cordova on a white mule.

"The one I should like best to have known of all the great men who ever lived at Cordova was the Caliph Abd-er-Rahman. What a man he was! Servant of the compassionate, they called him. That is his Mosque, those are his palms; he planted the great-grandfathers of those trees with his own hand. If you could make Seneca's toga out of that old beggar's *capa*, can't you see Abd-er-Rahman's bournous in that young fellow's cloak? He is as dark as an Arab; the red handkerchief knotted round his head under the sombrero makes a decent turban. He has the swagger of a *torrero*. Conqueror of bulls, conqueror of men, where is the difference? Toga, bournous, *capa*,—all three garments are practically the same."

"What do you suppose Gonsalvo de Cordova, El Gran Capitan wore?"

"A cloak like the rest of them, I fancy. There are a great many things named for him in the city over there: a theatre, a paseo, I don't know what else. In poetry they call him the Scourge of Islam. When I showed Don Jaime a rather steep bill, he whistled, and said 'They have made you out the account of *el Gran Capitan*.' The size of the bills he presented to Ferdinand and Isabel for scourging the infidel is the thing he is best remembered for in Cordova."

"That's gossip; history says he really was a great captain," I protested.

"According to the proverb, it is the blood of the soldier makes the great captain," said Patsy. "As to history, Martial says;—'Give up frivolous fable and read history!' He also says, 'Fool that I was! Why did I not follow the advice I gave Mamura?' But, truly, isn't to-day's gossip, to-morrow's history?"

"To-morrow's history will be rheumatism if we stay mooning here any longer," J. said firmly. "Right about face, homeward, march!"

After dinner, as he sat writing postal cards to be despatched to the four corners of the earth, Patsy made acquaintance, over the inkstand, with the Argentino. He was a tall man with a close-cut, pointed beard that had been gold and would soon be silver, and fiery brown eyes that would always be young.

"So you are an American, too?" I heard him say to Patsy. "Are you from the States?"

"Yes; I took you for a Spaniard."

"No, I am an American from the Argentine."

We left Patsy and the stranger plunged in talk. Half an hour later, Patsy brought his new acquaintance to our room.

"It's raining so hard we can't go out," he whispered; "this is the most comfortable place in the house—he is a kind of an American—"

"This is 'a good Son of the Way,' that is what the Arabs call a traveller," said the Argentino, looking at Patsy. "He makes a friend as a sailor makes a sweetheart, between tides, waiting for his ship to sail."

It was pouring now. Beside the noise of the rain on the roof we heard, every now and then, a strange sobbing sigh.

"Grrr! Isn't that a creepy noise? If I were not broad awake and looking at you all by electric light, I should believe those were the ghosts of the great men of Cordova lamenting the departed glory of their city."

"I wish they were," said the Argentino. "They could tell me just where the old Iberian village stood, when the Phœnicians came punting up the river and discovered it, just as our people poked up the rivers in America, and discovered the Indian pueblos."

"Tell them what you were telling me," said Patsy. "He has been here ever so long, and has ferreted out a lot of interesting things about Cordova."

"There is not much to tell that you don't know. The old game of civilization is going on in the world to-day just as it was then. You have only to cross the Straits of Gibraltar, and go over to Morocco and up into the Atlas Mountains to find a Kabyl village very like the primitive Iberian pueblo the Greeks and Phœnicians found here. The French may be a little quicker about civilizing Morocco than the Phœnicians and Greeks were in civilizing the Peninsula, though I doubt it."

"You said," Patsy insisted, "that you had seen some things in a museum that gave you a pretty clear idea of how they lived in Cordova, when it belonged to Carthage."

"I saw some recent finds made in a mound not far from here," said the Argentino. "A bust which they call the Lady of Elche that has something of the early Greek feeling. After seeing these things and reading all I could lay hands on about them, I came to the conclusion that Cordova must have been a pretty civilized place under the Republic of Carthage. The people had gold and silver vessels,—the Greeks have a story that the anchors of their galleys were gold. They certainly had ivory combs, for I have seen them, and Greek vases and Celtic pottery—geometric raised patterns and all—and coins stamped with a winged horse. Then we know all about their wool, what fine cloth they made, and that famous scarlet dye of the kermes that ran the Tyrian purple so hard in the markets of the East."

"Those markets of the East another republic hankers to supply," Patsy put in.

"Take up the white man's burden and put it on the back
Of every yaller nigger and kick him when he's slack.
They've got to wear our cotton, they've got to drink our gin,
And pay our missionaries to save their souls from sin."

He threw open the window and leaned out.

"It has stopped raining. My wig! do you smell the flowers? I can make out jasmine, acacia, and mignonette. Spanish flowers seem to grow with their perfume already triple distilled."

"They are the most fragrant in the world," said the Argentino. "Don't sleep with your windows open, if you are afraid of headache! Now you want to go to bed, this Son of the Way and I will say good night to you."

A few minutes later Patsy's laugh, a whiff of the Argentino's cigarette, some broken fragments of their talk floated in at the window, as they walked up and down in the garden outside.

"The original inhabitants of Spain—what they call the Iberians—" said the Argentino.

"Where did they come from?" Patsy interrupted.

"Nobody knows; they weren't Aryans. In the Neolithic Age a very dark race, with long heads, and thick curling hair inhabited the whole Peninsula—"

"I do not propose going back to the beginning of time to-night," said J. as he shut the window. "That boy's thirst for information—easily acquired—will get us into trouble yet. Don Jaime comes to-morrow. How will he and this new friend get along?"

I had already asked myself that question.

"Did the norias keep you awake?" Patsy asked at breakfast the next morning. "What we heard last night was not the sighs of ghosts, but the noise of the pumping machines that supply the houses with water!"

Our rooms looked into a walled garden, with flower-beds framed in geometrical designs, surrounded by nice thick box borders. There was a superb syringa in full bloom that looked like ivory and smelt like honey. The jasmines were trained against the wall. The roses were glorious. In an outer court, where the poultry lived, a patriarchal fig-tree shaded a row of old-fashioned wooden beehives. Under a pergola covered by grape-vines stood a tiny house no bigger than a sentry-box; in the house sat Vicente. His voice waked us each morning with a fierce but tremulous cry:

"*Andar*, Morisco!"

Close to the sentry-box was the noria. Morisco, a tall mule hitched to a pole, and blindfolded so that he should not grow dizzy, walked round and round in a circle, faithfully pumping the water, while Vicente alternately slept and exhorted him to "go!" The red-haired waiter told us Vicente's story. In his youth he had been head gardener on a Grandee's estate. For twenty years he had been attached to the hotel. He was now ninety-five years old. A few months before his wife had died, at the age of one hundred. Until then, Vicente had lived at home. Now that there is nobody to cook and wash for him, the proprietor gives him a room in the hotel, his food, his clothes, a little money for cigarettes; for his companion, Morisco.

As we entered the garden, Vicente awoke with a start, lighted a cigarette, and jerked the mule's bridle.

"*Andar*, Morisco!" The patient mule, who had worked while Vicente slept, trod his weary round a little faster, the clatter of his hoofs mingling with the droning creak, creak of the noria.

A brown girl passed from the outer court, where she had been taking down the washing, half hidden by the pile of linen in her arms.

"*Hé, hé! Basta aqua*, Vicente!" she cried, and went into the hot laundry with her linen.

"*Muy bien*, Rafaela." Vicente sneezed, relighted his cigarette, with trembling hands unharnessed Morisco, and toddled off with him to the stable. In a few moments the old man came back, and pottered about the garden, making his tour of inspection. Nothing escaped his wise old eyes. He crushed a snail that was devouring a velvety pansy, nipped off an overblown peony, stripped the buds and foliage so ruthlessly from a fine red carnation that I had to ask him the reason.

"This work should have been done in September, but I was not here then. We shall have poor carnations this year." From the look of them—they were only just coming into bloom—they would have taken a prize anywhere out of Spain.

"The carnation plant has need of cleanliness like a person. What I take off is its misery. See, these are nothing but leaves; they do no good, they only take the strength. These are children; there are too many of them! Sacrifice these three little buds, and in fourteen days this large one will make a carnation so big." He joined his palsied hands at the finger tips to show me the size. He had thrown some of the "misery" carelessly on the ground, some he had laid carefully in a pile.

"Those I threw away are nothing but leaves and children. These others are little plants, you see the difference? I shall plant all these; not one must be lost. It is so late many will not grow, but I shall get some good ones. Very soon they will throw out roots, then I shall transplant them; next season they will bear. The carnation is only good for three years; the second season is the best. See, this is an old plant. We will help it to give its last flowers. They will be small, but of a good variety." He stirred the earth about the roots, and mixed with it a trowelful of rich loam.

"One might almost live in a place where they grow such flowers!" J. began.

"No, one might not!" cried Patsy.

"Vicente has been a famous gardener in his day!" the waiter had said it more than once. That explains why the pear trees were so well pruned, the oranges so healthy, why the carnations of Cordova still bloom in my memory. A peacock strutted down the brick path, hopped on the wall of the noria, spread the glory of his tail, turned his proud head to show the sapphire sheen of his neck, and gave his strange cry, "mahor mahor."

The laundry window was open. We could see Rafaela's pretty head bent over her ironing, and catch the words she sang:

Contrabandista es mi padre,	Contrabandista is my father,
contrabandista es mi hermano,	Contrabandista is my brother;
contrabandista ha de ser	Contrabandista he must be
aquel á quien dé mi mano.	To whom I give my hand.

"The trouble with Cordova is, it is dead and not buried," said Patsy. "It may comfort you to know it was the first town in Europe to have paved streets. I believe they never have been repaved since." We were picking our way over the abominable pavement of the Plazuela de Seneca. A little farther on, near the Seven Corners, is a large house with carved stone façade, handsome iron gratings, and something distinguished about it that caught our attention. It stands in a deserted plaza where the grass grows between the paving stones. For five minutes we had met nobody, not even a cat or dog. We peeped into the patio. There was no living thing there except a fountain and a tame quail asleep in a cage.

"The palace of the Sleeping Beauty!" murmured Patsy. We went round behind the house to explore. The frowsy little street at the back was fragrant with a smell of new baked bread that made us hungry. Through a half-closed gate we saw a courtyard full of beggars. An inner door opened, and the lady of the silver curls whom we had first seen on Cordova Bridge came out followed by two servants carrying baskets filled with bread. The beggars formed in line and shuffled past the lady, who gave a loaf to each and received a blessing in return.

"Bread is given out at this house every Saturday," said a little gentleman in a black stock, who was passing. "Last year, when there was a death in the family, they gave alms for nine days. The *pordioseros* have no better friend in all Cordova than the mistress of this house."

As the last beggar hobbled from the court, a carriage drawn by a pair of sleek mules drove out, with two ladies and a gentleman. Just then Don Jaime came round the corner in search of us; he bowed to the ladies.

"Who are your friends?" Patsy demanded.

"The old it is Duquesa B. It is no longer young, but conserved very good, eh? Her daughter it is appelled Rafaela. Was Queen of Beauty at the *Yuego Florales*. To the elected poet she gave the prize, a natural rose."

"He means that they have a Contest of Poets every year here," said Patsy. "A theme is given out, a jury appointed, then the poems just stream in from all over the province. From what the Don says, this old dustheap of a Cordova wakes up a little at fair time. What luck that we saw the Beauty!"

"Did you see who was sitting opposite her?" asked J. "It was O'Shea."

"He's easily consoled for Trinidad." In spite of Patsy's natural jealousy, that meeting with O'Shea was a comfort to us all. It seemed to bring us out of musty, dusty Cordova's dead past, and link us with dear, living Seville. In the cool of the afternoon, the streets woke up a little; there were more carriages than one would have supposed possible in the Paseo of El Gran Capitan.

That evening we went to the theatre. The performance began at half-past eight. The price of box was five pesetas for each play. There were four different pieces, each lasting about an hour. The advantage of the system is, you can drop into a theatre early or late, and are not obliged to pay for more of the performance than you see. The first play, about a *contrabandista* and his sweetheart, a *cigarrera*, was full of gunshots and morality, and highly applauded, though the acting was mediocre. Patsy, who discovered several pretty girls in the audience, asked the Don if the women of Northern Spain were as charming as in the South.

"Not all women in Andalusia is beautifool," the Don admitted, "but *all* is gracious; the young gels have a naturality. The Madrileñas, it is affective their manniers for to speak, it is different from the Andaluz!"

J. and I were satisfied with two plays. Patsy and Don Jaime stayed for the last, an operetta.

"I like him better the music, it is the end representation," said the Don.

The next day Pasty had a great deal to tell us about Cordova. "There are about twenty of the old aristocratic families who still live here," he said. "There is literally nothing for the young men to do but loaf about the Club of Friendship, where, Don Jaime says, half the nobility of the province have been ruined by gambling. Some people he knows have had to sell their silver. They had a complete silver service, tureen, vegetable dishes, plates, platters, all the rest of it, for every day. They only used their English porcelain for best; now they have to use it every day. The same people had solid silver basins and pitchers, and dozens of those stunning old repoussé silver trays and platters they used to make here. You see the Don knows Cordova well; he can tell you more about it in an hour than you could get out of books in a year."

The Don twirled his mustache and ran his fingers through his hair. "I have a custom to come to Cordoba every winter," he admitted. "At that season all families is at their coontry place in the hills for the shootings. In the *coto* of my friend it is no luxury, all comfort. The ladies go very simple, put a handkerchief over the head, or an old hat; the children is dressed very plain, like the poor."

"Is the sport good?" asked Patsy.

"In my youth it was more plenty the black beasts (wild boar). Now is much deer, hares, rabbits, partridges."

"Do you care about shooting?" I asked. The Don never walked a step, if he could avoid it, and got up at two in the afternoon. I could not think of him in the light of a sportsman.

"It is the preferred sport of all Spanishes men as of the English," he answered. "The ladies like the coontry very mooch; some of them kill the game. We have large fires of great tree troonks, no small pieces of woods like in the city. In the evening it is very sociable; we gather at one house or another; there is singing and dancing. Ah, yes, the most pleasant life is in the coontry. If the guests come far, they spend the night. It is all so simply, no like England. One large room for all the ladies; one for all the gentlemen."

I asked the Don if they stayed in their country places in summer.

"No, in the spring they return to Cordoba. The hot is very strong; here the houses is prepared for the hot. All people sit out in the court. In soomer, they go to take another climate. The Sierra is not good for the health, it is very humid."

"He was telling me last night," said Patsy, "about the time Queen Isabel II came to Cordova. He was only a boy then, but his father was at a banquet the Marquis de Benemeji gave for her at Quita Pesares—Away Cares; isn't that a good name for a garden? The old gentleman must have plied a better knife and fork than the Don, for Jaime remembers to this day the way his father rolled up his eyes when he told them about the good things they had to eat. *Aroz a la Valenciana*—baked rice with fish, quails, green peas and artichokes; saddle of veal larded and roasted with aromatic herbs and manzanilla, rice boiled in cream with the name of the best guest at each table traced in powdered cinnamon, *natilla*, a wonderful kind of cream, and *ojaldres*,—a sort of pastry, light and brittle as a butterfly's wing, which they eat with chocolate. When they had eaten and drunk all that they could, the Queen said good-bye and started to go. What do you suppose she found at the door? A brand new coach, Andalusian style, with eight splendid *caballos antigrados* (Cordovan horses with yellow skins marked like tigers) harnessed Andalusian fashion, with silver bells and silken tags. The Queen hopped into the coach and drove away. She took it back to Madrid, where, the Don thinks, we can see it still in the royal stables. He says Cordova has traditions to live up to.

"When the Queen's son, Alfonzo XII, came here, the days of coaches were gone by. The Grandee at whose house the King stayed had the railroad tracks laid through the streets to his door, so that the King should not have the trouble of driving from the station to the house."

"Speaking of railroads," said J. "I think I've had enough of Cordova."

"So have I, this season," Patsy agreed. "Next year, when I make the tour of all the *ferias* of Spain, with my friend the Mountebank, I shall come back to Cordova and enter the Contest of Poets."

From that moment till we left, I spent every waking hour in the Mosque, the thing best worth seeing in Cordova. Outside, it looks more like a fortress than a sanctuary. It has battlements, towers and buttresses quite in character with the militant Mahommedan religion, and hopelessly out of character with the Christian. It is grim, forbidding, and tremendously impressive all at once! The gates, the gates alone, give a hint of the beauty inside! The light, interlaced, horseshoe arches resting on slender columns, and the rich mosaic over the Puerta Arabe are like a foretaste of a feast. In the splendid court of Oranges, where the trees are planted in long aisles (they originally were a continuation of the aisles of the Mosque), there are five fountains, and fifty beggars and guides. As we were making a bargain with the youngest guide to keep the others at bay, the Argentino came up and offered his services in the place of a guide.

"I have had them all," he said; "and picked their brains like a corbie."

We sat on a bench and watched the women drawing water at the fountain while the Argentino—he spoke English rather better than any of us—and Patsy talked like two Trappists, newly absolved from the vow of silence!

"Think of the Mosque first as the most perfect thing left of the Cordova of the Caliphs, the city of Abd-er-Rahman, whom you tell me you saw cross the old bridge the night you arrived. I have not been so fortunate, though I have had a sense of him more than once sitting here in his court. If it were not for the Mosque, the story of Moorish Cordova would be to me as the Thousand and Second Story of Scheherezade. Even so, I can hardly believe it. This, a city of a million inhabitants—think of it! Those silent, God-forsaken streets full of people, the place fairly humming with business. Thousands of looms weaving stuffs, tissues, carpets. You know what Cordova leather was? It has never been equalled. As to their blacksmiths, their silver and goldsmiths, there are none like them in the world to-day that I know."

Patsy took a brown paper parcel from his pocket. "Here are some rather nice bits I have picked up." He showed a close silver chain, supple as a serpent, and a fascinating pair of gold filigree earrings studded with small emeralds.

"You're in luck. These look like real old Cordova

THE MOSQUE, CORDOVA. LA PUERTA DEL SOL, TOLEDO.

work. The jeweller's art is the hardest to kill of all, except the cook's. They make nice jewelry here still; the pastry and the orange flower sweetmeats of Cordova are the best I have eaten in Spain. Of all the arts of Cordova, the cook's and the jeweller's alone survive! Man is still greedy; woman—may I say it?—still vain."

"But wasn't the University the great thing after all?" said Patsy.

"Right! You can't say it too often or too loud. When you hear the Jews abused, speak up, tell the old story over again. In the Dark Ages, when in the rest of Europe, Greece and Rome were forgotten, asleep, seemingly dead, the spirit of Athens and of Rome was alive here in Cordova. Art, philosophy, science,—our great inheritance from the older civilizations— were held in trust for you and me right here by the Jews and Arabs of Cordova."

"That won't be forgotten while Dante is read." Patsy quoted a line from the Inferno:

"Averrois che il gran commento feo."

"No, six words from Dante give a man a patent of nobility in the Republic of Letters that outlives any title an emperor confers. Well, that Averroes, that same Hebrew Jew whom Dante met along with those other Cordovans, Seneca and Lucan, in the place of the sighing, unbaptized spirits, lived and wrote his great Commentary on Aristotle here in Cordova. He probably walked through this court every day, he washed perhaps in that fountain; ate oranges, may be, from those trees—how should I know the life of an orange?"

"Those two men," said J. to me, "would rather talk about a thing any day than see it." So we left Patsy and the Argentino reconstructing old Cordova, and went to look at the Mosque.

Inside we soon lost ourselves in a forest of columns, with long aisles running in every direction. Every path we chose led to beauty. The columns are of many different marbles, porphyry, jasper, Africano, alabaster, verde antique; of all styles, and many periods. We found some from the old Roman temple of Janus; some with smooth polished shafts; some twisted, with Roman, Arab, Byzantine or Visigothic capitals. The mosque has been compared to the bed of Procrustes,—if the column was too short, it was lengthened by adding a base; if too long, it was sunk into the ground. Whatever the columns might have been originally, they now are all of the same height, and serve to hold up the beautiful double arches that support the roof.

We found our way to the Mihrâb, a wonderful little octagonal chapel. The roof is a shell hollowed from a single block of marble, the walls are of marble finely carved. A deep groove is worn in the pavement by the knees of the pilgrims who made the tour of the Mihrâb seven times, for in those days a pilgrimage to Cordova was as good as one to Mecca.

"Los Moros que te labraron
capilla del Zancarrón
merecián ser Cristianos."

"That means the Moors that made you, chapel of the bare bone, deserved to be Christians," said Patsy, coming up behind us. "Bare bone, because one of Mohammed's shin-bones is supposed to have been worshipped here."

"Si hoy mismo resucitaran
aqui en Cordoba los moros
cada cual se iba á su casa."

the Argentino capped the *copla.* "That means if to-day the Moors here in Cordova rose from the dead, each could go to his own house,—because the houses are so little changed, I suppose, and because their descendants have kept the keys."

As if in answer to the challenge, there came slowly towards us, down a narrow aisle of flanking columns, two tall Moors, dressed all in white.

They had left their shoes at the door of the Mosque; each carried a prayer rug. They entered the small, seven-sided chapel that leads to the holy of holies, and placing their rugs upon the ground stood under the pineapple dome with bowed heads. There we left them on the threshold of the Mihrâb, in the Mosque of their fathers.

"Haven't we seen the impossible thing?" cried Patsy. We were outside the church in the hot sunshine, having left those grave Moors undisturbed in the shadowy mosque.

We had seen the impossible thing, the only thing worth seeing, as the only thing worth doing. Since the Conquest of Granada, it is as difficult to see a Moor in Spain as to meet an Iroquois in Broadway, but, we had not dreamed them! They were real Moors in the suite of the envoys of the Sultan of Morocco at the Algeciras Conference, who had taken advantage of a few days recess, and come up to see Cordova.

As we stood absorbed in thinking of those Moors, whose red morocco slippers lay before us on the steps, we did not notice what was happening just behind us.

"Off with your hats, heretic Jews!" The words were hissed in Patsy's ear,—he stood nearest the church door; his hat was knocked off his head. "Take that, and that, and that!" He was hit in the face three times with a fan by a small lady in black satin.

The Argentino drew us quickly aside, as a procession of priests came out of the door. One carried something that was hidden by the rich vestment hunched over his shoulders and covering his hands.

"They are taking the sacrament to some sick person," the Argentino explained. At that moment Don Jaime, who had come up without our seeing him, tried to pour oil upon the troubled waters.

"These are strangers, Señora, they did not know that his divine majesty was about to pass."

The little old lady was nothing appeased; she gave us one last furious look, and muttering "Accursed heretic Jews!" followed the priests with the sacrament.

"That's the same spirit that more than once has drenched this city in the blood of its best people," said the Argentino. "In Abd-er-Rahman's time the church of St. Vicente that stood here, on the site of the Temple of Janus, was divided between Christians and Musselmans. They worshipped under the same roof till Abd-er-Rahman bought the Christians out and built this Mosque. The Christian priests left the church peaceably, in procession, carrying the pictures and relics of the saints. Afterwards the

Mohammedan Marabouts and the Christian fanatics stirred up all the strife; they are equally responsible for the throat slitting, burning, and torturing; there's not a pin to choose between them. That old lady would send us to the stake to-day if she could. Priest and woman, the old allies! Do you know, Señor, that the future of Spain depends upon the education you give your women." His eyes flashed as he asked Jaime the question. The Don looked back at him with withering scorn.

"The *ladies* of Spain receive the education best suited to them," he said gravely.

"They know how to use their fans," said Patsy; his nose had begun to bleed. "That I should be assaulted for the first time in my life by a little old lady with a fan,—wonderful! I will say she's the livest thing I've seen in Cordova."

"You saw who she was?" said J. "The lady with the silver curls who didn't want to pay duty on the ham, and who gives bread to the beggars of Cordova every Saturday."

GATE OF JUSTICE, ALHAMBRA.

VIII

GRANADA

Quiero vivir en Granada	I like to live in Granada
porque me gusta el oir	Because it pleases me to hear
la campana de la Vela	The bell of the Vela
quando me voy a dormir.	When I am going to sleep.

"Who's there?"

"People of peace."

Encarnacion opened the door of the bell tower just a crack. Though the sun had not set, it was already dark inside the watch-tower of the Alhambra. The walls are six feet thick; the windows, narrow slits on the winding stair, let in very little light. Encarnacion carried a classic brass lamp for olive oil. She shaded the flame from her eyes with a long, hairy hand, and the light shining through showed how thin it was. Maria, the younger sister, as grim looking, though more timid in her bearing, stood behind, peering over Encarnacion's shoulder.

"It is the young *caballero* and his friends," she whispered. Encarnacion threw the door wide open, the two sisters smiled hospitably upon us like a pair of kind ogresses.

"But come in."

"Come in."

They echoed each other as if they were singing a perpetual duet.

"They are welcome."

"Welcome."

"Will they be pleased to enter?"

"To enter!"

We followed the sisters to a square room with enormously thick walls. A range was built into one corner, a charcoal fire smouldered under a tiny grate, where something that smelt very good bubbled in an earthenware pot. Four cages of canaries hung against the wall. A brindled cat stole in behind us, licked its whiskers, fixed fierce, unwinking eyes on the birds. Maria threatened him with her finger.

"Bad little cat! Who killed the young robin in the myrtle hedge? And now you make eyes at these? He knows too much to touch them; he looks and looks at them, and then goes out and chases the wild birds."

In the middle of the room stood a round worktable covered with sewing. A jacket, half cut out of red cotton, lay near a pair of shears. From an

COURT OF LIONS, THE ALHAMBRA.

GARDEN OF THE GENERALIFE, GRANADA.

opening in the dark, vaulted ceiling over the worktable, dangled a long knotted cord.

"That is the rope of the *campana de la Vela*!" said Encarnacion.

"Is it true that it is you who ring the bell of the Vela?"

"Yes, once every half hour, from eight o'clock in the evening till four in the morning, we ring the bell in the watch-tower."

"You sit up all night to do it? Isn't it dreadfully cold?"

"Yes, it is often very cold. In winter we have a fire." Encarnacion drew aside the chintz curtains that hid the lower part of the table, and showed a copper brazier covered with a wire netting that stood underneath.

"We kindle the charcoal, put our feet close to the brazier on this wooden shelf, and wrap ourselves up in heavy shawls and hoods. We manage very well, we are so used to it."

"What do you do with yourselves through the long winter nights? How do you pass the time?"

"There is always plenty of work; we take in sewing. Sometimes one of us reads aloud to the other."

"Do you two live here quite alone?"

"Sometimes our brother is with us, not always," sighed Encarnacion. "I have been the portress of the Torre de la Vela since the night the tower was struck by lightning and our father and mother, now in glory, were killed."

"Now in glory were killed!" echoed Maria.

"What a terrible thing! When did it happen?"

"Long and long ago,—the year Maria made her first communion. We were waked by a great crash. The tower shook, the bell rang as never before, there was a thick smoke. It was easy for us to escape, we slept below; our brother slept above, near our parents. He saved his life by clapping a towel over his mouth, and creeping down-stairs on his hands and knees."

"On his knees," Maria crossed herself. "Virgin mine! May the Lord receive them into Paradise in their shoes!"

"The bell gives the signal for opening the sluices," Encarnacion went on; "it regulates the irrigation of the vega. Each piece of land has its hour for letting on the water. On still nights you can hear the bell thirty miles away."

High up in the Sierra Nevada Mountains over Granada, the Darrow, a mountain torrent flowing down from the eternal snows on the summits, is caught, tamed, and led off into small channels that spread, like the veins of a man's body, all over the vega. Moors' work this; perhaps the greatest part of their legacy to Spain, for water

WINDOW, TOWER OF CAPTIVE, ALHAMBRA.

is wealth. Thanks to the Moors, the vega of Granada is the garden of the Peninsula; the hemp grown here is the finest, the olives and grapes are the best. The land bears three crops a year in succession,—wheat, beans and corn. Part of it is now given over to the new sugar beet industry; the beets grown here are enormous. The soil is light and clean; you will not find a stone in a whole field. The regulation of the complicated system of irrigation, the life blood of Granada, is in the hands of Encarnacion and

Maria. To live in a tower, of all others in a tower of the Alhambra, and spend your life helping to make Granada green and beautiful, seems a pleasant existence, even if it be a lonely one. To wake when others sleep, and sleep when all the world's awake, always seems a hard fate.

"Your birds must be a great company to you," I said to Maria.

"*Claro*. We raise them ourselves. Would you like to see the little ones? We keep them in our bedroom where it is warmer."

"Do me the favor," Encarnacion relighted the lamp, and showed the way up the heavy stone stairway.

The neat upper room where the sisters slept had three beds. In spite of the thick whitewash on the walls, we could still make out the graceful lines of the old Moorish arches and windows. A palm branch, a crucifix, and a chromo of the Madonna of Lourdes appearing to Bernadette, hung between the beds. At one end of the room was a long table with the breeding cages of the canaries, whose loves and nurseries the sisters of the tower guard so tenderly.

"See this little one;" Maria put her face close to the cage and made a little singing sound. "He's getting strong now; he was weakly at first, and I thought we should lose him. It would be a pity; his father is our best singer." The canaries, all in a flutter at being waked up, chattered and scolded at her.

"Maria will take them up to see the view," said Encarnacion; "if they will excuse me, I will go down in case some one else should call." I am afraid Encarnacion knew we liked Maria best.

Down in the town of Granada the bells were ringing like mad, the nightingales were singing in the Duke of Wellington's elms, that shade the long, steep road leading from the town to the red city of the Alhambra, perched high above it. At the foot of the tower was a carpet of wild flowers, anemones, wild callas, and many other blossoms I did not know.

"Is the snow always there?" J. asked, pointing to the Sierra Nevada.

"I was born in the tower," said Maria; "I have lived here all my life, and I have never seen those mountains without snow. That is the *campana de la Vela*," she pointed to a huge bronze bell hanging in the turret. "You should see the tower on the day after New Year. How many girls come up to see the view that day! They believe, foolish ones, that she who rings the bell on the second of January will get a husband before the year is over." Maria smiled, with grim close-shut lips. Had she ever been weak enough to try the charm? For Encarnacion it was unthinkable.

"When Don Alfonzo was here we asked him to ring the bell. Though he laughed very much, he would not. From what we hear, he will be married before New Year all the same."

In the Torre de la Vela they know all that is going on. It was growing dark; the stars were pricking through the blue; down in the city of Granada the lights seemed to reflect them.

"Is that the Gypsy quarter?" I asked Maria. I could just make out doors like the one leading to Aladdin's cave, in the face of a hillside far below.

"Yes, that is the Albaicin. You have been there?"

"Not yet; to-morrow we shall go to see some Gypsy dancing."

Maria shrugged scornful shoulders. "Take care they don't pick your pockets. The Gitanos are great thieves; they are taught to steal from the time they are babies. You may like what you will see. When there are no ladies," she held up her hands in horror, "their dances are not to be imagined or described. Do not let him go by himself." She looked at Patsy, leaning over the parapet absorbed in the view. "They are deceitful hussies! The dances they dance when men go alone are very different from what you will see!"

"That would be a hot walk without the shade of those trees," said Patsy. "Pleasant that we should remember the Iron Duke in Spain most of all for his elms. Who loves his fellow men, plants trees. The English *are* civilized, confound 'em! The longer you're in Europe, the more you have to think of England as the Great Friend."

There was no excuse to linger longer. The sisters had invited us to sup, and we had declined.

"Go you with God," said Encarnacion, she came with us to the door. "To-night when you hear the *campana* de la Vela, think of Maria and me in the tower."

"In the tower," echoed Maria over her shoulder.

The next day we drove to the Albaicin, by the road of the Sacred Mountain. The base of the mountain is honeycombed with gypsy cave dwellings. The caves are built, or rather excavated,

GIPSIES OF GRANADA.

at four different levels, and entered from rough terraces. The gypsy settlement seemed a sort of primitive community, like those from which Tangiers and Naples must have developed into the terraced cities they are to-day. Higher up the mountains are the sacred caves where hermits once lived. On the summit is a large church and a religious house.

"That old gentleman Don Jaime gave me the letter to," said Patsy, "told me that the priests who live up there are no end of swells. They can't 'get in' on anything but merit, not even royal patronage. They must show that they have the goods; must pass a stiff examination. Each one has his separate establishment, with his own house and garden and servants, and draws a pension of from three to five thousand pesetas a year. Most of them are great 'orators'; they are sent for from all over Spain to preach, and jolly well paid for it. They always get twenty-five dollars a sermon, and have been known to get forty! Spain's the place for priests; when I take orders I shall come here to live!"

The gypsy King met us at the entrance of his cave; a swart hulk of a man, with the voice of a bull and bold piercing eyes. Behind him stood his son, looking just as the King must have looked at twenty. The boy had a mop of coarse black hair—the King's was iron gray—low forehead, strong white teeth, that curious veiled eye that later in life grows fierce and bright; body, hands, feet, exquisitely turned, color a rich olive, the look of race that is better than beauty, and the glow of youth that is best of all. It was small wonder the two ragged girls plaiting straw in the dust of the hot yellow road looked at him with longing eyes.

The door of the cave, fitted flat against the hillside, seemed to lead into the bowels of the earth. The cave, literally scooped out of the mountain, was divided into four decent whitewashed rooms, comfortable and clean enough. We went directly from the road into the largest; it was of fair size, with rough beams running across the ceiling and with a tiled floor. We were expected; great preparations had been made for our visit. A row of rush-bottomed chairs stood against the wall. Beautifully polished copper saucepans of many sizes were placed on a shelf, with some wild peonies stuck in a beer bottle. I somehow fancied that the saucepans would be for sale if we took a fancy to them. A small inner room, perfectly dark, led from the living room; it had a bed with a white crocheted quilt. On the left of the entrance was a cave room that served as a kitchen; on the right, a sort of property room,—where half a dozen women and girls with powdered faces and fresh flowers in their hair were waiting. The eldest, a fierce old woman with a beak like a parrot's, dusted a chair for me.

"This is my house," she said. Pointing to the King, "He is my son, these are all my family." She seemed surprised at my asking if there was any other cave as good as hers.

"No," she said, "this is the best; cool in summer, warm in winter, and clean, as you can see."

The musicians, the King's son and another youth with oiled hair and clean new jackets, took their places, twanged their guitars and the *fiesta flamanca* began. First a dance by two women, while the others sat by, clapping their hands, tapping with their feet, keeping time to the music.

"More power!" cried the King.

"*Dalé, dalé,*" droned the chorus. The guitars twanged louder, the hand-clapping redoubled. Little by little the dancers woke up. The youngest woman was sixty, the oldest girl ten. This was a little disappointing to Patsy, though they all did their best and gave us good measure. The children were evidently students being carefully trained; the old women were all good artists, and intent on preserving and handing down the traditions of their art,—but the thing was somehow curiously academic! The old mother took a tambourine from the wall and shook out the music from it in fine style. "Tire yourselves!" she cried. After the second dance, she handed a tray with glasses of wine. Each succeeding dance was better than the last. The best of all was the one the old woman gave us at the end. Only once was there an approach to what Maria had hinted at. A woman with a bad face gave us a Jaleo, a gross, wriggling dance with unpleasant contortions of the body, wonderful as an exhibition of skill and strength, but not quite decent, and lacking the grace, the beauty, and the dignity of the old woman's performance.

"Haven't we had enough?" said Patsy, at the end of half an hour. "You saw those men tip the wink to our coachman as we passed? The whole village is on its good behavior. We are not to be shocked, annoyed, or begged from; it's all put down in the bill we must pay the ruffian King for protecting us from his tribe, preventing us from seeing the real thing and giving us this fake show."

Patsy was all wrong—because he was disappointed in the age of the performers! You can see a young and handsome Spanish dancing girl in any music hall in Madrid. The gypsy cave in the mountainside, where the dancers of the past and the dancers of the future meet, was worth a trip to Granada!

LA PUERTA DEL VINO, GRANADA.

A COURT OF THE ALHAMBRA.

Of course we spent most of our time in Granada at the Alhambra. Some things must be experienced to be understood. Falling in love is one, Niagara Falls another, going down a toboggan slide a third, the Alhambra a fourth. The old simile of the oyster came to mind as freshly as if we had invented it,—just as every pair of young lovers imagine they have invented love! The heavy walls are the outside of the oyster; the fairy courts and halls painted with the tints of rainbow, dawn, sea, and moonlight are the inside of the shell. The pearl? In the room of the Two Sisters the winter apartment of the sultana, I had a vision of Irving's Linderaxa. I could not remember how he described his pearl of the harem, but the face I saw or dreamed of as I sat in that fairy palace was the fairest woman's face I ever saw. Her skin was like warm ivory, her hair an aureole of flame, her eyes, gray stars, her smile, the smile of the imperishable child.

I asked Patsy if he was disappointed in the Alhambra.

"Yes," he said, "disappointed the right way. After the Acropolis, it is the best thing I ever saw. The lovely color, the movement of it all! Will you tell me how any people could invent a written language as decorative as this?" We were in one of the great halls looking at the Cuffik inscriptions that form one of the most fascinating and characteristic of the wall ornamentations.

"It is all based on Persian art, but it is even more joyous, don't you think? You know the Koran discourages, if it does not forbid, the representation of any living creature in art. That is like the 'Thou shalt make no graven image.' Man and beast are practically ruled out of Arab art. Do you miss them? I don't. After the gross use of men and animals,—remember the great bearded bullmen of the Assyrians, and the hawk and cat headed gods of Egypt,—this endless variation of leaf and flower and geometric design is refreshing. Why it is like a vegetarian diet to a sailor man who has had scurvy from living on salt beef."

The guardian, who had long tracked us, here buttonholed J., and poured out a flood of familiar information. We listened mechanically, as he talked, until he said something we had not heard twenty times before.

"Last week two Moors from the Algeciras Conference were here. I myself took them about. They showed no enthusiasm. In this room the older one said to me, 'These are sentences from the Koran,' as if I did not know that before! In spite of all their pretended indifference, I knew very well what those Moors were feeling. It is a very deceitful race; they always hide their emotions." The guardian spoke as scornfully of the Moors as Maria had spoken of the gypsies.

"Do you notice how they all dislike what they call deceit? The Spaniard is a truthful person, and honest. I don't know why it is surprising, but after some of the countries we have traveled in, it comes like a shock!" said Patsy.

A long straight path of gold sand between two lines of tall, black cypresses leads to the old Moorish garden of the Generalife, near the Alhambra. Every other tree is clipped square at the top, the alternate one towering to a pointed spire. There is always a sound of gliding waters; in the early morning and evening, when the birds' matins and lauds are sung, you can hear the nightingales and the merles. In the patio of the cypresses, under the shade of immemorial trees, is a great sheet of still green water like a vast chrysophrase, where you can study the cloud shadows, or your own reflection—if you are handsome—like Narcissus, or watch the greedy gudgeon and gold fish devour the bread you throw them. We passed through a long, flower-bordered path with a thicket of laurel, aloes and pomegranate for a background. A hundred tiny jets of water, like white aigrettes, waved among the green, and lost themselves in the shrubbery. We climbed the long Stairway of the Cascades, cheered by the babble of the little streams of water that run down the tops of the balustrade on either side. In the mirador at the top we rested, and looked down on the wonderful garden with its terraces, cedars, clipped myrtle hedges, thousand and one fountains.

"The Bankshires are only beginning here; in Seville the rose madness was at its height," said Patsy. "We have travelled with the rose; we couldn't have managed better if we had tried."

From the mirador you see the Sierras with the eternal snow fields glistening on their summits. "The Moors certainly understood the use of water," said J. "I have never seen anything quite so good as this garden even in Italy."

There was music in the air, the rushing sound of water from those melting snows cunningly led down the mountainside and set here to dance and sing, to cool the heat and beguile the leisure hours of long, hot, summer days. Patsy watched with fascinated eyes a joyous *saldadore* of water leaping and singing under the shade of an oak.

"Water is to these people of the south what fire is to us northerners," he said. "They are the two living elements, and they both dance. Dancing is the natural expression of joy in life; it is copied from dancing spray and dancing flame. David was quite right to dance before the ark. I had a

RETABLO, CARVED IN HIGH AND LOW RELIEF. *Roldan*

Shaker nurse who danced with me when I cried; I suppose that is why I'm so fond of it."

Granada cathedral is so hemmed in with trumpery little buildings that it is impossible to get an impression of it as a whole. The mushroom growth will have to go. Each succeeding tourist wave sweeping over Europe, as the Goths and Vandals swept before them, sweeps away some such trash, and uncovers hidden gems of architecture. The interior of the cathedral, though over ornate, has some splendid architectural effects, and is rich in every sort of treasure ecclesiastical. I remember a curious white marble statue of the Virgin with a black marble cloak, and a very charming painted wood group of St. Anne, St. Joachim and Mary, a good example of one of the arts you must come to Spain to see. Painted wood statuary, wrought iron work, ecclesiastical embroidery and—dancing have all been carried farther in Spain than anywhere else in Europe. Montañes, Roldan, and Alonzo Cano, succeeded in making their painted wood statues and bas-reliefs as dignified as if they had worked in bronze or marble. Just as Luca della Robbia did with terra cotta. There is a polychrome carved retablo of the Entombment in Seville, by Roldan, that is a true masterpiece of sculpture. The outer figures are modelled in such high relief they seem almost free; those in the middle distance are in ordinary high relief, the more distant in low, almost flat relief; the background is a painted wood panel. This does not sound encouraging, but the material a masterpiece is made of is of little consequence; it may be wood, marble, iron, gold or woven wool,—if a master uses it, a masterpiece is produced.

As I was sketching the wonderful wrought iron screen that shuts off the tombs from the main part of the chapel royal, I heard two women's voices: "You have made a mistake, I think. The tombs of Ferdinand and Isabel are on the right," said an alert, gray-haired woman.

"Thank you; I know," said a clear young voice. The last speaker, caught red handed in the very act of laying flowers on a tomb, was annoyed. She saw that I, too, looked with disfavor on the alert gray-haired lady with the guidebook, and by mutual consent we made acquaintance beside the tomb of Juana la Loca, the daughter of Ferdinand and Isabel, and her husband, Philippe le Bel.

"Poor things!" said the girl who had laid the flowers between the two marble figures lying side by side.

"Poor things! Tell me their story if you remember it."

"They were married when Juana was seventeen, and Philippe eighteen. She was very pretty, but he was the handsomest man in Europe. They only had each other ten years; even then they were not allowed much peace! At first they lived at his court in Brussels where they were very happy; life was not quite so strict and straight laced as at the Spanish Court. Isabel was a great queen, but I don't think she could have been a nice mother. She sent a priest to be Juana's confessor, a grim Spanish bigot. Phillippe laughed at him so much that Juana refused to confess to him. That was the beginning of all their troubles! The priest came back to Spain and told tales, set her mother against Juana. When she came home, to be with her mother when her child was born, Isabel tried to prevent her returning to her husband,—locked her up. Did you ever hear of such a thing?"

She spoke as if it was happening now; her face was flushed; she clinched and unclinched her hand.

"But they couldn't keep Juana; she was like a raging lioness; they had to let her go back to her husband. Then Isabel spread the report that Juana was mad,—and made arrangements in her will to prevent her ever reigning. Juana wouldn't have cared about that; all she wanted was to be let alone, to have a little peace and happiness in her life. After Isabel's death, those two poor things made their great mistake,—they came back to Spain. Somebody who was jealous of their happiness poisoned Philippe. Nobody knows whether Juana's father Ferdinand was responsible for the murder or the Inquisition. I think it was the Inquisition; those cruel inquisitors did not want anybody to be happy, and Philippe was too liberal, too open-minded to suit that terrible Cardinal Jimenez. Juana and Philippe were at Burgos at the time. When it was all over, the friends who were with her at the deathbed told Juana that her husband was dead.

"No," she said, "not dead, asleep!" You see, then, she really did go mad. They had Philippe embalmed and put in a leaden coffin; from that day Juana was never separated from his body. Wherever she went she took it with her; for twenty years she travelled all over the country with it. I saw her coach, the first that ever came to Spain, in Madrid. In those days, when royalties travelled, they stopped at convents or monasteries, if there was no royal residence near. Poor Juana was so jealous she would never go into a convent, for fear the nuns might look at her beloved! Philippe dead had his pages and his suite just as if he had been alive. Finally, Juana was shut up at Tordesillas. There she had the coffin placed in a chapel leading from her room, where she could always see it.

MOORISH COLUMNS IN THE ALHAMBRA.

Here is a photograph I bought of Pradilla's picture of Juana."

The picture shows the sad procession on a windswept hillside outside Burgos just before dawn. The coffin stands on an iron bier, with two wax candles at the head and foot. A priest reads the service from his book. Juana's ladies stand or sit exhausted on the ground. A group of pages and gentlemen in furred dresses stand near a fire kindled in the open. Juana, in a long black dress, stands beside the coffin looking down. "Dead? No, asleep!" she seems to say.

"For forty-seven years Juana watched beside the body of her husband. He died at twenty-eight; she lived to seventy-four. Their son, Charles V, gave Juana as fine a tomb as Isabel's. I think she deserved it. A great lover is as rare as a great queen. Come with me and see the vault. That old battered coffin is Philippe's, the very one Juana carried about with her. I touched it the other day. It made it all seem so real!"

We were standing by the royal vault, looking down through a grating at the coffins, when a fair young man with blue eyes strolled through the chapel and joined us.

"Haven't you been here long enough, Joan?" he said. "Let's get out of this stuffy old church."

"All ready, Philip; I was only waiting for you." She looked at him with adoring eyes, smiled kindly at me, and went off leaning on his arm. They were as pretty a young couple as you could see, and their names were Philip and Joan! It could hardly have been by chance that they were here. I fancied that the bride had contrived to include a pilgrimage to the tomb of the true lover, Joan the Mad, in their wedding journey.

Amor es como el vino	Love is like wine;
guárdate á tiempo	Guarded with time
y te sabrá más dulce	It shall taste to thee sweetest
cuanto mas viejo.	When it is oldest.

IX

TANGIERS

WE sailed from Algeciras for what Don Jaime called our "little crusade to Morocco." The Don could not go with us; he was called to Madrid, he said, on important business. Patsy, who went down to Algeciras a day or two before us, had something to tell about the Conference then in session. The Moroccan delegates had arrived at night, bringing the ladies of their harems with them. They had landed between two and three in the morning, so the few curious persons waiting on the dock only caught an unsatisfactory glimpse of muffled figures passing from the vessel to the waiting carriages. Private houses had been prepared for the Moorish delegates; most of the Europeans, and Mr. Henry White, the American delegate, stayed at the Hotel Maria Cristina.

At the opening meeting of the Conference on the sixteenth of January, 1906, the president, the Duc d'Almodovar, declared that the reforms to be introduced into Morocco must be based on the triple principle of the sovereignty of the Sultan the integrity of his states, and the open door. The poor Moroccan delegates, who did not want any reforms at all introduced into their country, were only allowed to read their little speech at the second session, and as it was in Arabic, nobody understood much of it.

We had a perfect day for our trip across the Straits of Gibraltar from Europe to Africa. It took two hours and a half, and seemed much shorter than crossing the English channel. At one point we could see at the same time the white houses of Tangiers, and the gray Moorish fortifications of Tarifa, the southernmost point of Europe. The currents are very strong between the two coasts. A French steamer lay wrecked upon the rocks close to Tarifa Point light. The sea was like a silver shield. On the Spanish coast there were long stretches of tawny sands among the gray and purple rocks, with here and there an ancient Saracen watch-tower.

"Trafalgar Bay lies in that direction," said Patsy, pointing to the northwest. "Nelson must have looked at these yellow cliffs, as he lay dying on the deck of the Victory, thinking, perhaps, of the white cliffs of England."

The winds that blew over Trafalgar Bay caught the great Admiral's last command, "Anchor,

TANGIERS.

Hardy, anchor," and his last request whispered to his trusty Captain, "Kiss me, Hardy!" If you ever sail that way, listen to the wind whistling in the shrouds. If you have ears to hear such things, you may catch the echo of that whisper.

The coast of Africa, as we approached it, was not more arid than the opposite shore.

We anchored in the bay far out from Tangiers, a white town set like a pearl on the edge of an emerald crescent. Near the right point of the crescent, Tangiers climbs up the hill from the yellow sea sands to the green heights of the foreign embassies and villas; at the extreme point stands the lighthouse. America cleared the Mediterranean of Barbary pirates; and the great European powers built the lighthouse, as they have built the post-offices, the hospital, and every other modern thing in Morocco. While waiting for the health officers, we watched the fish darting through the clear, beryl-green water. Presently a lighter with a load of bulls closely wedged together drew up alongside the steamer. A rope was passed round the horns of two of the bulls, and they were hoisted on board in pairs, in what seemed a cruel manner. The whole weight came on their horns, their necks were stretched out, their poor, frightened eyes, blank with terror haunt me still. They made no noise; most of them hung limp; a few struggled and only succeeded in kicking each other.

We and our luggage were rowed ashore in a small boat. The sea was alive with half naked bronze men in sacking bournouses, who waded back and forth, carrying enormous loads of terra cotta tiles from a lighter to the land. On the pier a splendid person in a long blue garbardine, white turban, and yellow slippers, met us with a card and a bouquet of flowers.

"My name is Ali," he said; "I am your friend." He laid his hand to his lips, then to his forehead with the grave and lovely salutation of the East.

Ali led us before three magnificent, white-robed Moors, sitting cross-legged on the floor of the custom-house, smoking long chibouks. These officials paid no attention to us; indeed, they seemed unconscious of our presence. The two younger men went on with their conversation; the elder, kingly as Saul, looked silently across the sea towards that lost paradise of his race, Andalusia. Our luggage was laid down at their feet; they did not even glance at it. After a few minutes, the youngest Moor took his pipe from his mouth, and waved his hand slightly in our direction.

"All right," said Ali, "good custom-house, yes?"

The bearers took up our portmanteaus, and we passed into the narrow crowded street where no vehicle can go, and where Ali had hard work to protect me from the surging crowd of heavily laden porters and donkeys. It was market day. Ali piloted us through a maze of narrow, twisting lanes, and markets thronged with strange figures: Moors in white bournouses, Jews in black caftans, negro slaves with gashed faces, wild looking hill men with blue eyes, who looked at us more fiercely than all the rest. The buyers and sellers outshrieked each other. The long sharp cry of the water-carriers, the braying of donkeys, the yelling of man, woman and child, mingled with the hammering of the tin and coppersmiths in the bazaars.

In the vegetable market we met a tall old Sheik with a long beard, dressed in a lovely pea-green *jellabiyah*, with turban to match, and salmon colored undergarments. Ali salaamed to him.

"Health be with you!"

"And with you be peace!" The Sheik's voice was like distant thunder. He carried a large basket. The seller of vegetables received him respectfully, if less cordially than Ali. The Sheik cast a critical eye over the vegetables, then laid his hand on a bunch of young carrots, a string of fresh onions, some ruby radishes and some long green beans. Whatever he touched, the dealer put into his basket, saying, "Take it," each time more faintly.

"God increase thy goods!" said the Sheik, when he had considerably diminished them by half filling his own basket.

"And thy goods, also," answered the dealer cheerfully, as the old man pottered off to the butcher's, next door.

"He is holy man," said Ali; "they all give to him."

The butcher's gifts—a skinned sheep's head, with awful staring eyes, and other gruesome things, were too horrid to look at. We waited till the Sheik passed on to the bread sellers, a group of white shrouded women sitting against a wall. They were as carefully veiled as if they had been young and lovely ladies. Each had a cushion before her with flat loaves of bread. When the middle one gave the Sheik a loaf, there was the rattle of bangles, and a glimpse of a hand that might have belonged to the Cumaean sibyl.

Outside the market, in the midst of the mad hurly-burly, there appeared an incarnation of that Oriental calm we had begun to believe the Moors had left behind them in Cordova. Down the middle of an evil-smelling lane, a man on horseback rode slowly towards us. The squalling crowd made way for him, flattening itself against the wall.

"Welcome!" said Ali, as the stranger passed in the odor of sandalwood.

"Twice welcome," answered the horseman. He was fairer than many Spaniards; his brown beard and moustache were beautifully combed and curled, he had a high aquiline nose, eyes like dark jewels, thin pencilled eyebrows. He was dressed all in white; his *sulham* of finest wool had a silk braid round the edge, and tassel hanging from the hood drawn over his head. He turned his horse to avoid us. Except for that slight motion of laying the reins against the animal's neck—the action showed a slim brown hand with an ancient turquoise ring—he gave no sign of having seen us. It is a sign of Arab as of British breeding, not to look too much at strangers.

"That was an Arab gentleman," said J.

"Now I know just how Abd-er Rahman looked!" murmured Patsy.

The horse was a spirited chestnut, with a skin so thin the veins showed under it, and delicate, proud feet that he planted scornfully in the unspeakable filth of the lane. Later, in Blacksmiths Square, where we lingered to watch two men shoe an old white mare—one held her foot, the other put on the shoe—a servant led the chestnut up to the smith. The man stopped work, patted the chestnut and kissed it, while his helper fed it with little cakes. Though there were a dozen horses and mules waiting their turn to be shod, the chestnut took precedence over all.

Ali explained this favoritism. "That horse, he have been to Mecca," he said. "That make him very holy."

For all his holiness the homely smell of the chestnut's scorched hoof when the hot shoe touched it was in no wise different from the old white mare's!

Seeing the horse fitted with a set of new shoes reminded J. and Patsy that while in Morocco they must each buy a pair of real Morocco slippers. Ali had a friend who was a slipper seller, so we hunted him up in the quiet, back street where he lived. We found him in a tiny bazaar like a big box, hung with slippers of every size and color. The others were so long choosing their shoes, the street was so deserted, that I ventured to walk on alone. From an open doorway came the drone of childish voices reciting a lesson; an Arab school was in session. Twenty very little boys sat upon the floor, rocking slowly back and forth, reciting verses from the Koran in a sort of singsong chant. The schoolroom was a dark, dank hole, its only light coming from the door. Dazzled by the blinding light of the street, I did not at first see the schoolmaster, a young man of eighteen. He sat near the door, writing out sentences from the Koran with a reed pen, in a large book like a ledger. He had just reached the bottom of the page, had dipped his reed in a fascinating bronze inkstand worn in his sash, and I was silently admiring his beautiful Arabic handwriting, when he looked up and saw me. A tiny boy, who could not have been more than three, just then smiled at me. He was such a bonny child, so like one of the children at home, that I kissed my hand to him.

"Christian dog!" The master's rattan whizzed through the air, and came down whack, whack, on each side of the boy's head. Then all the little children scowled and bit their thumbs at me. The master tore the neatly written page from the book, crumpled it up, threw it at me, and retreated across the room, the book under his arm, cursing me as I believe I was never cursed before.

At that moment Ali came running up, and after a few angry words with the schoolmaster, hurried me away.

"They no like you," he said. "I am your friend; I take care of you."

The page had been torn from the book because the shadow of a Christian had fallen upon it! After that, Ali became as my shadow. When I wanted to stop and admire the tower of the great Mosque,—it has a poor, far-away likeness to the Giralda—he would not let me stay, telling me that it was not safe for Christians to linger near the mosque or the tombs of saints.

The Great Socco, the big market-place outside the city gate, is the most Oriental thing you can see without going to India. The bazaars of Constantinople, the Muski of Cairo, even the streets of Jaffa, are European compared to it. The Socco lies on a bare hillside; it is shut in with walls, and entered through a handsome Moorish gate. A restless stream of camels, asses, beggars, traders, fruit-sellers, veiled women, jugglers and snake charmers pulses ceaselessly back and forth. A caravan from Fez was starting that day, another had just arrived. The camels snarled and grunted as the drivers unloaded their bales of merchandise and dates. Near the gate, in a corner of comparative peace, an audience had collected about the one-eyed story teller. He beat his drum as we came up. Ali gave him a piece of silver, and we were allowed to stand on the edge of the crowd and listen to the tale of the Fisherman and the Genie told in Arabic with dramatic gestures, and listened to with breathless interest.

There was an encampment at one end of the Socco, extending outside the gate along the road to Vez. The tents were small and poor, the people who lived in them wild, and, at the same time, wan

STREET IN TANGIERS.

- 127 -

looking,—the most wretched of all the wretched people I have ever seen. They belong to a tribe of Berbers from the country, driven by famine into Tangiers. The blue eyes of those half-naked, half-starved hillmen shone with a fierce light; the black-eyed Moors looked gentle beside them. Blue eyes mean white blood! The wild hillmen have not forgotten where it comes from. They remember that long and long ago, in Roman days, a tribe of Vandals and Alans—some say eighty thousand people—crossed the straits to Morocco and never came back, though three hundred years later some of their descendants came over to Spain with Tarik, our old friend of Tarik's Hill, and conquered Christian Spain for the Crescent.[2]

Outside the Socco, on the road leading up to the villas, we came upon a white umbrella with an artist we knew by sight sketching under it, guarded by a soldier. His was the first Christian face we had seen since we left the steamer; it seemed an age, it was but a few hours ago. We greeted each other as if we had been old friends! He knew Tangiers well, had been here three months sketching, therefore he had a great deal to tell us about Morocco and the Moors. I noticed during all our stay that the people who had lived longest in Morocco were the least positive in what they said about the Moors! My first question to the artist was about the Berber tribe.

"During the Algeciras Conference," he said, "the Sultan feeds them with bread every day, so that it may not be said that he cannot take care of his own. They tell me here that the day the Conference adjourns, there will be no more bread given away in Tangiers."

Before lunch time J. and Patsy adopted, or were adopted, by a Hebrew Jew. Israel was his name; Christian, compared to the fierce Moslem horde, was his nature. He was a neat young man, educated at the school of the Israelite Alliance in Tangiers, pleasant and well mannered, his chief defect being that he wore silly European clothes, when he might have worn lovely Oriental robes. He quickly confided to us that he was engaged to be married, and that his Rachel was suffering from acute dyspepsia. He didn't *say* dyspepsia, but he illustrated it with unmistakable sounds and gestures.

"Let her take one of these after every meal." Patsy handed Israel a bottle of soda mint tablets. Israel bent himself double with bowing. Meanwhile he and Ali gabbled together; the word *hakem* (physician) was repeated several times. The soda mints worked well; they suited Rachel, and Patsy's reputation as a physician was made. That was the beginning of all his glory, and our discomfort.

At luncheon there was quail for him, larks for us. When we rode out, he had the best mount. The pillows of his bed were soft as down, ours hard as brickbats. That night Ali consulted him about his daughter, who seemed to be suffering from bronchitis. A box of Brown's bronchial troches was unearthed from my medicine chest and given to Ali. Though the troches were mine, the credit was Patsy's!

I saw three prisons in Tangiers: the prison of the Moors, the prison of the Jews, and the prison of a Prominent Citizen's wives. In the first two, hideous and squalid past belief, criminals are kept; in the third, the mothers of the prominent citizens of to-morrow, in whose hands lie the future of Morocco. This prison, called a harem, was the most dreadful of all, though it was clean, handsome, had a large patio, marble columns, and whatever else passes in Morocco for luxury. I was received by the Prominent Citizen's four wives. The favorite, an enormously fat young woman, sleek and sleepy as a cat, had painted eyes and finger nails reddened with henna. After the first greeting, the other women paid little attention to me; the favorite, who was younger, had some questions to ask.

"Are you married? How many children have you? I have a son. She"—looking at a woman who sat near, a sour-faced creature of Chinese type—"has only daughters. This morning we saw you pass in the street. I know that everything is different in your country. You travel, we stay at home; you go out unveiled, we may not show our faces to any strange man. There were two men with you this morning; were they your two husbands?"

I tried to explain Patsy. It seemed stranger to her that he was only our friend travelling with us, than if he had been an extra husband.

A servant brought in a copper machine like a Russian samovar, and the Chinese looking wife made tea for us with fresh green tea leaves and mint. It was very sweet, and not just what I am used to in the way of tea, but I managed to drink one small tumblerful; the ladies of the harem drank glass after glass. I had brought a present of some goodies, and when these had been distributed the conversation became more animated. The women all examined my dress, hat, gloves and jewels, with greatest interest. The favorite cried out at the close fitting French waist, held her hands to her own fat sides, and shook her head at the very thought of confining those Atlas mountains of flesh with stiff whalebone. I told her that I thought her dress much more comfortable, and far prettier than mine; this pleased her more than anything I said.

From the corridor round the patio heavy green doors led to the women's sleeping rooms. They had no windows; no light or air could ever penetrate those dreadful places, quite empty save for the beds,—mattresses laid on the floor covered with gay quilts,—and several large clocks hanging on the walls. In the part of the harem I saw there was literally nothing except divans, beds, and little stands for trays,—things to sit on, to sleep in, to eat from. There must have been rooms where the cooking and housework goes on, but I did not see them. The rooms were empty, the faces of the women were empty. It seemed the height of irony that where time is of so little value there should be so many timepieces. The English lady who arranged the visit for me goes often to this and other harems.

"The women's lives are so dull, any visitor is welcome," she said. "One rule I have had to make. I must choose the subject we talk about,— otherwise, they would talk of unspeakable things. They are so coarse and dull. Poor things!"

The poorer women seem better off than the well-to-do, because they have more occupation. They cook, wash, and make the clothes for themselves and their children. They must be very strong, for I saw women carrying the most enormous loads of faggots. Divorce is not uncommon among them; the divorced woman is always given back her dowry. A bride is brought to her husband's house heavily veiled. It is for her to lift the veil; if she refuses, the marriage does not go on. I heard of a girl who for three days kept her veil down, and was then sent back to her parent's house.

It was pleasant after a day spent in the muck and confusion of Tangiers, to mount Zuleika, the big gray donkey, and ride up to the European quarter for the sunset. My saddle was like a little chair set sideways on the mule, with a swinging board to support my feet. Ali walked by my side, Abdul, the mule driver, just behind.

"Arrree!" Abdul cried, and twisted Zuleika's tail till the poor creature screamed.

"Stop!" said Ali. "By thy head, do not that again. Dost thou not know that Christians would rather see a man beaten than a beast?"

"*Mashallah!*" muttered Abdul. Israel, running beside Patsy, holding his stirrup, told him in French what the other two said, so they were usually silent in Israel's presence.

SPANISH PEASANTS.

ALI AND ZULEIKA.

We were on our way to see our friend Mme. Hortense, whom we found waiting for us on the terrace of her pleasant house. She had kept her word, and provided a characteristic Moorish entertainment for our afternoon's visit,—a snake charmer. His long bag of snakes moved as the mass of serpents writhed and wriggled. One after another he took the long pythons from his bag and let them coil and twist about his body. Last of all he took out a small, vicious looking serpent, and held it to his mouth. The snake bit his tongue, or appeared to do so, for drops of the snakecharmer's blood fell on the white marble pavement.

"You've seen enough?" asked Mme. Hortense. She spoke to the snake charmer with the voice of authority; he gathered up his dreadful linen bag and departed.

"*Allahu akbar!*" The cry of the Muezzin in the minaret of the mosque came faintly up to us on the heights.

"Progress?" said Mme. Hortense in answer to my question, as the ridiculous shambling figure of the snake charmer left the terrace. "Among the Jews, yes, if you call it progress! When I came here, thirty-four years ago, your boy Israel's father and all the rest of them, wore the fez and the kaftan. Now many of the younger ones wear straw hats and trousers. They have built themselves comfortable houses in the worst possible taste. The schools of the Israelite Alliance have really accomplished a miracle. For the Moors there is no progress, believe me. In all these years they have not advanced one step. Here in Tangiers they are on their good behavior, of course; the city is well policed by the European powers. There is no public slave market here, you must go to Fez to see that; but as to real advance,—look at that blind man! His eyes were put out for stealing."

Down the hot road under the blue cactus hedge a poor pock-marked blind man cried for alms. Mme. Hortense threw him a coin, a tall, shrouded woman who was passing, a bare brown child astride on her hip, picked up the money and gave it him.

"God increase thy goods," said the blind man. Then as he wandered down the hill led by his dog, tapping with his cane, "God vouchsafe thee a good evening. May thy night be happy!"

"He is my cook's son," said Mme. Hortense. "All my servants are Moors, except my Jewish chairmen,—no Moor will carry a Christian. I like the Moors best. At the time of the last uprising I asked my favorite servant what he would do if our house were attacked. He said, 'I would lie down on the ground before you. That means that you belong to me and that they must kill me before they touch you.' I think he would have done it, too. A good Moor has no vices; he neither drinks nor smokes. The doctors will tell you what good blood they have; a wound heals with them in half the time it does with us. Of course I know the servant class best, that is natural. The better class do not like us,—can you blame them? A man my husband knew, quite a great personage in his way, got into evil ways from associating with Christians; in fact, he drank himself to death. He was a sacred person, of the family of the prophet. The faithful believed the liquor he drank was turned to milk as it touched his lips, and that he died without sin; all the same, the wise ones hold us at arm's length."

"Progress!" Mme. Hortense came back to my question. "Last week a man from the interior came to Tangiers on business. It turned out that it was important for him to stay here longer than he had planned; but, at some sacrifice, he persisted in returning to his home on the day originally fixed. It leaked out through his servants that before leaving home he had walled up the door of his house. There was a well inside, and the house was provisioned, as if for a siege, but the women would grow restless if he delayed his return too long!"

While Mme. Hortense talked, there appeared before us on the terrace, as if by magic, a lean man with very few clothes and bare, sinewy arms. He was a juggler, and as we sat there looking down on the flat white houses, the minarets, the sea beyond, listening to Mme. Hortense's stories of life in Tangiers, the juggler pulled from his mouth length after length of rose-colored ribbon, till he stood in a pink bower miraculously produced from his interior. A string of large, dangerous looking needles followed the pink ribbons from his inexhaustible maw.

"*Baraka, baraka!*" Enough, enough, cried Mme. Hortense. The juggler bowed and was gone as he had come, silently, and as if by magic.

I never knew where Ali slept or when he ate. If I wanted him at the most impossible time, he was always there! One morning when the voice of the sea and the song of the birds called me out into the garden for the sunrise, I thought I had escaped him. Before I reached the end of the oleander walk he was at my side. Then came the natural, if unreasonable, demand: "Ali, I am so hungry, get me something to eat."

"He cook, he hurry up; lady, wait ten minutes."

"I can't wait. Get me a glass of milk."

"Pick your pardon, lady, no can squeeze the buffalo before he had his breakfast."

Such strange and interesting creatures lived in that garden: wonderful long-tailed Japanese cocks with their neat little hens, a lame gazelle, a white peacock, some blue Australian pigeons, and many other birds,—and they all had their breakfasts before I had mine. When Ali finally brought it on a tray and set it on a table under a mammoth mulberry tree, I was so busy with the bread and honey—orange blossom honey; when I took the lid off the jar, the perfume was as strong as if I had held a bunch of orange flowers in my hand—that I did not notice two gentlemen who were waiting for their breakfast. The buffalo had been squeezed by this time, for the gentlemen's servant brought them dates and milk.

My neighbors were an odd pair: an old man who looked like Jumbo, with wise small eyes, and gray wrinkled skin like an elephant's, and a young man, his son or grandson, who could not have been more than twenty, though the lower part of his face was covered with a full soft beard. They were Orientals, I thought, and they would have looked better in turbans and robes than in European dress. They talked together in a language whose very sound was unfamiliar. They seemed so remote, so unconscious of my presence, so much more like figures out of the Arabian Nights than fellow travellers, that when the older man came up to my table, spoke to me in perfect English, and asked me if I would like to see *La Dépêche Morocaine*, the French daily newspaper, I was as much astonished as if the Sheik of the market-place had spoken to me in my own tongue. We talked about the weather, the view, the picturesqueness of Tangiers; when the ice was well broken I found that he wanted to talk about things at home.

"It is many years since I was in America," he said. "I rarely meet an American." Where *did* he live? "When I have the good fortune," he made me such a bow as Solomon might have made the Queen of Sheba, "I like to hear how the Great Experiment is working out." Then followed a searching examination about affairs at home. His questions showed a complete ignorance of detail, a good grasp of large issues. He read me as if I were a book he only had time to skim through. After I had told him what I could about "the working out" of what he called "the Great Experiment," I asked him to tell me something about the Sultan of Morocco and his brother Muli Hafid. He asked permission to smoke; an Indian servant brought him a nargileh. When it was drawing nicely, and the smoke came cool to his mouth after passing through the water in the crystal jar, he spoke as one who speaks with authority.

"I have known Abdul Aziz and Muli Hafid since they were boys. They are both weak men; there is little to choose between them. I knew their father, Muli el Hassan, before them. He was a strong man; he ruled this people by might, the only way. He was clever, too, pitted the strong tribes against each other so that they punished one another: thus all were kept in order, and the balance of power preserved. When he died, the power remained in the hands of the young Sultan's mother and the Grand Vizier: people said he was her lover,—that is as it may be. Then the Vizier died, the young Sultan took the reins, and everything was changed. The English got hold of the boy, as they have got hold of so many a weak young ruler before him. Abdul Aziz became so completely under English influence that it was said in the bazaars he wore English clothes under the native dress. He is not only a weak, but a pleasure-loving person; the two things usually go together. His favorite amusements are playing polo and going out at night in one of his many automobiles." This he said scornfully, and pulled so hard at his pipe that the water bubbled in the vase.

The young man looked at me and laughed. "Would you rather he took to ballooning, father? Even a Sultan of Morocco must amuse himself. I knew a fellow the Sultan took a fancy to. One sign of his favor was that he accepted my friend's riding crop and cigarette case and forgot to make any return present. He told me a good story about Abdul Aziz: One day he was riding with him, when they met the Sultan's caravan on its way from Tangiers to Fez, bringing Abdul Aziz a grand piano. It had come on to rain, as it sometimes can rain in Morocco! The Sultan insisted on having the piano unloaded from the camels' backs and put together. Then he sat down and strummed on the piano in the middle of the pelting rain, and the camels and the camel drivers and all the escort stood round, or sat on their horses, and waited, on the road to Fez."

"That was like him," said the old man. "It was when he had become so unpopular with the people on account of the English influence that he remitted the taxes for four years as a bid for popularity. Taxes once lifted from a people like this are not easily put on again. The country was nearly bankrupt; the Sultan was at the last gasp financially. As usual he appealed to the English for help. Just then the understanding between England and France was complete: France was to withdraw from Egypt and leave England a free hand there; in return for this, England was to withdraw her influence and support from Morocco. Egypt was worth more to England than Morocco; the Sultan was sold for forty pieces of silver."

"More than he is worth!" said the boy. "France or England, does it matter which? They are the only two civilized countries in Europe."

"There is only one country that can civilize," said the old man,— "England!"

"It would have gone on well enough, if William the Wilful had not put his finger into the pie," said the boy resentfully. His sympathies were evidently with France.

"We were in Fez when the German Emperor made that famous visit to the Sultan," said the old man. "I have never seen the people so moved. They were in a frenzy of joy; they thought they were saved!"

"That bubble was soon pricked," said the boy.

"Perhaps, but the Conference sitting over in Algeciras would never have come off, if it had not been for his visit."

"What will the Conference accomplish?" I asked.

"It will insure what the diplomats call 'the integrity of Morocco' for a little longer, that is all."

"How will it end?"

The old man stroked his long gray beard with a truly Oriental movement of the hand. "Keep your ear to the ground," he said; "the end of Islam is not yet. There are more Mohammedans than Christians in the world; they still make converts. I myself knew an English Lord who became a musselman."

"Instead of quarreling among themselves, let the Christians unite!" said the young man.

"Strife there must be. The young tigers wrestle together, or they would not be strong to wrestle with the enemy when it is time to go out into the jungle and kill!"

We might have gone on gossiping till dinner time,—*they* were in no hurry,—if Ali had not reminded me of an engagement that could not be postponed; I had been invited to tea with the Lady of Tangiers.

The house of the Lady of Tangiers is set on the edge of a high cliff. Far, far below, at the foot of the cliff, the waves break into white foam flowers, and the seagulls flit and swoop in restless flight over the emerald sea. House and garden are shut in by a high wall. A man on horseback was waiting in the road outside the gate, surrounded by a horde of beggars and cripples. A pair of white shrouded women stood a little apart, each with a child on her shoulder. The horseman was armed: a pair of pistols and a knife were stuck in his sash, a rifle was slung over his shoulder; at his left side hung a long sword. Man and horse were both of pure Arab breed; there was a certain likeness between them. Both were thin and wiry, with delicate feet, fierce, flashing eyes, thin, quivering nostrils. The man sat impassive as a bronze statue, and gave no sign of having seen our queer cavalcade as we rode up,—Zuleika, the big gray donkey, with me in my ridiculous chair saddle on her back, Ali running beside, and Abdul hanging on to her tail. The horse pricked its dainty ears, whinnied, and turned its head to look at us.

"*Es-salem alekum!*" Health be with you, said Ali, who never allowed himself to be ignored.

"*U alekum es-salem!*" and with you be peace, answered the Arab on the horse.

The sound of footsteps inside the garden caused great excitement among the cripples. The gate was opened and a servant came out leading a beautiful little boy of four or five. At the sight of the boy, a fair child, with brown curls and pretty, gracious manners, a howl arose from the beggars and cripples. They tried to get hold of him, to kiss his hands or touch his garments. The servant and the man on horseback kept them back as best they could. The horseman laid about him with the flat of his sword:

"By the life of the prophet, room there for my lord the prince! *Yalla!* Go on!"

"I am under thy protection, save me!" cried the oldest beggar; he was rather cleaner than the rest, and was allowed to touch the little foot before the horseman caught up the child, set him before him, put spurs to the horse, and galloped off joyously in a cloud of dust.

"*Al Allah!*" cried the old beggar.

"*Al Allah!*" echoed the cripples, waving their crutches and their maimed stumps after the pretty child.

Ali gave my card and letter of introduction to the servant. I was invited to enter the garden. Ali waited for me in the road outside. Near the house was a little flower bed, with a few homely English flowers; some one had been at work among the marigolds. Outside the door stood a large rocking-horse, a drum and a toy trumpet. I had not long to wait in the reception room, before the Lady of Tangiers appeared. She greeted me heartily.

"Come in," she said, and led the way to a large comfortable, English drawing-room. I suppose I showed some surprise at finding myself in so thoroughly British an interior, for she said:

"I lead a double life. With the Arabs, I am an Arab; with the Europeans, I am a European. We will have our tea here first,—you will like my tea better than my daughter-in-law's; then I will take you into the Arab part of the house and introduce you to my son's wife."

At the first glance the Lady of Tangiers looked the full-blooded English woman she is by birth. As I talked with her, I felt something Oriental in her expression. You cannot live three parts of your life among an alien race without catching something of the racial look. First, and last, and all the time, I felt her to be a woman of power. The servant who brought the tea said something to her in Arabic.

"Were there many children waiting in the crowd outside the gate?" she asked.

I told her I had seen only two.

"They can wait, or come to-morrow," she said. "Their mothers have brought them to be vaccinated. When I first came here I once spoke to my husband about a child I thought should be vaccinated, as there was so much small-pox about."

"How is it done?" he asked.

"I know how it is done," I said, "and I can do it. That was the beginning. Now I vaccinate hundreds of children every year. That is the sort of missionary work I believe in. There is not the slightest use in sending Christian missionaries to any Mahommedan country, unless they are willing to work without direct religious teaching. Civilize first! Teach the women and the girls to cook and sew, something about the laws of health, and the care of children."

The Lady of Tangiers is a member of the Church of England, by the way.

I asked about the pretty boy I had met at the gate.

"That was my little grandson, Muli Hassan, going out for his afternoon's airing. All those people hanging about were waiting to see him start. To them he is not only a noble, but a sacred person. My husband was of a great family. He was descended from the Prophet,—but I am of the oldest family in the world; I am of the Adam and Eve connection!" Her eyes danced as she said it. "In certain respects, my grandchildren are brought up English fashion, as my children were. When my oldest boy was perhaps twelve days old, my mother, who had come out from England to be with me, thought that it might please my husband's old nurse to see the baby have his bath; so she called her into my room. My husband was asleep in a neighboring room. Suddenly he was waked by the old nurse, she was past eighty, shaking him by the arm—usually she would not have dared to disturb him—and crying:

"Come, come quickly! The Christians are murdering your son, they are drowning him!"

My husband hurried to my room. "What does this mean?" he cried out. When he found out what it meant, he threw himself down on the divan and laughed till he cried.

When we had finished our tea, my hostess took me into the part of the house where her son's wife, the mother of Muli Hassan, lives. As she was receiving native visitors in the reception room, the Lady of Tangiers showed me into the bedroom; a large, handsome, airy room with windows opening seawards, and comfortable brass beds. We had not been there long,—I had not had time to take in half the beauty of the outlook from those windows,—when I heard behind me the soft patter of bare feet on the tiled floor, and the daughter-in-law was at my side. She was a pretty woman, with a refined, intelligent face, who received me with a charming Oriental reverence. The nails of her hands and feet were reddened with henna, otherwise she was not painted. She wore a pretty, simple, green tissue robe, with a robe of dotted muslin over it.

"May thy day be white as milk," was her first greeting. Then, "How is thy health?"

"She is sorry she cannot speak your language," said the Lady of Tangiers, "you must not think her an uneducated person on that account. She reads and writes Arabic beautifully."

The young woman was in mourning for a relative: she would wear it for forty days, she told me. Her mourning consisted of not wearing silk or jewels,—the most sensible mourning I ever heard of. She was so fair, except for her melting eyes and coal-black eyebrows, that in European dress she might easily have passed for an Italian. As the other guests were waiting for the daughter-in-law, our visit to her was short.

"*Yalla bina*," now let us go, said the elder woman.

"To Allah's protection," said the mother of Muli Hassan.

We returned to the English drawing-room, where I stayed as long, perhaps longer, than good manners allowed, while the Lady of Tangiers told me things that I hope she will some day tell the world. While I was listening, entranced, there came the sound of a childish voice crying "Grandmama!" The little Prince Muli Hassan had come back from his ride. I had stayed an unconscionable time, and my visit, the most interesting episode in all those interesting Moroccan days, had to come to an end!

While in Tangiers our party was much broken up. J. and Patsy made several riding trips with Israel, leaving me to potter about the Socco with Ali, or to prowl with Mme. Hortense in the bazaars, where I bought a long, salmon colored cloth gabardine with wide sleeves and fascinating silk buttons and loops; and a fine *sulham* like the one the Arab gentleman wore. Both are men's garments, though they pass muster very well, on the other side of the Straits of Gibraltar, for a woman's.

Our greatest pleasure we all enjoy together,—a dinner at one of the foreign villas on the heights. It was nearly dark when I mounted Zuleika and rode under the stars and a thin crescent moon to our friend's house. All the company except ourselves belonged to the diplomatic circle. They were as agreeable, well dressed, and well bred as such people are the world over. The dinner was excellent, the talk, for me, of absorbing interest. After dinner, as we were sitting talking together in the pretty drawing-room, admiring the Arabic curios our host had collected, we heard, faintly first, then gradually growing louder, the sound of a shepherd's pipe, like the flute in Tristan and Isolde.

"I thought you might like to hear a little Arab music," said our host, leading the way to an open-air concert room. In the corner made by two sides of his house, rugs were spread upon the ground, lanterns hung among the rose covered walls, and six native musicians squatted on the ground. Their instruments were a lute, a tambourine, a reban,—two-stringed fiddle—and the shepherd's pipe. The leader was a handsome dark man with dreamy eyes, and the face of an enthusiast. He threw back his head and began a song that was like a wail; the others joined in from time to time like a chorus.

"They are singing," said the host, "the Lament for Granada!"

When anybody says Tangiers to me suddenly, *this* is what I see! The Arab musicians sitting cross-legged on the ground under the stars, and the thin crescent moon. I hear the high wail of the Moorish pipe, the throb of the drum struck by the hand, the voices of the Moorish minstrels mourning for the Moors' lost paradise, singing the Lament for Granada.

X

MADRID

"SEÑORA, this is my mother," said Pedra the Vestal, who took care of our sitting-room fire.

"I am glad to make your acquaintance," said Pedra's mother; she shook my hand heartily, and looked at me with keen, kind eyes. "In regard to the washing, I will call for it on Mondays and bring it back on Fridays. If mending is required, there will be an additional price."

"Where do you wash the clothes?"

She was astonished at the question. "In the river, where else?"

"And where do you hang them out to dry?"

"On the river bank, near the palace of the King."

When Pedra the Vestal knelt on the hearth blowing the bellows, she looked more than ever like a Tanagra figurine. She built up the fire with odd little chunks of dark red wood that give out a strange perfume of the forest, and burn as slowly as soft coal.

"What sort of wood is that?" I asked.

"Who knows? The wood of a tree," Pedra looked over her shoulder with the flashing smile that made everything she said pass for wit.

"I know; it is ilex," said her mother. "In Segovia I used to gather it on the mountain. Here it costs too much, we burn charcoal."

"Is Madrid dearer than Segovia?"

"Madrid is the dearest place in the world, and the coldest." She wrapped her faded plaid shawl about her shoulders. There had been a slight snow flurry that morning; it was proper Christmas weather, but Pedra and her mother took it as seriously as we take a blizzard. Pedra was straight as a lance, hard as marble, built of stuff that wears well, judging from her mother. The elder woman was not one of those mothers who serve as a dreadful warning of what a daughter may become, if she had lost youth and freshness; she had kept her health and strength, a fiery spirit, a tough fibre.

The next time she came in to mend the fire, Pedra's bright eyes were dull and red. It took only a little coaxing to find out her trouble.

"My mother brought bad news," she said. "My brother has married a girl who is not worthy of him. Though we are poor, Señora, our family is an old one; there is none more respected in Segovia. After all the sacrifices we made for Juan to keep on the little shop that was my father's,—to marry beneath him, it was unworthy, it was ignoble!" The tears came to her eyes again. Here was Castilian pride, indeed.

We had come to Madrid meaning to keep house for six months or more. We soon found that a furnished apartment at a moderate price in Madrid is as rare as a roc's egg. We spent several days driving up and down the streets of the quarter where we wished to live, looking up at the houses. A large sheet of blank paper hung at the end of a window or balcony means unfurnished apartments to let, in the middle, furnished. We could find nothing available. It seemed as if we must give up our plan of passing the winter in Madrid. Then came the great invitation. Our old friends Don José and Doña Lucia Villegas asked us to share their large comfortable home. When we found they really wished us to accept this unparalleled hospitality, J. and I moved over to their delightful apartment, and Don Jaime found a modest hotel for Patsy.

The Villegas' house is opposite the handsome new National Museum on the Paseo Recoletos, a wide avenue laid out in the grand style of the Champs Elysées.

Madrid is a modern capital; at first it seemed as if we had left picturesque Spain behind us and come to a modern European city, a little like Paris, a little like Brussels, and not at all like the Spain we knew. Then, as we began to learn our way about the city, we found that beside the new Madrid, with its splendid boulevards, its conventional new houses and cafés, its air of prosperous business, there was an old Madrid, full of quaint corners and picturesque buildings.

The palace of the King stands at the edge of this old Madrid, boldly planted on the high land above the river, where the old Moorish Alcazar once stood, a magnificent situation for a royal palace. The façade fronts and dominates the city; the rear looks out on vast stretches of royal demesne.

"This looks more as a palace should look than any I ever saw," said Patsy. We had driven over one sharp clear morning to see Guard-mounting. "All grand and white and shining. The sort of a palace where lovely princesses with golden hair always live in poetry,—sometimes even in history."

On the right of the palace is the noble Plaza de Armas, where, besides the guards pacing up and down their beat, there was a continual coming and going of all sorts and conditions of men. In a sheltered corner, under the very palace windows, two boys were playing at marbles. This was all in keeping with what we had seen and heard of the democratic character of the people. At one end of the Plaza, the long narrow arches of the peristyle frame a stupendous view. Behind the palace runs the river Manzanares; beyond lies the royal park of the Casa de Campo, with its masses of green trees, broken here and there by the glint of a lake, or the spire of one of poor Isabel Second's expiatory chapels. Beyond the park, the bare plains of Castile sweep grandly to the north, rising to the stern snow-capped range of the Sierra Guaderrama.

It was all dearly familiar, because Velasquez has painted that blue-gray landscape, that silver light sometimes hardening to steel, those snow mountains, not once, but many, many times, as the background of his pictures.

"The Manzanares is not much of a stream compared to the Guadalquiver," said Patsy. "That must be the bridge the Frenchman meant, when he advised the King of Spain either to sell his bridge, or to buy a river!" He pointed to a big handsome bridge, curiously out of proportion to the size of the meagre river.

Not far from the palace, along the river bank, was a gorgeous, tremulous, swaying mass of color,—scarlet, blue, orange, every tint of the rainbow.

"That," said Patsy, "looks like the Field of the Cloth of Gold. Those might be the fluttering pennons of Leon and Castile, Navarre and Aragon."

"Don't look too closely, or you will lose the illusion. That is the drying ground, where Pedra's mother and the other washerwomen of Madrid hang out their clothes."

"Standards of heroes, standards of heroines, what's the odds? They *are* heroines. I stood and watched them yesterday, their petticoats kilted up to their knees, rubbing and scrubbing and singing at their work."

A young American artist painted an admirable picture of the drying ground with its many-colored garments not long ago. He worked in summer, close to the river when the water was low, and caught a fever that put an end to all his painting!

Fronting the palace is the large oval Plaza del Oriente, with a good equestrian statue of Philip IV, surrounded by a circle of quaint marble statues of Visigothic and Spanish kings and queens, from Berenguela to Isabel the Catholic.

"We know Philip IV better than all the rest of them put together!" Patsy exclaimed, as we walked round the royal group. "Thanks to the genius for making a likeness of that young man shown by Velasquez, whom he engaged as his *valet de chambre* at a salary of eleven dollars a month. Philip young, thin and cadaverous, Philip old, fat and blowsy; I know his face as well as I know my own. People who want to be remembered by posterity should be very polite to the painters and sculptors—even to the writers— of their day. Strange they don't realize it!"

Madrid was gay with Christmas bustle; streets and shops were crowded; Pedra was busy with the presents that poured into the house for Lucia and Villegas. From Granada came a cask of oil, from Malaga a small barrel of grapes, from Jerez a cask of olorosa, from Tangiers a box of oranges, from Seville a flagon of cologne, the finest in the world,—it smells of fresh orange blossoms.

One morning, a few days before Christmas, I heard a strange hob-gobbling noise outside in the passage. I opened my door; there was Pedra, flushed and out of breath with the effort, trying to get two large speckled turkeys up the terrace stairs.

"*Miré*," she said, "observe these fine birds, Señora, a present from the country. I shall mix a dish of corn meal and hot water for them, that will be the food of luxury, fattening besides. Poor animals! they shall live well until Cisera wrings their necks."

Cisera, the Tuscan cook, followed the procession up the terrace stairs, and felt the larger turkey.

"In a week," she said, "he will be fit to kill, perhaps sooner."

When the turkeys had been fed with the food of luxury, Pedra showed me another gift that had just come for Villegas. "Don José will like this more than all the rest, you will see!" she said.

Villegas is the Director of the Prado Museum. What Pedra called the best present was a "testimonial," with his photograph and a complimentary address signed by all the employees of the Prado. He gave the dreadful thing with its impossible plush frame the place of honor, and hung it up himself in the hall.

Cisera killed the larger turkey, and stuffed it with pistacchio nuts for the Christmas eve dinner-party. As we were all sitting together, waiting for the last guest to arrive, Gil, the melancholy Gallegan man-servant, threw open the door and announced:

"The Bohemian Gentleman."

A big blond man with dancing blue eyes and a ruffled shirt came in, followed by Pedra, carrying in her upraised hands a tray with two enormous hams (she looked like the picture of Titian's daughter with the fruit).

"A good Christmas!" the Bohemian made Lucia a grand bow. "I have brought you a pair of hams from Prague!"

"The best hams in the world," Villegas patted one of them. "I was afraid you had forgotten this year!"

"They should be good; the pigs were raised on

DETAIL FROM "THE MAIDS OF HONOR." *Velasquez*

my father's farm, and, I was assured, were fed on nothing but milk."

Before the turkey made its appearance, Villegas had discovered that among his guests were people of seven nationalities, and that four languages were being spoken at the table.

"This," he said, "is the Tower of Babel." The name stuck for as long at least as that hospitable house was our home.

"What," I asked Don Jaime who sat beside me, "is the Bohemian gentleman's name?"

"Of baptism or of family?"

"Both, particularly of family."

"Ah!" the Don relapsed into Spanish, "nobody can pronounce it; it begins with a cough and ends with a sneeze. He is called Don Carlos the Bohemian, because he comes from Bohemia. He copies royal portraits in the Prado for the Archduke Eugenio of Austria; no one has made such copies of Velasquez since Villegas left off painting them!" The Bohemian saw we were speaking of him, for he looked over at us.

"This lady, whose name I did not catch," he said, "is an American?"

"Oh, no!" cried little Serafita, who gives music lessons to the Infanta; "she is English, Yankee, from New York." In Madrid, American means South American, unless the contrary is stated.

I asked Serafita, a sparkling Andaluz with a drop of Hebrew blood in her veins, if many of her pupils worked seriously. "Only a few," she said, "more give up their music when they marry. It is the same with their other studies. The women I know drop their reading and studies when they leave school. If one cannot talk with them about the fashions or the last ball, they have nothing to say. You North American women can speak on every subject. Our women are not less clever, but our men do not wish us to be improved, for they know that we are naturally more intelligent than they themselves, and if our minds were cultivated they believe we would not be content always to stay at home."

Villegas had lately sat for his photograph, and as Lucia wished opinions on the likeness, the photographs were handed round the table. When they came to Don Jaime he counted them, and told me that there were twelve, and all alike, adding with a sigh that if there were only twelve Villegases, all alike, and he could dine with all of them, he could then be sure of twelve such dinners a year!

Before Villegas came to Madrid, and took Don Jaime under his wing, the Don often had no dinner—so he confided to Patsy. One does not exactly dine when one spends two cents a day for food. "Under such circumstances," the Don said, "it is best to invest all your money in bread of the day before; it costs less than fresh bread, and goes farther."

While we were still at table, there came a tremendous ringing at the door-bell. There was a lull in the conversation as Gil opened the front door. "A message and a box from the bedchamber of the King for Don José!" cried a loud voice in the hall outside.

"Put down the box. Don José is dining," Gil replied firmly.

"Give him the message then as I give it to thee. Here are the pantaloons of his Majesty the King. They must be returned by the fifteenth of the month, when his Majesty wishes to wear them."

We looked at each other in astonishment.

"I am painting the King's portrait," said Villegas; "as he is not very fond of posing they have sent me the clothes to work from before the next sitting."

"The Infanta's wedding is on the eighteenth," said Lucia; "perhaps they are wanted for that. Be sure nothing happens to them at the studio."

It was nearly twelve when the Bohemian, the first to make the move, rose to go. They keep late hours in Madrid, even later than in Paris. Don Carlos was reproved for breaking up the party so early.

"I promised," he said by way of excuse, "to be at the Countess Q's for midnight mass."

"I should not have thought that *misa del gallo*—cockcrow mass was exactly in your line!" said Don Jaime. "You grow devout with years!"

"Ah, well—I know the music will be good, they will give selections from Carmen. Besides, I promised I would stay and help them out with the supper and dance after the mass."

Just then Gil brought in a curiously shaped old bottle covered with dust and cobwebs.

"Try this before you go," said Villegas; "it is Trafalgar 1805, the year of the great vintage of Jerez and of the great battle." He himself poured out the wine, with greatest care not to shake the bottle.

"It is good enough," said the Bohemian, with another of his grand bows, "to drink to Doña Lucia's health, and," raising his glass, "to the portrait of the King."

"The portrait of the King!" We drank the toast standing.

The next morning we walked over to the studio with Villegas and Lucia, Gil following with the box from the bedchamber of the King. As we left the Tower of Babel, Cisera came running after us.

"Don José, you have forgotten your brushes," she put a bundle of paint-brushes done up in a newspaper into his hand. Villegas tucked them in his pocket and thanked Cisera; it is her privilege to wash the brushes, and she allows no one else to touch them. The studio is in the Pasaje del Alhambra, rather a picturesque place for Madrid, not more than half a mile from the house. Though it was late, after ten o'clock, the streets were very uncomfortable on account of the floods of water pouring through them. The extreme dryness of the soil and the air makes it necessary to flush the streets twice a day! A pair of wild looking gypsy girls were standing by one of the corners, watching the water pouring from the hydrant. The taller girl was very handsome, the shorter one seemed older, and had an ill-tempered face, with a head shaped like a snake's. They stood gaping at us with the dazed look of country people unused to a city. They were so poorly dressed I rather thought they would beg of us.

"What a type!" said Villegas, looking at the handsome girl, a beauty with rough black hair hanging over the eyes, and a half fierce, half shy expression.

"What character in that head, eh?"

"She has exactly the face you have been looking for," said Lucia. "Ask her to come to the studio and pose."

They spoke to the handsome girl, who seemed to agree. At this the elder girl caught her by the arm and dragged her back.

"No, no, you shall not go!" she cried. "Do you know what he will do? He will look you in the eyes fixedly, fixedly, like this, and while he is looking at you, he will suck your blood!" At this the two took to their heels and ran for dear life.

"You see how difficult it is to get models in Madrid!" Villegas laughed. "One is driven here, by force, to paint portraits!"

We were passing a house in a garden where an old retired General and his old wife sat opposite each other on the porch in large covered invalid chairs, keeping a sharp lookout on all passers-by. They were both deaf, and imagining other people heard no better than they, talked quite audibly about the people in the street.

"There goes Villegas, the painter," said the wife. "He seems amused about something." (Don José had laughed to tears over the gypsy's warning). "What do you suppose his servant is carrying in that big box?"

"What ridiculous curiosity," growled the General; "isn't it the same old box?"

"No, I never saw it before. I wonder what he *has* got in it!"

As we reached the corner of the Barquillo, Villegas exclaimed: "There's the Novio. He must have been ill, he looks rather pale; I haven't seen him for a week." The novio, a pallid young man in a plaid suit, stood in a protected angle of the side-walk, looking up at a window at the top of a high house where a roguish girl's face looked out from between the curtains. The young man was talking with his fingers in the deaf and dumb language.

"He talks so fast I cannot read what he says," said Villegas. "But one can guess; one has either heard or said such things oneself, is it not so?"

At the opposite corner the old flower woman, who sat stooping and huddled under her black shawls like the eldest of the Fates, chose from her stock a white hyacinth and silently handed it to Villegas, who gave her a coin, took the flower and walked briskly on. The old woman sat up a little straighter, after he had passed, and set her flowers in better order. It is characteristic of Villegas that people always sit up straighter and put their affairs in better order when he has passed their way.

Angoscia, the glove-maker of Granada, who takes care of the studio, and serves as a draped model, opened the studio door: it is almost impossible in Madrid to get either male or female models to pose for the nude. Angoscia is a pretty young woman with an almost perfect face, beautiful hands and feet, but with a tendency to grow stout.

"You have been eating maccaroni again!" said Lucia.

"No, no, I swear by the Virgin I have not. I eat nothing, I starve myself, I am hungry always."

"Or *torrones*. You are much fatter than before Christmas; that comes of giving you a holiday!"

Poor Angoscia, looking worthy of her name—it means anguish—made a diversion by asking what we had brought in the box. Lucia, with her help, then unpacked a fine cocked hat, a red and blue military coat and waistcoat, a pair of short white cloth knee breeches, the belt linings and pockets of heaviest satin, a dainty sword and sword belt. Angoscia drew the damascened Toledo blade, pretty as a toy, cruel as death, from its sheath; it glinted in the sun and flashed its reflection in her soft brave eyes. Everything in the box was most carefully packed, each silver button and bit of silver lace separately wrapped in black tissue paper to keep it from tarnishing. At the very bottom of the box was a long thin morocco case. This I opened, gave a scream, and almost dropped the case that contained the ensign of the Order of the Garter. The garter was of dark blue velvet bordered with gold. The letters were separate, of very thick gold, attached by invisible rivets to the velvet. After the legend "Honi Soit Qui Mal Y Pense" the velvet strap was heavily embroidered in gold thread, the tab and buckle were finely chased gold.

"A beautiful piece of work!" Villegas turned it over in his hand and nodded approval. How all good workmen feel a good piece of work!

"Edward the Black Prince was made the first knight of the Order of the Garter after Crécy, when he brought the great ruby back from Spain," said J.

"Where is it worn?" That was a serious question. By this time the clothes were on the mannikin, the palette was set, Villegas unrolled the great sheaf of brushes, and was ready to go to work.

"On the left leg below the knee," said J. There was some argument on the point, finally settled by appeal to a Van Dyke portrait in the Prado.

"They have forgotten the shoes!" cried Angoscia.

"There is nothing remarkable about them: any low evening pumps will do till the next sitting," said Villegas.

"Mariano Benlliure has a pair!" cried Jaime, and went off in a cab to borrow them. He came back with two pairs of patent leather pumps nicely fitted on wooden lasts.

"Mariano must be very rich," said Jaime. "I will pawn the pair you don't use, send him the ticket, and when he wants to wear them he can redeem the shoes."

At last the mannikin was dressed with the King's clothes and put in the right pose and Villegas got to work. He did not like to paint from the mannikin; he said it looked too stiff, and would spoil the portrait, but that it would be impossible to put the King's clothes on a model!

"If Don Alfonzo had only given me a sitting instead of going hunting to-day!" he sighed, squeezing more yellow ochre on his palette to paint the garter; "I should like to have gone into the country too!"

"A hundred years from now who will care whether the King went hunting to-day or not? Somebody may be glad that you stayed in your studio and worked."

"*Quien sabé?*" sighed Villegas.

"He is never satisfied!" said Lucia.

"The day he is satisfied, he will be finished!" laughed J. Villegas, who likes company when he works, and can endure a dozen people talking in the studio without listening to a word that is said, went steadily on with his painting, laying on the bold, firm strokes of color in a manner all his own.

In those days there was much to do in Madrid about the Infanta Maria Teresa's wedding. The trousseau and presents were exhibited in the great dining-hall of the palace. The jewels given by the King, Queen Maria Cristina, and the bridegroom, Prince Ferdinand of Bavaria, were said to be fabulously fine. There were fifty dresses with shoes to match, among other items, and all the rest of the outfit was on the same scale. The bridegroom and his parents arrived in Madrid some days before the wedding. His mother, the Infanta Paz, was the sister of the bride's father, Alfonzo XII, so it was a family affair and a deal of entertaining went on in the palace of the King. Prince Max of Bavaria, the bridegroom's father, took little part in the merrymaking, but slipped off whenever he could to the hospitals to have a look at the interesting cases, and compare notes with his confrères, the surgeons. The story was told of his coming home late to lunch one day, and saying to the guests invited to meet him, "I have made such a successful operation this morning; cut off a man's leg. It all went well; the patient stood it admirably!"

"Even royalties are becoming emancipated," said Patsy; "they have practically gone on strike. Can you blame a man for refusing to spend his life standing round waiting on the chance that he may be wanted to fill a throne? Here you have a royal explorer, like the Duke of Abruzzi, and a royal surgeon, like Prince Max, real professionals, not amateurs; what are we coming to next?"

We were driving along the gay crowded Calle Acalá, on our way to the wedding.

"They have a fine day," Patsy went on. "I saw a few icicles on the fountain of Cebele this morning, but they're all melted now. At home we should call this mild weather for January; here they act as if it were ten below zero."

Every carriage or automobile we passed was hermetically sealed; not a crack of a window was left open, and the Madrileños were muffled in furs to the eyes. The climate of Madrid is not half so black as it is painted; half the bronchitis and lung troubles we hear about come from too much wrapping up and too little fresh air! The only open carriages to be seen in Madrid at this season belong to the royal family. They set a good example in that direction, at least.

The chapel royal of the palace, where the wedding took place, leads from the glass enclosed gallery that surrounds the courtyard at the second story, and communicates with the bedchamber of the King and the other private apartments. Each door is guarded day and night by two tall halberdiers, in whose hands lies the safety of the King. They are picked men, the very flower of the army, the type of Spanish soldier history and romance have made familiar. They look as fierce, proud, and terrible as the men who marched with Cortes. The young officer in lovely white broadcloth uniform and shining feathered helmet, who took us in charge at the palace door, delivered us over into the hands of a halberdier in a cocked hat and short clothes, who led us through the gallery, empty save for the guards pacing up and down. The four men on duty at the chapel door stood like breathing statues; they never moved their eyes; they hardly seemed to wink. Though they were relieved every fifteen minutes, as long as flesh and blood can stand the strain, one of the big handsome fellows fainted, before his quarter of an hour was over.

Our halberdier—his name was Pedro—led us up a private stairway covered with a blue Aubusson carpet, sprinkled with roses and lilies so lifelike that you could almost pick them, then to a little, dark, secret stair leading to the grated balcony, where we were to sit, as if in a private stage box, and see the royal wedding. We were spectators, not guests, as only the Court and the diplomatic circle were admitted to the floor of the chapel. Don Jaime soon joined us; he had made the unprecedented sacrifice of getting up at ten o'clock, so that he might tell us who all the great personages were.

"To the left sit members of Government and his wifes. Next Greats of Spain"—usually called Grandees—"Major-domos-de-semana, Gentilhombres, *corps diplomatique*, authorities, mayor and members of city, dames of court, generals, chamberlains, suite of bridegroom."

"*Solo Madrid es corte;*" only at Madrid is there a court, according to the old saying. The arrival of this famous Spanish court was the most impressive feature of the whole gorgeous pageant. The ladies, wearing long velvet trains and white mantillas, entered the chapel one by one, bowed before the altar, crossed themselves, and with consummate grace and dignity, above all with perfect calm, made their way to their places, where they spread out their trains and settled themselves like so many brilliant birds of paradise. There was no noise, no confusion, no crowding; it had all been calculated to a nicety. There was plenty of time, and plenty of space for everybody; this above all else made for the great distinction of the ceremony. The Chinese minister and secretary, in their embroidered silk gowns, their mandarin caps and peacock feathers, were the most picturesque figures in the diplomatic tribune. Chief among the Grandees were the Knights of the Golden Fleece. Patsy asked the name of one whose face seemed familiar.

"Is Pidal, Duke of Veragua," said Jaime. "He receive the order on the anniversary of 1892, as proof of worthy to be descendant of Columbus. He is the elevator of the finest bulls in Spain; you will see them at the next *corrida*."

"Are all the seven Spanish Knights of the Golden Fleece here?"

"No, not Count Cheste. Has nineteen seven years, is more ancient of army and of literature. It is a poet."

The King's clothes had been returned in plenty of time for the wedding; care had been taken of them, they looked as good as new when, to the music of the Lohengrin march, Don Alfonzo walked into the chapel, leading the bride with one hand, the bridegroom with the other.

"It's just like the opera," Patsy whispered. "Wagner made no mistakes in his stage directions; he knew all the traditions of the Bavarian Court, and must have seen a royal wedding or two."

The bride wore orange blossoms in her hair; the front of her satin dress sparkled with diamonds, the train of white velvet, bordered with ostrich feathers, hung from the shoulders and was carried by a page.

"Her code is three metres long," the Don told us.

The bride knelt at the altar, made her first prayer, then crossed the church, passing the three officiating cardinals in their arrogant scarlet robes, to the prie-dieu where her mother knelt apart from all the rest. She stooped, and raised the Queen's hand to her lips. The Queen, who wept openly throughout the ceremony, kissed her cheek; the bride then rejoined the bridegroom, a kind looking, round-faced young man, with thick brown hair. The ceremony was performed by the Archbishop of Toledo, Cardinal primate of Spain, a subtle-faced old man with silver hair and benevolent manners. The King knew his mass perfectly; he kissed his prayer-book and crossed himself at all the proper times, and throughout the service prompted the bridegroom, who seemed ill prepared and had evidently not been so well drilled.

"*Mea culpa, mea culpa, mea maxima culpa!*" the King struck his breast three times with his clenched fist, as he said the words.

"What do you suppose Don Alfonzo's *maxima culpa* is?" murmured Patsy. "I don't believe he has had much chance to commit one. Villegas might say it is his not liking to pose. Some old fogy might say it was his habit of riding his horse up the palace stairs. I would not give a fig for a young man in his position who didn't do that; it is a time-honored custom of gay young princes! It wasn't *his* fault that he was born a king; he can't be expected to forfeit all the fun he might otherwise have enjoyed as heir to the throne!"

While the Archbishop knotted the white satin scarf, symbol of the marriage tie, about the young couple's shoulders, Don Jaime hurried us down to the gallery to see the cortége pass from the chapel to the private apartments. Our halberdier, Pedro, had kept us a place opposite the chapel door. The gallery was lined with these superb guards. They stood shoulder to shoulder, their steel halberds flashing in the sunlight that streamed through the glass sides of the gallery.

"The *alabardaros*," Don Jaime explained, "are a particularity, all must be of so great length." He added that they all held rank two grades below what they had held in the army; that the soldiers had been sergeants and the general formerly a field marshal.

The fateful music of Mendelssohn's march thrilled through the gallery, the waiting crowd behind the halberdiers swayed at the sound as wind-flowers shaken by the wind.

The wedding party came out of the chapel behind four mace bearers, stalwart men in black velvet, with gold maces over their shoulders.

"The Infanta Isabel, the King's aunt, *es muy Española!*" she is very Spanish—whispered Jaime as a gray-haired, hearty-looking woman passed, bowing and smiling.

"I like her," said Patsy; "she looks a thoroughly good sort; she has twice been heir to the throne, before the birth of her brother Alfonzo XII, and again after his death, before our Don Alfonzo was born. Trying, wasn't it? She seems to be the most popular of the elder members of the family."

The Infanta Eulalia is not so well known as her sister, the Infanta Isabel, because she has been little in Spain and prefers to live in Paris. She looked very much as she did when she was in Chicago, at the time of the World's Fair, very elegant, very graceful, more cosmopolitan, less *Española* than her sister.

The Queen walked with Don Alfonzo. She wore a long ash colored dress, a white lace mantilla, a diamond diadem, and the finest pearls I ever saw. She neither bowed nor smiled.

In the clear sunlight of the gallery, at a range of ten feet, one saw the dreadful look of suffering in her face. It must have been a trying day for her. Her eldest daughter, Princess of the Asturias, had died only a year before, leaving four little children: *her* marriage had been so unpopular that it nearly caused a revolution, and there had been none of the rejoicing and merrymaking her sister, the Infanta Maria, was enjoying. Besides this recent grief, what bitter memories must have surged up in the Queen's heart. Her own marriage and all of the tragedy and suffering that it held. Hers had been a state marriage; her bridegroom met her at the altar with a heart still sore for his adored Mercedes, his first wife dead in the first year of their marriage. Then came her husband's early death, after a cruel, lingering illness; the summoning together of the ministers, to whom she announced that there was still hope of an heir, for besides her three daughters, she was again with child: the birth of that child, Alfonzo XIII, one of the very few who have been born King, twenty years of passionate devotion to the care of the delicate boy's health, his education, his religious training. Twenty years of intense, unresting effort to keep the throne for her son,—all this among a people to whom she was ever "the Austrian," is still the Outlander. And now, after all that she has done, another woman is to usurp her place. Her son will marry within the year a woman who has been bred a Protestant.

As she passed, without a look at the people, it seemed that for once the mask of the Queen had dropped from the grief-ravaged face of the woman.

The young people were in the gayest mood. Don Alfonzo nodded and smiled to right and left, the bride and bridegroom came along, laughing and talking together, like any other happy young couple. There was youth and hope in their faces; they were still far from the stereotyped bow, the dreadful mechanical smile of the elder royalties.

"*Felicidad eternal!*" said Don Jaime, as the bride passed us.

"A good word," Patsy echoed it as the doors closed behind the wedding party. "Eternal felicity, may they be as happy as if they had not been born in the shadow of a throne."

DETAILS FROM "THE SURRENDER OF BREDA." *Velasquez*

XI

THE PRADO

<table>
<tr><td>Por las calles de Madrid</td><td>Through the streets of Madrid</td></tr>
<tr><td>se pasea un valenciano</td><td>A Valencian was straying</td></tr>
<tr><td>con un clavel en la boca</td><td>With a pink in his mouth</td></tr>
<tr><td>y una rosa en cada mano.</td><td>And a rose in each hand.</td></tr>
</table>

LITTLE Don Luis the Valencian took the pink from his mouth, when he met Villegas coming up the steps of the Prado Museum. "I was going away," he said, "but I will turn back with you. Anything for an excuse not to go to work!"

"Work!" Villegas fairly snorted! "You call painting work, when it is the only thing you like to do? Caramba! There are some things in this world hard to understand!" Villegas was disappointed. He had waited an hour at the studio for Luz, who never came for her sitting; this was quite natural the day after the court ball.

The head porter met us at the door; any of the famous painters whose pictures hang in the room of the great portraits might have been glad to have him for a sitter. He was a handsome man of the grave Castilian type, with a big, square black beard and skin like alabaster. He wore a broadcloth overcoat down to his heels and a gold laced cap.

"These are my friends," Villegas introduced us. "You will give them any help they may need."

The porter bowed gravely and we all followed Villegas into the Museum. He had come to make his morning rounds, and little Don Luis offered to be our guide while he looked over his mail.

"I was too discouraged to paint to-day," said Don Luis, "so I came for help to the great artists, whose work is here. They seem to hold out their hands to me, and say: 'we have travelled the road you find so hard; we, too, have known discouragement and despair!' I always go away from the Museum as from the company of my best friends, full of courage and hope."

"The way I feel, after seeing a play of Shakespeare's," murmured Patsy. "Clever work discourages you; great work puts heart into you, makes you feel you can go home and do something as good, that you might even have done that."

Villegas, who loves the pictures under his care as if they were his children, is not satisfied with the Prado, and is always hoping they may some day have a museum worthy of them.

"The three arts should be united, as they were in Greece," he said. "Oh, for a building that should be as a perfect casket for the two jewels, painting and sculpture. Other museums may illustrate the history of art better than the Prado, none possesses more masterpieces of painting!"

"He has performed miracles since he became Director," said Don Luis; "not only in the care and hanging of the pictures, but against the risk of fire. He has put in all the latest fire extinguishing apparatus. He is right, though, we must have a new building, and, it appears to me, he will get it for us!"

The Prado was built for a Natural History Museum, and the light in many rooms, especially on the upper floor, is very bad. Many valuable pictures cannot be shown for want of space, others can hardly be seen for lack of light. In spite of these drawbacks, the Prado is the most delightful Museum I know. It soon became to us, as to Don Luis, a second home. The first impression is of an immense hospitality; there is no entrance fee to pay; the Museum is free to all. Then the guardians are all so kind and, nearly all, so good-looking. The man who takes your umbrella or walking stick treats you with courtesy and respect, not, as in some galleries, as if you were a criminal or a lunatic bent on poking holes in the canvases.... Every museum has its climate or atmosphere; the climate of the Prado is genial and cordial beyond compare.

The first impression we received of the pictures was a great joy that there are so many surprises among them. A few of the Velasquez and the Murillos we knew already, but as a whole the collection is less familiar than any other I have ever seen. The vast majority of the pictures were new to us. No work of art that has become well known through endless copies and reproductions can make the impression these undreamed-of splendors make. As Patsy said, "they hit you hard like love at first sight!"

Last, but not least, the Prado is comfortable! It has wood floors, and is properly warmed. You can spend a morning there without that fear of catching cold that haunts you in the chill marble-paved galleries of Italy.

In the long hall of the Spanish School, Villegas joined us. We were looking at a portrait of Marianna of Austria, the second wife of Philip IV.

"This is a copy of the Velasquez made by his son-in-law, Maza," said Don José. "It formerly passed as a replica by Velasquez himself."

"And how do you know now that it is not?" asked Patsy.

"You shall see." Don José called an attendant, and ordered that the copy be carried into the

THE TIPPLERS. *Velasquez*

Velasquez room and placed beside the great original.

"Observe that it lacks the extraordinary silvery tone peculiar to Velasquez and, besides, is too accurate a copy! Velasquez would never have had patience to copy mere accidents of brush-marks, or kinks in the folds of the dress, if he had been copying one of his own pictures. He would preserve the tone, the spirit, the pose of the original, but he would not go seeking to make the same strokes with his brush. The very mechanical accuracy helps to prove this a copy made by a faithful pupil; thus it is!"

The sixty-seven Velasquez pictures are all together in one room. They are admirably hung, in the chronological order they were painted, so that you can follow the painter's work from the beginning to the end. The impression produced is of a wonderful living autobiography. Every picture is a page on which you may read some momentous event in the artist's life. You trace his development from the Adoration of the Kings, the earliest picture, to St. Anthony the Abbot visiting St. Paul, perhaps the latest. It is an autobiography that cannot be read at a glance. In that first visit, made in the company of artists to whom the Velasquez room is holy as Mecca to the Mahommedan, I was introduced to the genius who, for the next six months, I was to study and try to understand.

"Why did Velasquez paint so many pictures of fools, dwarfs and gabaloonzy men?" Patsy asked. We were looking at the portrait of El Primo, the dwarf, holding in his tiny hands a big book, looking out from under his slouch hat and long feather with the humpback's sharp, uncanny eyes.

"Because he could always get one of them to sit for him when the royal sitters disappointed him," sighed Villegas; "they had more time than the courtiers, and were perhaps the most vigorous and characteristic subjects for painting of all the people he lived among."

We passed on to the idiot Child of Vallecas. The poor, vacant face seems to flicker at you from the canvas, the weak, wasted hands with the pack of cards never took hold of anything, not even life itself, save with a faltering grasp. At first, when you begin to study Velasquez, you feel it monstrous that his genius should have been wasted on such ridiculous deformities; in the end you accept them all, for the sake of the genius that has immortalized them.

"Look at that hand!" said Villegas, as we were standing before the portrait of Montañez, the sculptor. "How it is painted! With nothing, you may say—zip-zap, two strokes of the brush, and it is a

DUKE OF OLIVARES. *Velasquez*

hand. To create something out of nothing—colossal!"

"That is a good copy," said J. A canvas, still wet, stood on an easel near the Montañez.

"Ah, yes—you may say so. That is made by an American—a certain Hibson; he has talent if you will; he will arrive! notice what I say, that man will go far."

In Spanish G is pronounced H. The "Hibson," of whom Villegas foretold great and serious things, the new star on the artistic horizon, in an earlier incarnation, achieved fame as the creator of the Gibson Girl!

"I saw that effect of sky this morning. Velasquez painted that background on a day like this."

We were standing before the portrait of the Duke de Olivarez, with the bare blue plains of Castile and the snow-capped Guaderrama behind him. You feel the keen, clear air with the bite of the wind from the snow mountains, as you look at that picture of the Duke on his prancing war-horse of the best Arabo-Velasquez breed!

"Look at that dog! It is nothing, painted with nothing, when you look close at it; take two steps backwards, and it is everything."

It was the dog in the Meninas, one of the details Villegas never failed to look at as he passed.

"That is a canine dog," said Patsy. "Dogs in pictures almost always have a human expression. These of Velasquez look as dogs must look to each other; it is as if they were painted by one of themselves!"

The Meninas has a separate room to itself. Look at the picture long enough, and the illusion seizes you that you are really looking into a room of the gloomy old palace of the Alcazar, the Court of Philip IV, where Velasquez lived and worked the greater part of his working life. You can walk into that room where he stands at work before a big canvas, look over his shoulder, see the portrait he is painting of the King and Queen; you can even touch him on the arm that supports his palette.

"He paints pictures no longer," cried little Don Luis the Valencian. "Like a god he creates a world with light and atmosphere, plains and mountains. Into that world he puts kings and queens, buffoons and beggars."

"And soldiers and horses!" said Villegas, stopping before the "Surrender of Breda," a great spacious picture with a gray-blue sky, and room enough in it for all the sublimity of victory, the tragedy of defeat. In the background the distant town of Breda still smokes from the besiegers' shells. In the nearer distance, marching up the hill, is a company of the victorious soldiers armed with the long lances that give the picture its nickname. The men's faces are grave, they show no exultation to the group of the defeated enemy standing opposite to them. In the foreground Justino de Nassau, the defender of Breda, offers the key of the city to the victorious general Spinola. De Nassau's knee is slightly bent—it is a stubborn knee and hard to bend—as he holds out the key. Spinola has neither hand free to take it; one holds his baton, the other is laid in what seems almost an embrace, on De Nassau's shoulder. "Take back your key," he seems to say. "To-day it was our turn to win; to-morrow it may be yours."

What was it Grant said to Lee about needing the horses for the spring plowing? There you have the magnanimous spirit of Velasquez's "Surrender of Breda" in a nutshell.

"My friend," said Villegas to a stout German artist, who was working away in grim earnest at a copy of the "Lances"; "your color is too hot, remember the cool silver-grays; always try for them!"

"*Ach Gott*, you have said it!" cried the poor man, squinting from his copy to the original; "why could I not myself before have seen it?" Then he broke into profuse thanks to the Herr Director, who hurried on to escape them.

"I have a plan," said Villegas, "for a new arrangement of this room." We had passed into the long gallery of the Spanish School, from which the Velasquez room opens. "Here, opposite this entrance, I shall hang the Titian portrait of Charles V on his war-horse; it is too much sacrificed where it is now. Near this I shall hang some Tintorettos and some Grecos. In this way it will be possible to trace the influence of each of these masters on the other: the influence of Titian on Tintoretto, of Tintoretto on Greco, of Greco on Velasquez."

The head porter, who had come hurrying up to Villegas, now delivered his message.

"They have telephoned from the Palace that the King of Portugal will be at the Museum in half an hour."

These sudden entrances of royalty upon the scene added enormously to the interest of our life in Madrid. The marriage of the Infanta, the betrothal and the marriage of the King brought more royal visitors to Madrid that season than usual, and they all came to the Prado. The Museum has for them an especial attraction apart from the artistic interest. The Prado contains portraits of the ancestors of most of the royal personages in Europe, and they are naturally interested in seeing their family portraits. The collection begun by Charles V, and constantly added to by his descendants, is essentially a royal collection. Isabel II generously

VENUS AND CUPID. *Velasquez*

- 162 -

gave the pictures to the Spanish nation. How generously that gift is shared with the artists and art lovers of all nations, every visitor to the Prado knows.

Villegas hurried off to prepare for the visit of Don Carlos, the King of Portugal, and little Don Luis, still glad of an excuse not to go back to work, offered to take me to see Don Carlos the Bohemian. We found him in a big barrack of a lumber-room smelling of paint, turpentine and varnish, at the top of the Prado. He was at work on a copy of the disputed portrait of Don John of Austria. He threw down his palette and ran to meet Don Luis, rumpling up his hair with desperate hands.

"Was I mad to undertake it?" he cried. "It is the fourth Antonio Moro I have copied. Not another, not for a million."

"Not for a million, no; what couldst thou do with it? But for—well, something else—yes, as many as thy grand duke will find room for in his museum!"

"The work that accursed Fleming put into a picture. I tell thee it is brutal to work so hard; he had the patience of a saint!"

"Or a Coello or a Pantoja. It is not a Moro! Thou hast some patience thyself; it is not bad, thy copy!" Don Luis looked critically at it; "a little crude. How many glazes hast thou given it?"

"Only eight."

"Ah! thou seest? thou wilt get the tone soon. There is nothing wrong with the drawing; the worst of the work is over with that."

"Blessed be thy mouth!"

Don John, the Conqueror of Lepanto, is a young man standing with the lion of Alcazaba at his side. He wears a shirt of mail the rings as fine as those of a lady's purse, and every ring is painted. The fringe of the cushion is painted thread by thread, you can almost count the hairs in the moustache.

"How can you know where to begin?" I asked. The copying of this life-sized full length, painted with the detail of a miniature, seemed a desperate undertaking.

"I know how the devil worked! I studied and studied him till I got his secret; ah, there is no one like him; he is a despair! See, first I draw everything in black, white and gray, down to the last detail, then I get my tone with a series of thin glazes. Each one must be quite hard and dry before I give it the next. It takes a lifetime, you may say!"

A delightful copy of the Velasquez portrait of little Prince Baltasar with the gun and the dog stood against the wall. "Thou hast a good thing there," said Don Luis; "and once Velasquez was hard for thee to copy!"

DON BALTAZAR CARLOS. *Velasquez*

"How he baffled me! Now I have learned as much of his secret as a man can learn; rather twenty-five Velasquez than one Moro. This is the last, if I live to finish it!"

I told Don Carlos about the King of Portugal. "He always comes to the Prado when he is in Madrid," he said. "He is a fair painter himself, for a king. There is a portrait of his worth seeing in the Museum of Modern Arts."

"I think he once complimented thee on a copy thou wast making?" said Don Luis.

"Perhaps he did," growled Don Carlos. He smoothed out his towsled hair and went back, grumbling still, though less violently, to his work. Somehow the energy of despair had become the energy of courage; little Don Luis the Valencian with the pink in his mouth had turned the water of drudgery to the wine of work!

Madrid was perpetually *en fête* during the visit of the King and Queen of Portugal. We had visions of them flitting by like figures in a panorama, on their way to the bull-fight, driving to the gala performance at the opera, reviewing the troops. The review began with an open-air mass, the salute of the flag by the new recruits, and the defile before the two kings, Don Alfonzo and Don Carlos. The artillery was much applauded, especially the mountain battery, a troop of mules with cannon on their backs. The cavalry, a fine body of men and horses, galloped by the grand stand at breakneck speed. One company, all mounted on white horses, preceded by two lines of buglers, came flashing past with a splendid dash and brilliancy that pleased Don Carlos, for he clapped his great hands and cried "Bravo." After the review the two kings rode down the Paseo de la Castellana side by side. Don Carlos, an immense man with a strong likeness to his uncle, Victor Emanuel, was in uniform; he wore the broad blue ribbon of Charles III, and a row of other decorations on his coat. He rode a gigantic sorrel horse. He seemed very popular, for there was a deal of hand clapping and hurrahing as he passed. The young King rode beside him, looking gallant and boyish; he had a happy genial smile for everybody. Queen Amelia, a beautiful woman, built on a generous plan to match Don Carlos, followed in a *daumont* with four horses and two postilions. How often I have remembered the answer of a Spanish diplomat to my question that day:

"Is Don Carlos as popular at home as he is in Madrid?"

"I fear not. He spends too much money. If the things were done here that go on in Portugal, Spain would be in revolution from one end to the other."

Don Luis had more time for Patsy and me in those days than any of our friends. He was always ready to take us to see sights or studios. One day we surprised him in his own studio, an eyry at the top of a tall building. A card pinned to the door by a thumb tack told us where to knock. A little old lady with a white cap tied under her chin opened the door. She had a kind face, wrinkled like the skin of a late russet apple, and eyes like Luis'. She led us along a narrow passage—so low Patsy was forced to stoop—to a little door where she tapped.

"Is it thou, Mama?" called Luis from inside. "Come in, if thou art alone." When he heard Patsy's voice he ran to let us in. The studio, an attic with a slanting roof, was filled with piles of canvases stacked against the wall.

"Ay! *Virgincita!* don't sit down on the palette," cried the old lady, "nor on that sofa; this chair is quite safe!"

On an easel stood the picture Luis had been working on, a palace interior. There were flowers, jewels, light, warmth, and atmosphere in the pictured room, above all there was luxury; that was the thing most insisted upon.

"This is the papa, and this is the mama." Don Luis' mama in her cotton cap hung over the picture as she described it. "How it is painted, this lace! And the jewels, they shine as if they were real; is it not true?"

When we had admired all the pictures Don Luis would show us, they were not many, he was afraid of boring us, Patsy reminded him of his promise to take us to the Rastro.

"Go thou with them now," said mama. "He has not been out to-day; he needs the air." She pushed him from the studio.

"If thou wilt promise not to dust"——

"*Ojala!* what a son I have! I promise, if thou wilt go, nothing shall be touched. I swear thou shalt find the studio as thou dost leave it."

The Rastro is a vast rag fair, a city within a city, where the poor of Madrid who cannot afford to buy at first hand may buy whatever they need at second hand.

"We will go first to Las Grandes Americas," said Don Luis, leading the way into an enormous enclosure surrounded by high brick walls. "This is the quarter of the building materials. Here you can buy doors and windows, girders, ceiling beams, stairs, everything necessary to build a house. Across the way are fittings, fireplaces, stoves, gas fixtures, plumbing. Here you can furnish your house, your studio, even your church!"

If we had been bent on picking up antiquities, we might have found some nice things in the quarter where the refuse of the churches is gathered. There was a Madonna dressed in a fine silk robe, standing in a little shrine, a cherub's head in carved wood, a gilded ciborium, a carved bas-relief of Santa Justa and Santa Rufina, the patrons of Seville.

It was a sharp, clear day, we stopped to warm our hands at a fire of fagots kindled on the bare ground in the middle of an old book stall. A pale, near-sighted priest, on the other side of the fire, stood first on one leg then on the other, drawing up one foot at a time under his gown for warmth. He had his long nose between the leaves of a parchment book, and looked absurdly like a learned crane as he shifted from foot to foot.

The firelight brought out now one name, now another, as the flames flickered and the light played along the backs of the old books. On a sudden the immortal name Don Quixote leapt from the shadow in letters of gold. You can always pick up the best books cheap because, like bread, they are among the necessaries of life.

"Bayard Taylor's Voyage to Japan! I never knew he went to Japan. It looks so lonely among all these Spanish books, I must rescue it!" said Patsy. Don Luis bought him the volume for three *perros chicos*.

"Here's your Spanish and English dictionary," said Patsy, who has the scent of a ferret for old books. "How much for the dictionary?" The dealer, a lean, dyspeptic man in black, who looked like his kind the world over,— the old bookman is a type apart,—sold us the dictionary, a large, clean and most precious book, for four pesetas. A shabby photograph album stood on the shelf next the dictionary. As Patsy opened it, a photograph fell from the torn leaves. Don Luis picked it up.

"*Pobrecita!*" he showed the faded photograph of a young girl in the dress of thirty years ago. He turned it over and read what was written on the back.

"*Mi Corazon!*"

"What a lovely face!" said Patsy.

"Too lovely to be sold for old paper!" Don Luis crushed the photograph in his hand, threw it on the fire, and watched it burn till nothing was left but blackened cardboard.

In an old print shop, among heaps of dusty engravings, stood a picture of a Roman model in a *ciociara* shirt. The canvas had a hole knocked in it and lacked a frame.

"Manuel's Rosina!" sighed Don Luis! "Painted the second year we were at the Spanish Academy in Rome. He died last summer and all his things were sold for his widow!"

"Come away," I cried, "it has grown cold!"

On our way from the Rastro to the Tower of Babel we passed through the Pasajé del Alhambra. Villegas and J. were just leaving the studio, so we all walked home together. It was the hour at which the old General and his wife (the couple who always watched for Villegas as he passed their house on his way to and from his work) usually started for their afternoon drive. The proud porter stood at the gate in his best uniform, with all the General's coats-of-arms and his wife's woven into the yellow galloon trimmings. A carriage with two men in livery drove up to the door. A young woman came out of the house, followed by three flossy white poodles, their topknots tied up with strawberry and buff,—the General's colors.

"We call her the dog governess," J. explained.

"You are to take the dogs out, Tomaso," she said; "nobody will drive to-day. *They* are both ill; I am going for a walk."

Tomaso, the coachman looked exactly like the eldest poodle; he glanced scornfully over his shoulder at the dogs sitting up grandly, with their dear little paws in air. Their manners showed a martinet's training. The governess held up a warning finger.

"Sit up, Prim," she said. Prim gave a reassuring bark, and the General's carriage drove solemnly through the big bronze gates, on the way to the Park of the Buen Retiro.

"How horrible to have to drive every day!" said Patsy, "as if it was not enough to have to eat and sleep away so much time. If anything is to be exercised, rather my body than my horses!"

"*Se sabé!*" Villegas agreed.

"The General was well till he was put on the retired list," said Don Luis. "People say he is only ill because he is idle."

"Moral, don't let yourself be put on the retired list," said Patsy.

"What a great, big, beautiful profession is art!" cried Villegas; "a man is not retired till he goes blind or loses his wits! Titian was at work on a picture when he died, at ninety-nine. If the pest had not carried him off, he would have been alive now, is it thus?"

"*Claro!*" Don Luis agreed. "The artist's is the only calling for a man of sense and imagination, except, of course," with a bow to Patsy, "the writer's."

"For us," said Patsy, "the race-course is never closed. Heat after heat may be lost, the Great Futurity Stakes always remain open! Don Luis knows his picture may end up with a hole knocked through it in the Rastro, but he hopes, in his heart believes, that it will one day hang in the Prado. And, who knows? a generation or two from now, some traveller may pick up my book in Las Grandes Americas for three *perros chicos!*"

XII

CARNIVAL

"TO-DAY is the *fiesta* of San Antonio the Abbot," said Pedra, when she came in to light the fire. "The Señora should go to see the blessing of the animals at his church."

Fasts, feasts, everything connected with the Church has far greater importance in Madrid than in Rome. One gets some idea here of what the power of the church was in Italy before 1870. Pedra, who was very devout, never let me forget a saint's day. It was like living in ancient Rome, this strict observance of the days of *fest* and *ne fest*.

"Then this must be your mother's *fiesta*, her name is Antonina," I said.

"No, Señora. There are two San Antonios and two religions; the patron of my mother is San Antonio of Padua,—see, here is his picture; his *fiesta* comes in June." A photograph of Murillo's Vision of Saint Anthony hung on the wall.

"How can you tell the difference between the two?"

DETAIL FROM "MOSES." *Murillo*

"But it is so easy! San Antonio the Abbot is an old man with a beard; he is always represented with a pig; he carries a bell. It is said that whenever he rings his bell all the animals kneel down. San Antonio of Padua is young, and has no beard. It is he who grants so many favors. To him I burned the candle when the Señora lost her brooch; she found it the day after, she remembers."

Don Jaime, old pagan, took me to see the blessing of the animals. He brought me a little image of the saint with a pig following at his heels, as a dog follows.

The Abbot was very wise, Jaime explained; he knew, good man, that in case of hunger, pig is better eating than dog. In Madrid people are rather indifferent to him. All the Antonios the Don knew claim San Antonio of Padua for patron because he is more aristocratic. Only the peasants will have the Abbot for their patron, because he takes care of their animals.

As we drew near the church, we met a great number of horses, mules and donkeys on their way to be blessed. A white horse with the *paso castellano*, a beautiful silky mane braided with bright ribbons and a pretty silk head-stall, was so exactly like the horse the young dealer from Ronda showed at the Seville fair that I half believed it to be the same animal. The man who led him wore Andalusian dress, and a carnation behind the ear. Man and horse picked their way through the crowd of loafers, women, children and sweetmeat-sellers, to the church. A priest soon came out followed by an acolyte all in scarlet like an embryo cardinal, and from the church steps the priest sprinkled the horse with holy water, the acolyte swung his silver censer, the incense rose in a blue cloud. From a side window a sacristan passed the young man a bag of fodder that had been blessed, and with the payment of a little money, the ceremony was over.

The church was full of kneeling people; the altars were ablaze with candles. I wished to go in to see the Goya, a picture of the Last Communion of Saint Jerome.

Don Jaime said I had better see it another time; to-day there were too many people. There was some small-pox about—not enough to be nervous over—but to avoid contagion it was well to keep out of the churches. If there is a desperately sick child in the house, of course one goes continually from the bedside of the child to the church and prays for its recovery. The old grandmother, or the little children who can do nothing to help, can at least spend the morning in the church, out of harm's way, praying for it!

At dinner Antonina, a fairy of five who lived next door, brought in a plate of *rosquitas de San Antonio*, delicious little crisp cakes baked only this day in all the year. Jaime, who had come in while we were still at table, ate one of the cakes as a reward for having been to church.

"In England," the Don remembered, "they eat hot cross buns on Good Friday and pancakes on Shrove Tuesday; they have forgotten the *rosquitas* of Saint Anthony and the *tortas* of San José."

On the nineteenth of March, the *fiesta* of San José and of all his namesakes, I asked Pedra if we should have one of the tarts of St. Joseph for dinner.

"In all Madrid there is no house so poor that the *torta* of San José will not be eaten to-day. He is the patron of the church, and as such we all must venerate him." It was a busy day for Don José Villegas; a flood of visitors, cards, letters, telegrams and presents poured through the Tower of Babel from daylight till midnight. He sat in his study busy writing notes of congratulation and sending despatches to all the other Josés of his acquaintance. I looked over the cards; there were the names of statesmen, artists, poets, singers, musicians and bull-fighters, all linked together into a sort of fraternity, because they bore in common the name of good Saint Joseph.

In almost every circumstance of life or death, the Church plays a leading part. The wife of a friend of Don Jaime died while we were in Madrid, and the Don arranged that I should see the funeral procession and one of the many services. The cortége was headed by four men dressed in white broadcloth short clothes and Louis-Seize coats, white wigs, silk stockings and three cornered hats; each carried a long white staff. The hearse was a gorgeous white affair, drawn by four white horses with sweeping ostrich plumes. It was preceded and followed by a large company of priests, monks and choristers carrying wax candles and chanting a miserere. The mourners followed on foot. More than a week after the lady's death I went with Jaime and his sister Candalaria to the house of mourning. In the private chapel we listened to a long service lasting over an hour. The chaplain of the family officiated, reciting the rosary, the litany and many prayers. This was the last and ninth day of these services. When it was over, I went home, Don Jaime and Candalaria remaining behind to speak with the mourners. Afterwards they told me something of the visit. Candalaria found the ladies of the family in one room surrounded by a crowd of women friends dressed in mourning.

"They all talked at once," said Candalaria, "saying the same thing over and over again. 'Poor soul! So young to die! So good, so devout! What will her husband do without her?'"

The Don had found the widower in another room with his men friends about him. He told the Don that his greatest grief was that his wife had died suddenly, without having time to make a confession or receive the sacraments. The Don wondered what possible sin she could have had on her soul. Everybody said, and he believed, that the dead woman was very nearly a saint.

Candalaria—her name means Candlemas—is a Majorcan. When I asked Don Jaime to tell me something about the island of Majorca where she lives, he said: "In Majorca all properties is oranges. It has a fine weather as well." I said it must be a pleasant place to live.

"Candalaria she finds it so. She is bery clever, she plays piano and biolin." Jaime always assumed b and v to be interchangeable in English as they so often are in Spanish. "Her husband is topographic engineer. Candalaria helps him to draw the geographic carts."

Don Jaime's sister is married to an officer of engineers; she draws so nicely that she often helps her husband in making his army maps. She is a small, energetic woman with consuming eyes, fiery, energetic, practical, everything Don Jaime is not. She had come to Madrid to see her brother and the carnival. Jaime introduced us to her, and during her stay, we were often together.

"In your country, Señora," Candalaria said when we first met, "you have the largest of everything of the world. Is it rivers? The Mississippi. Is it a cataract? Niagara. Is it mountains? The Andes. Your fortunes are also the largest. Where we count in millions of *reals*, you count in millions of *duros*."

It was Candalaria who presented me to Doña Emilia Pardo de Bazan, one of the leading Spanish novelists, a gray-haired woman with a powerful face. Doña Pardo Bazan spoke with me about the position of women in Spain.

"I look for nothing from the women of my country," she said; "whatever is done to improve their position must be done by men. Our laws are good. Women have a right to enter some of the universities and some of the professions, but they take no advantages of these privileges. It is the fear of ridicule that keeps them back."

I told her that we used to hear a great deal about the fear of ridicule in the old days at home, and that it had been proved a bugbear. She went on to say that she had been asked to help form a woman's club and had refused; she knew it would be of no use, because it would be laughed at.

At the reception where I met Doña Pardo Bazan I was introduced to a pretty Marquesa Fulano and her prettier daughter. "Tell me," I said to the Marquesa, "the title of Doña Pardo Bazan's most important book."

"I do not know it," was the answer; "she writes for gentlemen, not for ladies. I will enquire, if, among the many books she has written, there is one that you could read."

Though I never saw the Marquesa again, I read *La Tribuna*, one of the writer's strongest novels, and I know the Marquesa and I should not agree about what books a woman may with advantage read. I know, too, that everything is to be looked for from the women of Spain, for whom Doña Pardo Bazan—I have heard her called the foremost literary woman in Europe—has done so much.

I asked Jaime how many children Candalaria had.

"Eleven," he said; "that gives me eleven to remember in my will. To whom God sends no children, the devil sends nephews and nieces."

The carnival Candalaria had timed her visit for, was well worth seeing. It was a famous year in Spain for pageants of all sorts. The King's engagement and approaching marriage put everybody in a good-natured, money-spending mood. Great enthusiasm was expressed for what was always spoken of as "the English alliance." Whenever the King gave his ministers the slip, and ran off in his automobile to see the Princess Ena at San Sebastián, everybody was delighted.

Carnival began the Sunday before Ash Wednesday. The chief feature was a parade of cars, or floats, competing for prizes offered by the municipality. The parade took place in the splendid avenue that, under various names, runs through the new quarter of Madrid from north to south.

Lucia, Patsy and I started from the Tower of Babel soon after three o'clock. We had not driven far, when we caught sight of Villegas in the crowd at the corner.

"I knew he was dying to come with us all the time," murmured Patsy; "in spite of what he said."

"Angoscia disappointed me; they are all mad;" sighed Villegas, as he climbed into the carriage.

"That is well," said Lucia. "Thou hadst need of a holiday; thou hast not taken a day of repose this year."

"Though the premium is offered for the best car, the best car will not get the premium, thou wilt see." Jaime called to Villegas from his cab, following at a foot-pace, along the Castellana.

"*Se sabé?*" Villegas agreed. The "best car" came creaking towards us, a vast float drawn by four gray oxen with gilded horns and gold-embroidered head-dresses. Two Catalan peasants

DETAIL FROM "MOSES." *Murillo*

walked beside, driving the oxen: they wore wide sombreros, and bright *mantas* folded over the shoulder. The car was an excellent representation of the House of Congress, with its Greek façade, white columns, timpanum, and bronze lions on either side the door. Behind the columns was a brazen pot filled with men dressed as locusts. The car was greeted with roars of laughter and applause.

"Thou seest?" said Jaime to Villegas. "The government devours the country like locusts! It is true! We have the best people in the world, and the worst government!"

"*Bravo! El Congreso!*" yelled the people in the carriages. "*Muy bien!*" The crowd that lined the sidewalks answered with cries of "*Magnifico! Bravo! El carro satirico!*"

Jaime was right, the prize was not awarded to the Congreso, but to the parrots. A mammoth cage in the middle of a float with a big sham parrot hanging on a ring and all around the cage a group of *señoritas* and *caballeros* dressed to look like parrots with green velvet coats, gray satin vests, red velvet caps and big beaks.

"It almost deserves the prize, only the Congreso should have had it!" said Patsy.

As the Government appoints the judges, that was hardly to be expected. The second prize was awarded to a wagon-load of toy soldiers in French uniform. They stood stiff as wooden dolls, till you looked close and saw, under the soldiers' caps, the faces of pretty girls and laughing lads.

"Seville, the Feria, Concepcion!" cried Patsy; "this is magic!"

It was little short of it. On the float coming towards us was the patio of an Andalusian house with Moorish columns and *azulejos*, from which a *maya* and a *mayo* looked out on the crowd. The *maya* wore a black chenille overdress with a yellow satin skirt and a rose in her hair like Concepcion.

Down the middle of the Paseo de la Castellana, the most fashionable part of the route, a line of gaily decorated tribunes had been built; these were filled with well-dressed people.

"That is the tribune of La Pena, the fashionable club in the Alcalá," Patsy said. "The next is the Press Club. This is the Artists' Club, and this last is the tribune of the French Colony."

The crowd of men, women and children in the stands were armed with flowers, huge sacks of confetti, and rolls of colored paper ribbons, which unwind when they are thrown, like rockets or lassos. In a white carriage drawn by four silver-gray mules with postilions and outriders, sat two beauties dressed in silver. Passing in the other direction was a car with a representation of Carthage. The Carthaginians were splendidly dressed. As car and carriage met, a pair of dark Carthaginian men lifted a bag of violet confetti and poured it down on the white carriage, so that we saw the beauties through a purple haze. The effect of the changing colors was dazzling. Violet, declared at Paris *the* color of the season, predominated over all others.

"This," said Patsy, "is like walking through a gallery of living impressionist pictures."

"*Maestro! Ay Maestro!*" we were passing the tribune of the Artists' Club, when, bifferty! a long yellow streamer coiled about Villegas' neck and flew out behind. Soon the landeau was hung in a maze of paper ribbons, every color of the rainbow, tangling in the wheels, wound round the hubs, filling the carriage, half strangling us. A fine victoria with a harlequin and a mask in pink satin, stopped close to us. A servant was sent to our carriage and presented Lucia with a pretty porcelaine *bonbonnière* of caramels. It was growing late and people began to be hungry. The flowers were exhausted; chocolates and candies hailed into the carriage. In the cab behind, Candelaria unpacked a box of sandwiches, a bottle and two glasses.

"*Un poco de ginevra de campana?*" said Don Jaime, offering a glass to Patsy.

"Luz, Luz, Luz!" The cry came from a box of caramels filled with young *caballeros* done up like bonbons in pink paper. Luz, lovely as daybreak, smiled as her carriage passed the caramels; we saw her through a storm of rosy confetti. We drove down for a last turn to the end of the Castellana.

The sunset was pink, gold and violet, to match the prevailing tone of the carnival. Against the sky the Guaderramas stood out boldly with the eternal white confetti on their summits. Our carriage halted by the statue of Isabel the Catholic, sitting on her horse between her good and her evil genius, Columbus standing at her bridle and just behind her the cowled, sinister figure of Torquemada.

"Don Alfonzo!" The young King in his automobile flew by, a dent in his bowler hat, his coat covered with confetti. He threw a bunch of roses to a *señorita* dressed like a strawberry, sitting in a basket of fruit, the other strawberries all answered with double handful of pinkish confetti, and cries of "*muy bien!*" He was supposed to be incognito and was throwing flowers and confetti just like any other jolly boy of nineteen. Of course everybody recognized him, but the fiction of the incognito was strictly respected, which seemed very sensible. It must be supposed that he needs a little fun for his soul's sake, like the rest of us. He got his full share that afternoon.

Last of all we drove through the Alcalá, Madrid's main artery, to the Puerta del Sol, the city's mighty heart. The rest of Madrid sometimes sleeps a little; here the life blood pulses ceaselessly to and fro.

"I have been in the Puerta del Sol at every hour of the twenty-four," said Patsy, "and I have never found it empty."

The streets were guarded by the Ramonones,—mounted police, polite, energetic, keeping an order that was wonderful, considering the vast crowd, and was most of all due to the crowd's desire that order should be kept.

It was growing dark, the electric lamps twinkled out of the lavender mist. Just ahead of us, on the prize-winning car of the parrots, they were burning red Bengal lights. At the corner of the dark street where we must turn to reach home, a fine carriage, full of elegant maskers, passed us. A Pierrot in green satin stood on one step flirting with a Turkish lady, a contrabandista on the other whispered to an Andaluz. As we drove by in our modest carriage, the red Bengal lights of the parrots lit up Don José's face. From the grand carriage came the cry:

"*Villegas! gloria de la patria!*"

"They are all mad!" said Villegas; "*vamos!* it's time to go home."

Ash Wednesday morning the streets were full of sweepers trying to get rid of the green, pink and red papers, the trampled débris of the last three days' frolic. We met Luz coming out of San Isidro Real. She was all in black, wearing the mantilla. On her forehead the priest had traced a cross of ashes. The church was filled with fashionably dressed men and women, many of whom we had seen the day before at the carnival. Each came out into the sunlight with the cross of dust and ashes on the forehead, in token of the day of mourning. In the stable-yard behind the church we saw the ruins of the second prize winner, the toy soldier cart. The little sentry box hung in the right place, the stiff green trees, the dummy soldiers in their smart French uniforms stuck up oddly from the cart. The merry group of live soldiers, the pretty girls and saucy boys were scattered; perhaps some of them were in the church. As we stood watching the wreck of the prize winner, men began to take the car to pieces and to pull off the remaining decorations.

"*Sic transit gloria mundi,*" said Patsy; "I'm for the Prado and glories that do not pass so quickly."

XIII

TOLEDO

OUR winter in Madrid wore pleasantly away; we basked in the Sun of To-day, gave hardly a thought to the Shadow of Yesterday. Fate wove the thread of our existence into her tapestry of life in the Spanish capital in the year 1906; a many-toned fabric with touches of gold and silver, sinister crimson and sombre black. Now that the web is finished and hung up in the hall of memory, I see that in the earlier part rose color is the predominating tone.

"It's as good for a nation as it is for a person, after they have been in mourning, to come out into the world again and take an interest in other people's affairs," said Patsy. "The Conference, whatever it may do for Morocco, is being very good for Spain."

The two absorbing topics of conversation were the Algeciras Conference and the King's marriage. From our friends in the diplomatic world we heard a deal of talk about what was going on at Algeciras, where the representatives of thirteen Powers were discussing the vexed questions of the State Bank of Morocco which it was proposed to establish under European control, the policing of the unhappy country by France and Spain, the administration of customs, and the various reforms proposed to the Sultan. On all sides we heard compliments for our representative, Mr. Henry White, *par excellence* the peacemaker of the Conference. I was told by a distinguished diplomat that Mr. White's exquisite tact and good feeling "saved the situation more than once."[3] Besides keeping the peace, the American delegate put in a good word for the Jews, asking that they might have religious tolerance in Morocco. His plea was seconded by Sir Arthur Nicholson, the English delegate, and the Duke of Almodovar who, ignoring the little detail of the expulsion of the Jews from Spain, reminded the delegates that his country had an especial interest in the Hebrews of Morocco, who still spoke the Castilian language, and were the descendants of Spanish Jews. The English, seconded by the Americans, made a plea for the gradual abolition of slavery in Morocco, against the public sale of men and women in the slave markets of the interior, and for the improvement of the prisons. It was pleasant to see England and the United States aiding and abetting each other in all these humane efforts.

The Moroccan delegate, Sid Hach el Mokri, Ancient Inspector of Weights and Measures at Fez, and his colleague did little but protest against the reforms the Powers proposed to institute at the expense of Morocco and under the direction of the Diplomatic Corps at Tangiers. Hach el Mokri cried out that he was there to see Morocco's income increased, not decreased, and that many of the proposed reforms had not been included in the programme of the Conference. Patsy, who had seen Sid Mokri and made an excellent photograph of the old man in his white bournous, with his long white beard and piercing eyes, had a sneaking sympathy for him.

"After all, the world will be a tame place when there are telephones and electric cars everywhere," he said. "If Morocco does not want to be civilized our way, or any other way, why should she be?" The Powers are cutting and carving the revenues, the commerce, the future of that unfortunate country as if they were masters of the situation. They are a long way from it! Before France gets the little Germany means to let her have, she must pay dear for it, even if England stands by to see fair play.

I had a sudden vision of the garden in Tangiers and the strange old man who had talked with me of Moroccan affairs. I seemed to hear his brooding voice utter, as if in prophecy, "Keep your ear to the ground; the end of Islam is not yet!"

Our Spanish friends were naturally even more interested in Don Alfonzo's affairs than in those of the Sultan of Morocco. It was wonderful how the courtship of one pair of lovers made a whole nation in love with life! There was a delicate thrill of expectation in the air. Spain drank deep of the three great cordials, youth, hope and love, forgot the old pain in the new rapture. Every detail of the King's wooing was eagerly discussed. The news that the Princess Ena had been received into the Church of Rome and renounced the errors of the Protestant faith was a "world event." Her decision to take the names, Victoria Eugenie, gave great satisfaction. It was rumored that the Empress Eugenie had given her a wedding present of a million *pesetas*, and would make the future Queen of Spain her heir. Older people recalled the poor young Prince Imperial's early attachment to Princess Beatrice, Princess Ena's mother.

"The Empress was a Spaniard," Candalaria reminded me; "a Montijo of Malaga. My parents knew the family. It is quite natural she should wish her money to come back to Spain. My father was at the funeral of her son, the Prince Imperial. He saw the great English Queen, Victoria, and her daughter, Princess Beatrice, when they drove over to Chiselhurst to lay a golden laurel wreath on the coffin of the young Prince Napoleon IV, as they called him, killed in the Zulu war, fighting for the English."

We had all become so absorbed in the pleasant social life of Madrid, so taken up with current matters of public and private interest, that the many journeys we had planned were put off and put off. Had it not been for a chance question of Patsy's, we might never even have seen Toledo, we were living—except for those golden hours in the Prado—so completely in To-day. One brilliant March afternoon Don Jaime greeted me at the door of the Museum with his cheery "Good day, Missis." The Don liked to go with us to the Prado; he was interested in Patsy's art education and, if neither Villegas nor Don Luis were present, would hold forth on the merits of the pictures.

"Good afternoon, Don," said Patsy; "what's the news?"

"There are very few news. You receive some lollipops?" The Don's intercourse with English-speaking people, broken off when he left school, led him to suppose that to be happy they must be continually fed with lollipops.

"Nuns of Concepcion Convent has secret of preparing those sweets, same like Benedictines' liquor secret."

Knowing his poverty, I was troubled by the little presents he was forever making one or other of us, of which Patsy's lollipops were an example.

"It's his way of keeping his end up," Patsy maintained. "The Don expects to die rich, to leave his family rolling in money. He has an invention for a flying machine half worked out. On his paternal *heredad*—a piece of waste land in the Sierra Rondina—there's a rich iron mine, and a spring of sparkling mineral water, better, he says, than apollinaris. The joke of it all is, I believe what he says is perfectly true. He will never 'realize' on spring or mine, though perhaps Candalaria's eleven may!"

"You look festive this morning, Don; where did that sporty rose come from?" Patsy asked. The Don always had a flower in his buttonhole, though he often had not a dollar in his pocket.

"It is monthly roses," said the Don, settling the bud in his coat; "they give every moon. Let us now to the parlor of the great Velasquez."

We always began with the Velasquez room, studying some one picture, and passing the rest in review. Don Jaime professed great admiration for the portrait of the Fool of Coria, one of the *hombres de placer*—literally, men of pleasure—of the court. The fool is seated on a stone, with a gourd on either side; his hands rest idly on his knee. It is a wonderfully pathetic picture, with a heartache in it for those who have some knowledge of those weakest of our brothers, the feeble-minded.

"How dreary Philip's court must have been," sighed Patsy, "if that pitiful creature could add to its gaiety."

"*Claro*," said Don Jaime, "but, *Canastos!* It is a most fine portrait. Look again, you will see in the face the idiotness of that man."

Canastos, baskets, was the Don's favorite oath; it was the only exclamation of impatience either he or Candalaria had ever heard their mother use. That morning the Don insisted on our looking more carefully at Ribera's pictures than suited Patsy. The Don himself felt little sympathy with them, but, as a Spaniard, it was his duty to interest us in all the well-known painters of the Spanish school. Ribera—we knew him better by his Italian nickname, Spagnoletto, little Spaniard—the Don said, painted for the Church. He was in no sense a court painter, was probably prejudiced against all court people on account of Don John of Austria's unhandsome treatment of his daughter in their unfortunate love affair. The Church at that time was under the sway of the Inquisition, where we must lay the blame, if the Ribera room was, as Patsy insisted, a little like the chamber of horrors.

"This painter," said Don Jaime, "lived in one epoca of inquisition and hell influences. In all his paintings are seen foreheads full of wrinkles for pain, eyes terrified by the fear, and naked flesh teared, or sullen martyrs, saints and gloomy friars."

"Why couldn't he always paint like that?" said Patsy, pausing before a fine poetic Magdalen. "The drawing is as good, the modelling as astonishing, the color as rich as in those morbid cruel pictures. The mission of art is to inspire, not to terrify; you can never make me like Ribera, Don."

The Don himself was more depressed than any of us by what he had seen. He mopped his bald ivory poll with his silk handkerchief—it was scented with orris—and sighed as we left the room:

"Everything it is so truthful, so to make fear, that everybody feel a relief, a joy of living, when he is gone from that parlor."

"Now let's go and play with the Venetians, as a reward of merit," said Patsy. "I have not seen those lovely Titians for a week." Patsy's beloved Venetians can be studied better in the Prado than anywhere outside of Venice. The Don, filled with a sudden access of zeal for the Spanish school, would not let us go until we had given some time to the work of El Greco.

"Here are seven paintings of the lifes of saints by El Greco," he said. "Every one so thin and transparent and of so greenish tones that they looks more than saints, like spirits who took the human form, notwithstanding they keep their impalpables. The intelligent people say that in this consist the worth of this painter, because he translated on the cloth the *asceticismo* of his *epoca*."

"You will never convince me that Greco is one of the world's great painters, however important he may have been to the development of the Spanish school," said Patsy. "A man who paints people eight feet high, who makes his angels goblins, his saints lunatics, is not sane; and without sanity there can be no great art."

"You must go to Toledo," said Don Luis, who had joined us, "before you can judge El Greco. You see his sacred pictures at a great disadvantage in a museum. They need the dim religious light of the churches or monasteries, for which they were painted. Only the portraits look well here; those, you must admit, are among the great portraits of the world."

Patsy was not quite ready to agree to this yet, Don Jaime meanwhile acknowledged that fashion in art is as capricious as it is in dress; perhaps the people who have made El Greco the fashion, not to say the rage of the moment, claimed too much for him. In spite of this, like Don Luis, Jaime considered El Greco among the first of portrait painters.

"Speaking of fashion in dress," said Patsy, stopping before an anonymous portrait of a lady in a yellow turban, "at what period did they wear that extraordinary headgear?"

"It must have been in the time of King Wamba," laughed Don Luis, as much as to say, "before the flood."

The name of King Wamba was like the kiss of the faithful hound on the cheek of the enchanted prince. Patsy awoke from the enchantment of To-day and remembered Yesterday, remembered Wamba and Wamba's capital, Toledo, remembered that all the records of that wonderful life of many yesterdays we call history was waiting for him to read, not three hours away from Madrid.

"I would not go to Toledo for the sake of El Greco," Patsy declared, "but for King Wamba's sake, and to buy a Toledo blade, I would go twice as far!"

So our trip to Toledo—one of the best of our Spanish adventures— came about. We cancelled all engagements, gave up seats for the opera, and the very next day started with little Don Luis for Toledo. The train took us past a small hillock, on which stands a church marking the exact geographical centre of Spain. Toledo is a walled town, built, like Rome, on seven hills. It stands high above the plain, surrounded on three sides by the Tagus, a rushing yellow river (Martial says its sands are of gold) that girdles the city, and keeps the *vega* around it a lovely green oasis in the arid Castilian plain. The road from the station passes through a rocky gorge and leads to the imposing bridge of Alcantara. From here the view of the stern fortress city is superb. We drove round the walls (Wamba's walls) and saw the towers, the splendid gates, with the portcullis in more than one still perfect; and finally climbed the height, to the commanding ruin of the Alcazar.

The hill of the Alcazar dominates Toledo, as the Acropolis dominates Athens. The Alcazar is an immense square building, with four towers surmounted by pointed roofs. Time, the supreme colorist, has laid on his matchless glazes of sun and shadow; the darker parts are rich saffron, the lightest, mellow gold. Seen from the distance, it is a broad imposing mass, simple, strong, overpowering all other architectural features of the city by its size and its situation. When you enter the splendid ruin, and stand in the patio with its fine double arcade of Corinthian columns, you are reminded of the courtyard of the Farnese palace in Rome, designed by Michaelangelo.

"If we could know the history of this old ruin," said Patsy, "we should know the history of Toledo. Here, where we stand, on the very highest point of this granite rock, the Romans built their *castellum*. From its ruins rose the Visigoths' citadel, and, still later, the Moors' Alcazar! The word means the palace of Cæsar: that shows the Moors did not forget! Kaiser means Cæsar, too; how many other things did the great Julius give his name to? I wonder. Think of the people who have lived between these four walls, and have looked out upon this glorious view! The Cid, Ferdinand and Isabel, Charles V and Philip II, just to mention a few stars."

As in some families the youngest child who can speak "asks the blessing," it fell to Patsy, youngest and most ardent of the party, to impart all inevitable information. The plan worked well, in spite of J.'s occasional restive "Use your eyes!" It was never necessary to tell *him* what to look at.

"That," said Patsy, map in hand, pointing to the lower levels of the town, "is the Bridge of Alcantara, literally the bridge of the bridge."

The great bridge leaps boldly across the river, supported by one large and one small arch. There

TOLEDO BY MOONLIGHT.

is a rugged watch-tower on the Toledo side; the tower that for so many centuries stood opposite has disappeared.

"The Bridge of San Martin is on the other side of the town. When you cross it, please cry out, 'My eye, Betty Martin,'—Yankee for *mihi Beato Martino*, to me blessed Martin, an old crusading war cry heard in Toledo before. The walls of Wamba extend from the Bridge of Alcantara to the Bridge of San Martin. The river runs round three sides of the city; the walls on the fourth make it impregnable."

"We may as well have Wamba's story now; we shall have to hear it some time," sighed J. "I want to sketch the bridge from here. Fire away, boy!" Patsy, loaded and primed with information, fired.

"There isn't much to tell! I always liked Wamba because, for a long time, I confused him with Wamba, son of Witless the Jester, in Ivanhoe," Patsy confessed.

"That's the way he always begins his longest yarns," J. groaned.

According to Patsy's yarn, this real Wamba was the last of the great Gothic kings, who, in spite of the tricks of his enemies, the churchmen, has left his mark on Toledo and on Spain. Wamba was an old soldier who lived just at the time when the Gothic power was on the wane, and Rome, for a second time, was becoming mistress of Spain. When the Gothic nobles elected him King, Wamba at first refused the throne. Then they gave him his choice of death or kingship, and he was finally forced to accept. He taught his people what they had almost forgotten, 'to fight the good fight'; in his time there was a last flicker of the old Gothic spirit. But Wamba was too free and independent to suit the churchmen, and they contrived to give him a sleeping draught that threw him into so deep a trance that his followers thought the King was dead. He was prepared for burial, as is still the fashion for great personages, as if he had been a monk, and a tonsure was shaved on his head. When he came to himself, the churchmen maintained that a man who had worn the dress and the tonsure of a monk could never again reign as King. So, having reigned against his will, wisely and too well, he was forced to abdicate against his will, and retire to a monastery where he ended his days. Staunch old fellow that he was, the Church was too strong for him, as it has been for most political reformers from that day to this.

The Visigoths laid hold upon our imagination at Toledo as the Romans had at Italica, and the Moors at Cordova. Those fair northmen came to Spain when Rome had grown old and feeble, her iron hand relaxed. The Romans had come as conquerors, carrying the eagles through Spain. They marched rapidly; twenty miles a day was their average. They smote Spain—Iberia they called it—hard, and left their imperishable mark upon her. The coming of the Visigoths was more a vast migration than a conquest. They moved slowly, wandered rather than marched, encumbered with women and children, flocks and herds. They wandered over Europe, crossed the Pyrenees and settled the Peninsula. The impress they have left on Spain is as different from the Roman as their coming differed from the triumphal progress of the Romans.

"It is not so easy to find traces of the Visigoths in Spain as of the Roman or the Moor," little Don Luis had assured us.

"That is a pity," was Patsy's answer, "for the Visigoths were the nicest people who ever came to Spain!"

They have not left so strong a mark on things material as Roman or Arab; they seem never to have held the land as firmly. Was it because they brought their wives with them, and neglected the dark-eyed Iberian women, skillful, like the dancing girls of Gades, in the dance with the castanets? To find traces of the Gothic occupation do not look for vast ruins of temple, circus, aqueduct or bridge. A few capitals in the Mosque of Cordova, the bas-relief of a hunting scene in the Museum, the city walls and the ruins of the palace of Wamba at Toledo—we saw little else to remind us of the Gothic rule in Spain, as far as material things go. The crown of King Swinthila at Madrid was the most impressive relic of the Visigoths we saw. It is of gold, surrounded by rosettes of pearls and sapphires, in a delicate red paste cloisonné setting.

The Visigoths' legacy to Spain was immaterial and immortal. Search for traces of the blue-eyed northmen, and you will find ideals that still survive in the Spaniards' deep inborn sense of the equality of all men (at least of all Spaniards), and in the Spanish woman's honesty. The Visigoths treated their wives as their equals, expected them to do their share of fighting the enemy and of providing food for the family, gave them control of their own property, and a right to half the common household stock. They only obeyed their King so long as they approved of him. "King shalt thou be as long as thou dost right. If thou dost not right, no King shalt thou be."

The influence of this immortal spiritual gift, these ideals of the independence of the individual and the equality of the wife with the husband, survive to-day in the temper of the modern Spaniard. I found them in Pedra's mother, Antonina, the washerwoman who so frankly shook hands with me on our first meeting; in the fact that in Spain to-day no man may leave more than half his fortune away from his wife; that the Grandee is free to wear his hat in the presence of the King, his wife to sit in the presence of the Queen. The legacy of the Goth survives in the ideals and the virtues of the race. The Spaniard has the virtues of the north as well as the ideals; he is truthful, honest, clean and, above all, he is independent.

The sketches were nearly done; we all had settled into silence, and worked, or dreamed half the morning away, looking out across that green *vega* or down at the old Moorish mills, far below in the Tagus, until Patsy, whose sketch was finished first, declared he could not live another hour unless he was possessor of a Toledo blade. Wandering in search of one, down into the lower part of the town, we soon lost ourselves in a labyrinth of narrow winding streets with high Oriental looking houses. At every corner we were brought to a standstill by some picturesque doorway, church or tower. These straight curving lanes, with scarcely one open square or space, must make Toledo a comfortable summer city. One has but to pass July in the modern quarter of Rome to know the folly of laying out a southern city with wide avenues and open squares, because they have proved comfortable and suitable for Paris or London. Every town has to reckon either with heat or cold as its chief enemy. Where heat is the more to be feared, as in Toledo or Rome, narrow streets with tall houses, where the shadows lie cool, are the best.

"Do you believe," asked Patsy, "that I shall find a blade 'with so fine a temper that it can be curled up like the mainspring of a watch?'"

Don Luis would not promise, but he guided us to the shop where we could buy the best wares for our money. The dealer welcomed us and invited us to examine his stock of swords, daggers, *cuchillos*, long pointed knives, *navajas*, clasp knives, and *puñalicos*, little deadly knives worn in the garter: one bore the motto, "I serve a lady."

Patsy had little money to spend; the edge of his enjoyment in spending it was keen as the blades he turned over so carefully. We were the only customers; the dealer seemed in no hurry, the shop—cool, comfortable and smelling of fresh mint—was a pleasant place. The sunlight, streaming through the windows, glinted on the weapons. Patsy handled the deadly things as skillfully as he had handled the scythe at Seville Fair. The dreadful inherited knowledge of killing was in his fingers; that strong, nervous hand could, if need be, use that rapier as it could use the scythe.

"How much for this dagger?" Patsy asked at last.

The dealer named a moderate price for the beautiful weapon. The handle and sheath were of iron, finely damascened with gold. The blade, sharp and flexible, as the dealer proved by bending it double, was of shining steel, a "Toledo trusty" such as Mercutio says a soldier dreams of. Patsy read the motto on the hilt; "Who lacks courage need place no faith in me!"

"Do you realize," he said, "that since the days of the Romans these Toledo blades 'with the ice-brook's temper' have been the most famous weapons in the world?" Then, in spite of my murmured, "Whatever will you do with it," he offered half the price that had been asked. We had done little shopping in Spain, and had come from a long stay in a land where the same article has many prices. The dealer stroked his pointed beard with a white well-kept hand, as if to hide the chilly smile that curved his thin lips, and politely repeated his price. Though he was willing to show his wares, he did not seem anxious to sell them.

"I had forgotten we were in Spain," murmured the crestfallen Patsy; "in Toledo, the 'Heart of Spain!'" Without more ado he bought the dagger and a lady's pocketknife with two sharp blades.

While the trade was making, I studied the tradesman. He might have been descended from one of the Toledan hidalgos, immortalized by El Greco's portraits. He had a thin nervous face, with great hollow eyes and a large sharp-cut nose. We got to know the type well before we left Toledo, for the citizens are of a distinct type. Just as in Seville we were always meeting Murillo Madonnas walking about the streets, and in Madrid Velasquez portraits, in Toledo we were continually meeting the hidalgos of El Greco.

From the shop where weapons are sold, we went to the Military Academy where soldiers are made. The cadets were just coming out from recitation as we looked into the courtyard to see the fountain cast from captured guns. They were gallant looking lads, full of pranks and tricks, as they streamed down the long staircase into the patio and out into the *calle*, past the wonderful carved stone doorway of the Hospital Santa Cruz. Don Luis sent in a message begging that a certain young cadet, Candalaria's son, might have leave of absence to lunch with us. Leave was granted, and the cadet, his name was Pepé, as smart a young blade as you could see, escorted us through the confusing labyrinth of narrow *calles* that lay between the Military Academy and our hotel. Pepé was well known at the hotel; after his visit we were even better treated than before.

"What is best worth seeing in Toledo, after the Academy?" Patsy asked.

"The Fabrica de Espadas, where your dagger was made," said Pepé promptly. So after lunch J. and Patsy, escorted by Pepé, went off to the Weapon Factory, leaving Don Luis and me to run lightly over "the chief attractions."

"Look up my brother, Gregorio," Pepé flung back over his shoulder, as they swung off together. "He is free this afternoon; he knows all about churches and museums, if you care such dull things."

"Yes," said Don Luis, "we will look up Gregorio. He knows a good deal about Toledo."

Gregorio, Candalaria's eldest son, was unlike any other member of that interesting family. He was small and fragile, with piercing brown eyes. He came, rather unwillingly, to show us the cathedral.

"Gregorio wished to go into the Church," Don Luis told us. "His father and Candalaria did not like the idea. They never opposed the boy, but sent him to Toledo to spend a year with a priest cousin, who is the greatest bore in the family; the plan was that old fox Jaime's, it's working out well. From what Pepé says, Gregorio is not so bent on taking orders now as he once was."

Gregorio took us to the cathedral, a fine building, so hemmed about by smaller ones that we could get no view of the whole. The exterior of a stone originally white, is now tanned by sun and weather to a delicious mellow tone. The ruddy tower faintly recalls that greater glory, the Giralda. Some parts of the cathedral are in severe Gothic style, some very florid; this shows that it was a long time in building. The main entrance is perfectly gorgeous, the stone fretted and carved like so much petrified lace; the outer gate is only opened to admit the reigning sovereign. The interior is marred, like Seville and Cordova, by the *coro*. The stained glass is sumptuous. Over the main door is a thirty-foot rose window, in each transept a smaller rose. The afternoon sun, pouring through these and the graceful pointed windows in the different parts of the church, did much to counteract the cold, whitewashed walls. The vast white stone columns, with their prodigal carving, were stained ruby, amber, emerald, the seven colors of the rainbow, by the sunlight falling through those jewel windows. The cathedral is a museum in itself. One of the treasures is a small carved wooden statuette of St. Francis, by Alonzo Cano. The saint stands with his arms folded; the marvellous face of carven ivory, the agate eyes, look at you from the dark shadow of his cowl. Eyes and face reminded us of a pair of Egyptian statues at Cairo, whose discovery Marriatt Bey described: the workman who first entered the tomb where they were found came hurrying out in terror, crying, "There are live people in there; I saw the shining of their eyes!"

Our first visit to the cathedral, with Gregorio to protect us, was the best. When we went back without him, we were harried by the *silencieros*, vulgarly called dog-beaters, fierce beadles with long staves who pursued us, would not let us look at what we wanted to see, and tried to make us look at things we did not care for.

From the cathedral Gregorio took us to the Archbishop's palace, connected with it by a covered bridge, high up in the air, like the Bridge of Sighs at Venice.

"The Cardinal Archbishop of Toledo, Primate of Spain, lives here," said Gregorio. "He passes through that bridge when he goes from the palace to the cathedral. I would take you to call upon him, but we should not find him at home. He goes every afternoon to the new convent he has founded, to see how the workmen are getting on."

"Let us follow him to the convent," said Don Luis, an adorable cicerone, bent on showing us all sorts and conditions of men and works. After a little coaxing, Gregorio agreed to take us to see the Archbishop. We must not object, he stipulated, to stopping for a lady, he mentioned her name.

"You will be doing our friends a great service," said Don Luis, "for she is not only very distinguished and beautiful, but exceedingly kind."

She was all Don Luis said, and more! Among the visions that arise when the magical name Toledo is spoken, none is more vivid than Engracia's dark, mobile face. She was one of those women born to command. From the moment she appeared to us, standing on the steps of the old Toledan palace, daintily holding up her white linen skirt, embroidered with purple grapes, we all, even Gregorio, obeyed her.

We drove directly to the convent where we were promptly admitted by one of the sisters of the new order founded by the Cardinal. She wore a simple black gown with a thin lace veil, not unlike those of Spanish women of the lower class,—the best dressed women in the world to-day, from the artist's standpoint. The sister showed us into the parlor, and went to announce our visit to the Cardinal. From the adjoining room came the sound of sweet high voices singing the rosary; we caught a glimpse of rows of little girls sitting demurely with folded hands.

Gregorio explained that this was a teaching sisterhood. He wished to interest Engracia in the convent. There was still room for a few more novices. Each novice must bring a dot of four thousand dollars, which insured her support for the rest of her life. While Gregorio was describing the joys of life in a Toledo convent, the Cardinal sent for us. We found him in the garden, attended by his secretary and the Lady Superior. They had been inspecting some mason work. The Cardinal was a fine subtle-faced old man with an authoritative manner, and a straighter, more dominating eye than any Roman cleric I know. Though he wore a simple black habit, with only a thread of scarlet and the scarlet moire skullcap under the shovel hat, I recognized him at once as the splendid prelate in the vermilion robes who had officiated at the Infanta's marriage, and who would, Gregorio said, celebrate the marriage of the King.

Imperious Engracia knelt before the Cardinal, and kissed his emerald ring. He asked about her husband and parents, whom he had known, and then began to talk with her about his convent. He had founded this new order to resist the teaching of socialism and atheism to the masses. He had talked the plan over with Leo XIII, "a fine, great pope," who had sympathized deeply with his scheme. Pope Leo, however, had feared it would be difficult to carry out the plan. It was a moment when convents and religious orders were being broken up everywhere; those already existing could only be maintained with the greatest fostering. He hoped, however, that the Cardinal might succeed, and blessed his undertaking. The whole idea of the new order was to teach the true value of the Church. The sisters were to have far greater liberty in coming and going than in the older orders. This was borne out by the free and frank bearing of the five or six sisters we saw. I was struck by the simplicity and directness of their manners. Compared to the Abbess of Ronda, who might have belonged to the time of Santa Teresa, the Superior of the Toledo Convent *seemed* a modern person belonging to our epoch. Was she? To this day I cannot make up my mind! Can we pour new wine into old bottles, and mend the old garment with new cloth? That is the question!

We parted with the Cardinal at sunset. He shook hands kindly with us, and with old-fashioned courtesy invited us to come and see him again if we should return to Toledo.

We spent much of our too short time in Toledo in studying the pictures of that strange and interesting painter, Domenico Theotocopulos, called El Greco because he was a Greek, a native of Crete. The portraits in the little Museum of San Juan de Los Reyes are among the best examples of his individual and peculiar manner. Greco is a realist; he paints what he sees with splendid fidelity

DETAIL FROM "THE BURIAL OF COUNT ORGAZ." *Greco*

and power. His most famous picture, the Funeral of Count Orgaz, in the church of San Tomé, is a fine illustration both of his strength and his weakness. In the lower part of the canvas we have the dead Count, with the priests and the mourners about him. Here all is real; the dead man in his armor, the Bishop in his mitre and gorgeous robes, the long line of attendants and mourners, and the lovely head of the young boy are all portrait studies. In the upper part, where the heavenly vision is painted, Greco has left the realm of the real and entered that of the ideal. Instead of raising us to the seventh heaven, he lets us down upon the earth. Saints Augustine and Stephen, who appear in the clouds as a heavenly vision attended by a heavenly host—things imagined and not seen—are grotesque, almost ridiculous.

Don Luis was right; it is only at Toledo that one can really understand El Greco. The religious pictures at the Prado had offended us; they had seemed the work of a madman. At Toledo one gets a true understanding of his original and extraordinary personality. He neither saw nor painted as other men see and paint. There was much that was morbid, something that was mad in his vision; but there was, besides, much that was sincere, honest and lucid. El Greco, who is now ranked as second only to Velasquez by many critics, by some as his equal if not superior, seems to have become so thoroughly saturated with the Spanish sentiment that, though his name is a constant reminder of his nationality, he is invariably spoken of as if he were in truth a Spaniard. The strange and wayward genius, who has so touched and influenced the imagination of Velasquez, of Sargent and so many other famous painters, was a true son of Hellas. To Greece belong his glory and his laurels.

XIV

THE BRIDE COMES

IN   March Sir Maurice de Bunsen, the new English Ambassador, presented his credentials to the King. We went over to the palace to see what we could of the ceremony. There had been a sudden change in the weather. It was very hot waiting in the Plaza de Armas outside the palace. The *chicos*, playing at marbles instead of basking in the sun, had moved into the shadow. There were very few spectators; Mrs. Young, the wife of one of the English Secretaries, fair and cool in a white summer dress, her maid armed with a kodak, and perhaps a dozen other people.

"What do they mean," said Patsy, "by saying that in Madrid you must not put away your overcoat till the fortieth of May?"

"Wait a little and perhaps you will know," said a familiar voice. It was the Argentino, who had lately come to Madrid; the chance acquaintance begun at Cordova was ripening into something like friendship.

Two lines of soldiers in fresh blue uniforms with green trimmings and gloves were drawn up between the gate of the plaza and the palace. Punctually at the appointed hour the band struck up the Spanish national air, there was a ruffle of drums and a fine gala coach from the royal stables came rumbling along the Calle Bailen at the heels of four noble horses with head-dresses of long nodding blue ostrich plumes. The coach was of gold and crystal with beautiful painted panels. The liveries of coachman, postillions, outriders, palfreniers and men-in-waiting who walked beside, were blue and gold to match the splendid trappings.

"The coach is empty, there is nobody inside," cried Patsy. "What does it mean?"

"This," said the Argentino, "is the *coche de respecto* for the Secretaries of Embassy. In the days when people travelled by post or on horseback, important personages always had a led horse or an extra carriage in case of accident."

"What accident," laughed Patsy, "could happen between the Embassy and the palace?"

"One never knows; it is one of the picturesque old customs the Spanish Court preserves, even though the need of the *coche de respecto* may have been outlived."

In the second coach—as handsome in every detail as the first, the only difference being that the feathers and decorations were red instead of blue—rode Mr. Fairfax Cartwright, Mr. George Young, and two other English Secretaries of Embassy, looking magnificent and uncomfortable in stiff gold-laced court uniforms. Mr. Young made a little gesture of recognition to his wife, the others did not look out of the window.

The Ambassador's *coche de respecto*, drawn by six horses, was even finer than the other. The liveries, trappings and feathers were red and yellow, the Spanish colors. There were six coaches in all, four for the Englishmen, two for the escort. In the last rode Sir Maurice, a tall fair man, with the First Introducer, both radiant in court finery. They had driven down the Calle Bailen in single file; at the plaza the shining coaches were drawn up into two lines, three abreast, with an escort of mounted cavalry on either side. They advanced at a snail's pace, crossed the palace yard where the soldiers stood at attention, and approached the three doors of the palace to the music of the military march. The ambassador drove in through the middle door.

"That is the royal entrance," said the Argentino. "Sir Maurice passes through it to-day because he brings letters from King Edward; he is not likely ever to go through it again."

While we waited to see them come out, a private brougham with black and silver liveries drove up to the door by which the Secretaries had gone in. We caught a glimpse of Lady de Bunsen in a white dress with feathers in her hair, on the way to her audience with the Queen.

"She has come early," said the Argentino, "so that she may see the finest sight of the ceremony, the halberdiers guarding the grand staircase while the Ambassador passes in and out of the throne room. They stand two on each step in that old swashbuckler uniform, silver-buckled shoes, cutaway coats, knee breeches and cocked hats, holding their big halberds so that the blades touch. The Ambassador walks up and down the stair between two flashing lines of steel. It really is worth seeing."

We waited till the audience was over, watched the Ambassador and his suite drive away in the same state as they had come, and a little later the halberdiers march out of the palace and down the Calle Bailen to their barracks.

"There goes Pedro," murmured Patsy, as the halberdier who had made room for us at the Infanta's wedding swung by. "The soldiers on duty in the yard looked like any other soldiers. These chaps could only be Spanishers. The fire in the eye, the haughtiness, are perfectly colossal!"

"And the fierce curl of the *bigotes*. You know what *bigote* means? When the Spanish soldiers were in the Low countries, they fell in with the English—you remember Uncle Toby says 'our army swore terribly in Flanders.' Every time the British soldier swore he twisted his moustache and said 'by God!' The Spanish imitated him, twirled his moustachios and cried 'bigote.' By and by he connected the action with the words, imagined the oath had something to do with the moustache; to this day the Spaniard calls his moustache a *bigote* in memory of that swearing English army in Flanders—or, some people say, of the swearing German soldiers of Charles V."

We lingered after the other spectators had gone, and the *chicos* had begun their game again; palace and plaza had a strong fascination for us. We looked through the arches of the peristyle across the bare Castilian plain to the snow-capped Guadarramas.

"The Escorial lies in that direction," said the Argentino. "On clear days it can be seen from the palace. Do you suppose when he looks out of window, Don Alfonzo ever thinks about that black marble sarcophagus waiting for him over there?"

That seventh wonder of the world, the Escorial, palace, monastery and mausoleum all in one, was built by Philip II. It is a proper monument to a man who is remembered as having laughed rarely, and loudest when he heard of the Massacre of Saint Bartholomew. The Escorial expresses Philip's dour personality as no other building that I know expresses any other man's. From the moment you catch sight of the gloomy pile, built in the shape of a gridiron, in memory of Saint Lawrence, you feel if ever place was haunted, the ghost of Philip haunts that gray grim tragedy in stone.

"I am glad," said Patsy, "that I saw the Escorial; I shall be glad never to see it again. The places where people have lived for me, rather than those where they are buried. This palace is a thousand times more interesting than the Escorial. Think how much we know about the people who have lived here! When Napoleon first saw this palace, he said to his brother Joseph—he had just casually made him King of Spain: "You will be better lodged than I."

(Poor Joseph did not enjoy the lodging long; he was glad to escape from it alive and fly to Bordentown, New Jersey, where he lived in semi-royal state at Point Breeze. Here, an old letter preserves the fact, my grandmother Ward dined with him, and wore an "embroidered cambric dress and a lilac turban.")

"We are interested not only in the people who have lived here, but in those who live here now," Patsy went on, as a closed carriage drawn by four black mules dashed by. "There go the King's nieces and nephews."

The little Prince of the Asturias, the heir to the throne, bowed, smiled and waved his tiny hand in quaint mechanical greeting to whoever might be looking. The youngest child, still happily unconscious of his rank, wriggled in the English nurse's arms like any other baby out for its airing.

"The boy has learned his part well," said the Argentino. "He's not like the little prince Imperial: when the Empress Eugenie threatened to punish him, he made the dreadful counter threat, *'je ferai des grimaces au peuple'* (I will make faces at the people). There you see the difference between real and upstart royalty!"

The day after the Ambassador's audience seemed to us the coldest of the winter. The trees in the Recoletos had a wedge of snow down one side, the side that faces north and gets the full force of the wind sweeping down from the snow fields of the Guadarramas. Engracia's vivid face was tingling with the cold when she blew into the Tower with Don Luis that morning and announced that she had come to take us into the country for the day.

"The motor is at the door," she declared, "luncheon is ordered. We go first to El Pardo to see the royal hunting chateau, and then on to our own shooting box where my husband joins us."

From our first meeting at Toledo, not a week had passed without some pleasant incident for which we had to thank Engracia.

The city was soon left behind and we were bowling along a road smooth as a billiard table cut through the heart of a wood. The cool breath of the forest was in our faces, the smell of the woods in our nostrils, a mingled perfume of tree, moss, wild creature, and under all, binding them together like ambergris, the mysterious scent of decay. The air was full of wood noises, the peace and calm of the wilderness lay on either side of us not twenty feet away from a road as good as the Paseo Castellana.

"For the first time," said Patsy, "I envy Don Alfonzo. I should hate to live in a palace, to have the power of life and death, to pass my life under a microscope, but I must say I should like to own El Pardo."

"Velasquez often stayed here with King Philip and his brothers," said Don Luis. "No wonder they all liked it. Court etiquette relaxed, the artist was treated as the friend. One understands why he painted so many portraits of the royalties man and boy, in hunting dress, with gun and dog. They were not only tremendous sports, but caramba! in these woods there was freedom, even for a king, even for a genius!"

Engracia on the front seat scanned the covers with keen eyes.

"Look!" she cried. "There is a deer; if I only had my gun, what an easy shot! There goes a red fox scuttling across the road. Ah! that was a hare." A bright-eyed furry creature gave us one timid glance, flattened its ears and leapt into the bracken.

At the chateau we were refused admittance. Engracia, used to seeing all doors fly open before her, sent for the official in charge, an old friend of hers.

"Don Fulano, these are my friends; they are very anxious to see the chateau. Surely we may come in?" Engracia entreated.

Don Fulano, a grave Castilian, regretted, evaded, apologized, finally confessed. All ordinary rules should be set aside for Engracia, but he himself had received orders from His Majesty that no one should be admitted to the grounds. The work of putting the chateau in order for the bride had begun.

Engracia sparkled with excitement at the news. In that case, of course, we would not dream of asking; how natural, how charming of Don Alfonzo!

As we could not see the house, Don Fulano took us to a neighboring casino where, he said, the royal guests would go for tea. Here we wandered in the garden; Engracia picked a spray of orange blossoms, tucked it in her belt; then, like a fairy godmother, witched us away in her motor to the shooting lodge, where we found her serious husband and her five-year-old son. The shooting box stood on a piece of high cleared ground surrounded by a thick wood; it seemed delightfully sylvan and remote from feverish Madrid.

"We come here three days a week," Engracia said when we were seated at luncheon. "Whenever the pace gets too rapid in town, I fly out here for a rest."

Her husband laughed. "For a change of activities," he said. "Engracia is a good shot, these are her trophies."

The antlers of a stag hung over the fireplace, the floor was spread with skins. Engracia, pouring tea at the head of the table, nodded towards a shelf laden with silver cups.

"There are his trophies," she laughed. "I have not yet won a prize."

"You shot the birds we are eating," said the husband. "Isn't that more important?"

After lunch the people who knew how to shoot went off with guns and left me in the lodge with a bright fire crackling in the chimney and Engracia's little son for company.

It was part of our luck, as Patsy said, that we should have had that sharp crisp day for our expedition, our one experience of life in a Spanish hunting lodge. Even the weather was on our side!

We drove back through the town of El Pardo, a sleepy place on the bank of the Manzanares. Cattle were drinking in the river; in a meadow where we stopped to admire some fine oaks, a flock of half-tame magpies were hopping over the grass.

In spite of April hailstorms it was a forward spring, the fruit trees put on their bridal dresses early to welcome the bride. In the Buen Retiro purple and white violets bloomed so thick that the air was scented. The laburnums shook out long golden clusters, the wistaria unfurled amethyst blossoms. The honey-sweet smell of the acacias in the Recoletos came in at the windows and drove us abroad early and late. It was impossible to stay indoors with the trees in flower, the streets abloom with children and girls. The crowd of vehicles in the Paseo was so great that horses and automobiles moved at a foot pace.

In the noon hour the working men and their families, who in winter had sought the sunny corners for their out-of-door feasts, hunted for the shadow of tree or kiosk. We were on friendly terms with several of these family groups, and had often been invited to join them at their meal. Patsy, consumed with curiosity to know just what they had to eat, made an excuse to stop one day and talk with a mason, just as the man left off work.

"Not two minutes after twelve," Patsy told us afterwards, "the mason's wife and children came trotting up with the family dinner. The wife carried a kettle of hot *puchero*, the eldest girl a dish of sausage and garlic, neatly tied up in a clean napkin; one boy had the bread, another the fruit, a middle-sized child plates, spoons and knives for the party. The father said there were few days in the year when his children did not dine with him; he believed in family life. He could not give time to go home, so the family came to him and they all dined together in the open air at the nearest sheltered corner."

The house where the mason was at work was being swept, garnished and put in apple-pie order for some of the wedding guests, who were to lodge there. It was a good season for the working people. It may be that Madrid is always as fresh, smart and tidy as it was in that year of Grace, 1906, but it seemed to us that everybody tried to add to the general festive air by a little private gilding and varnishing on his own account. Don Jaime bought what he had threatened to buy for years, a new set of teeth. Pedra made herself a scarlet bodice, in which she looked prettier than ever. At the palace an army of furbishers were touching up, silver-plating, gilding and polishing. Work was pushed at the royal stables. The fifty state carriages needed for the wedding pageant, with the harnesses, liveries, and ostrich plumes for the horses, were renewed or furbished up to look as good as new, at a cost of half a million duros.

The hostlers at the studs of Aranjuez had extra work, for the eight cream-colored horses chosen to draw the bridal coach must have coats like satin on the King's wedding day. Aranjuez, a royal summer residence, is a place lovely with the noise of running waters and the songs of nightingales. The elms here were brought out from England by grim Philip II, who laid out the garden so well that I relented a little towards him when I saw it. The court no longer goes to Aranjuez, and the royal stud is not what it was in the days when camels and lamas were raised there; but it is still an interesting place, if I only had time to tell about it! During the wars of the last century the French destroyed the breeding stables, but in 1842 they were restored and stallions were imported from England.

Extra hands were taken on at the Madrid Tapestry Manufactory. "Everybody who owns a tapestry wants it in order of course," said the Director who showed us over the factory. A dozen men were at work upon a famous set of ruby velvet hangings emblazoned with silver, priceless things, not only unique but beautiful.

"You will see these hanging from the front of the Duke of Cestus' palace all through the fêtes," the director said.

"Suppose it should rain!" I cried horrified.

He shrugged his shoulders; "The Duke takes the risk," he said. "The king is not married every day."

The last Friday in May the Princess Ena, her mother and her two brothers entered Spain. We heard then for the first time that she wished to be known in future as Queen Victoria.

"That shows courage," was Patsy's comment. "A great name is a good thing to try and live up to, to be sure!"

Don Alfonso met the Princess at the frontier and they all travelled together to El Pardo. All Madrid, at least all fashionable Madrid, rode, drove, motored or ballooned out to meet them. Patsy of course managed to be there with Don Jaime. They described the arrival of the bride as a brilliant scene. All the great people were there in their best clothes; there was an overwhelming amount of gold lace; they all looked and behaved just as they should. "It was more than ever like Lohengrin," was Patsy's summing up.

I begged for particulars and learned that the Princess looked beautiful as she drove to the chateau in a carriage drawn by four mules; Don Alfonzo on horseback at her right, the Prince of the Asturias at her left.

"What did she wear?"

"Such golden hair, such a color, such blue, *blue* eyes!" That was all the satisfaction I got out of Patsy. Don Jaime was incoherent with enthusiasm.

"*Muy guapa, divinamente guapa!*" he kept repeating. "And what a health, grace heaven! Not only for a Princess but if only a simple gel!"

By this time Madrid was upside down with excitement. The hurry-flurry of the final preparations was contagious. Most people really were busy, the others thought they were. Don Jaime got up at twelve o'clock, instead of two, and Patsy insisted, sometimes forgot to go to bed at all. The wedding guests were pouring into the city by every train.

"I am becoming hardened to royalty," Patsy announced one evening. "I have seen three royal princes and four Ambassadors Extraordinary arrive to-day. The Prince and Princess of Wales and the Crown Prince of Sweden drove straight to the palace."

All the King's relations and the direct heirs to thrones stayed at the palace. The other visiting Princes and Ambassadors Extraordinary were lodged at the best private houses. We heard that the owners would accept no pay for the use of them; it was honor enough to be allowed to lend their houses to the King for the use of his guests.

"It may be the custom in other countries," said Patsy, "but I doubt it. There's something chivalresque and Spanish about it!"

One of the envoys let it be known that he wished to give various entertainments during his stay in Madrid. He was told that he had but to give his orders: the house and the corps of servants were at his disposal. Only, Spain reserved the right of paying all the bills. In a commercial age such things are pleasant to meet with.

The Austrian Grand Duke stayed not far from the Tower at the palace of the Duke of Medina Celli, the representative of an elder branch of the royal family. At every coronation, the head of this house makes a formal protest, and asserts his hereditary claim to the throne. He ranks next to the King and has the second place at all ceremonials.

When the great people had all arrived, Villegas took an afternoon off and drove us about the city to show us where they were staying. Outside each palace or house where a distinguished guest was billeted a sentry box, painted with the national colors of the guest, had been placed and a sentinel posted. Over the handsome house allotted to Mr. Whittredge, the American Ambassador Extraordinary, floated the stars and stripes; the sentry box before the door was painted red, white and blue.

The American Consul at Madrid was an angel. It may not be set forth in the civil-service examination papers that applicants for consulships must prove angelic character; it is probably one of those traditions mightier than law. How else could they face the cares of office without becoming hopeless misanthropes? Our Consul made us welcome at the Consulate, over whose door a rusty American eagle spread his painted tin wings. In whatever trouble J. or Patsy or I found ourselves, we rushed to No. 8 Calle Jorge y Juan and either the Consul, or his angelic clerk, or his cherubic office boy, rescued and comforted us, smoothed out our difficulties, set our erring feet on the right road. One morning when the pressure on every official in Madrid, even the officials of foreign governments, was almost at breaking point, Patsy dropped in at the Consulate. He found the Consul opening his mail.

"Isn't it a pretty large order to read all those letters, Mr. Summers?" he asked.

"Listen to this," sighed the Consul:

"*Dear Sir.* My daughter and I arrive in Madrid on Saturday morning. As I hear the city is full on account of the wedding fêtes I must trouble you to engage rooms for us. They must be in a stylish, but not too expensive house. We wish to go to the wedding, the ball at the palace, and all the other entertainments. If you should be unable to secure us invitations, kindly ask the Ambassador to attend to the matter.

Yours truly,
MRS. EMERALD GREEN.'"

Just then a telegram was brought in by Pepé, the cherubic office boy. The Consul sighed again as he read it aloud:

"Please wire answer to my letter immediately, stating address of rooms. Am sending large trunk to your care. E. G."

"Friends of yours?" asked Patsy.

"Never heard of them."

"Wife and daughter of Congressman?"

"Emerald Green, it's not a name I know."

"Do you get many such letters?"

"Tons of them; it's all in the day's work."

The ring in his voice was characteristic of the time. Nobody minded the extra trouble they were put to, everybody gladly lent a hand to help those two young people get married. If a household is turned topsy turvy when a daughter is married, it is not strange that a city should be turned upside down and inside out when a King is wed. Mr. Collier, the American Minister, must have been as much pestered as the Consul; he always had time for us though, and we brought away pleasant memories of him and of the Legation where we were hospitably entertained.

Of all our friends, the Argentino alone held aloof from the joyous bustle; a week before the wedding he left Madrid.

"I'm off for Barcelona till all this pother's over," he said. "Come with me. What interest have we republicans in royal marriages?"

"The interest of seeing what we cannot see at home."

"Ah! that's the difference between your republic and mine; we do not forget, be sure that you do not."

"Don't be cryptic," said Patsy, "I never knew what a good republican I was till I came to Spain."

"Though Spain is one kingdom, the more free people in the world is the Spaniard," Don Jaime protested. "If he have a little money he do what he like. United States is one republic; there no man can do what he like."

"He can think as he likes," retorted the Argentino, then persuasively to Patsy, "you've seen enough of old Spain and its pageants. Come with me to Barcelona, have a look at new Spain. There's a great fight on there, that really is the most important thing that is happening in Spain."

"What sort of a fight?"

"The eternal fight between Yesterday and To-morrow, between new ideas and old. The liberals are making a brave stand. They are trying to get control of the vast sums of money now expended by the Church, which they wish to use for the public schools. There are not half enough schools to go round even in Catalonia, the brains, the nerve center, the place that does the thinking for Spain. Only thirty per cent of the people can read and write; that's not enough."

"Too much monks, nuns and priests expulsed from France," sighed Don Jaime; "enough came before from Cuba and Porto Rico. The priest he know what happen in every man's house before the husband."

"Which is worse?" asked Patsy, "the rule of the priest, the soldier, or the shopkeeper?"

"We have not time to argue that question to-day," laughed the Argentino, "for the last time will you come to Barcelona?"

"No," said Patsy, "I can see enough of the sort of fight you speak of at home. I may never have another chance to see a king married."

XV

THE KING'S WEDDING

MADRID was astir early the King's wedding morning. We left the Tower at seven o'clock, in order to get to the Puerta del Sol before the cordon of troops was drawn. We were to see the procession from the Hotel de Paris which stands at the angle of the Calle Alcalá and the Carerra San Jeronimo. We should see the marriage pageant cross the Puerta del Sol, the bull's-eye of the city, pass down the Alcalá on the way from the palace to the church, and return by the way of the Jeronimo. Our friends, the Larz Andersons, had invited us to spend the day with them; we arrived in time for early coffee.

"How could you," said J, "ask Villegas to let us see the show from the Prado when you had this invitation up your sleeve? This is the best place in the city."

"I thought it would be so interesting to watch it from the royal museum."

"So did a few hundred other people! They have been worrying and harrying him for a month. No one is allowed inside the Prado to-day, not even the head porter."

"I think Don José might make an exception for his family and—for us."

"Not even for himself. He is responsible for the safety of the pictures. Do you realize what that means?"

Villegas is responsible for one of the world's greatest treasures, and is uneasy about the safety of the building that contains it. No wonder Lucia complains her husband does not sleep as well as he once did.

We waited for the procession in the dining-room of the Paris, a comfortable low-ceiled room with a suggestion of a ship's dining cabin about it. A table had been engaged for us in the window. The last guest to arrive was Don Jaime, who strolled in leisurely after the streets had been closed to other people for two hours. The Don had on a new coat, a white waistcoat and a gardenia in his buttonhole; it was pleasant to see him dressed for once as he deserved.

"I passed the nuncio of the holy Pap driving to the church," he said. "They will not tardy greatly now."

A few minutes later the first of the fifty gala wedding coaches came in sight. Though of varying degrees of splendor they were all on the same general plan of those we had seen when Sir Maurice de Bunsen presented his credentials. That day one Ambassador and his suite had been escorted in state to the palace; to-day the whole court and all the wedding guests must be transported from the palace to the church. Could the wonderful carriages, the proud horses, the ostrich plumes, the trappings, wigs, galloons and silk stockings hold out?

They did; they grew finer and finer. One coach was of tortoise shell, one blue and silver, one purple and gold lacquer. All the shining company of princes, grandees, ambassadors extraordinary, court ladies, maids of honor, was magnificently conveyed in gala coaches drawn by noble horses with nodding feathered head-dresses, all attended by grooms in satin liveries. It was a torrent of dazzling splendor that wearied the eyes and stunned the imagination.

"I have been forty years in diplomacy," said a dapper old gentleman with a single eyeglass, who sat at the next table; "I have seen most of the royal marriages of my time; I never saw anything to compare to this."

The bride rode with her mother in the tortoise-shell coach; they were talking together as they passed. Princess Beatrice looked pale and grave, the bride happy, expectant, calm, as every bride should look. In the last coach, a marvel of crystal and gold, rode the King behind eight proud cream-colored horses. They ambled daintily along, tossing and tossing their heads so the long ostrich plumes nodded in time to their high stepping. Where, when, had we seen horses like these before? While we waited for the wedding party to come back from church, I remembered.

It was in Scotland just ten years ago this August, the season when Ben Marone puts on his imperial purple veil of heather, that we stood together outside the inn at Braemar waiting to see the royal carriage from Balmoral pass. Soon four, perfectly matched, cream-colored ponies—very like the King of Spain's horses—came racing in sight at the top of their speed, drawing a large, plain, old-fashioned carriage. On the box sat a Highlander in tartan and filibegs.

"'Twull be the Queen and Princess Beatrice," said one of the villagers.

The carriage came within our line of vision. "Ay, 'tis her Majesty."

On the back seat sat an old woman in a shabby black cloak and bonnet, a younger lady in black beside her. The Queen was old and very tired of state and ceremony; she looked neither to the right nor to the left, but straight before her, as the villagers pulled forelock or curtsied. She seemed to be thinking deeply, was perhaps looking into the future. If she could have foreseen that her little granddaughter—the one for whose future she might have felt the most concern—would assume the name she had made illustrious, would she have been pleased?

"They will be coming back from church in a moment." Patsy, whom we had not seen that morning, brought the news. "I saw them go into San Jeronimo's. The bride wore a white dress like others I have seen, only longer; her veil was lace—not that flimsy stuff; it did not cover her face." He was proud of having observed, and remembered so much.

Soon after we heard the joyous marriage music, and the long, glittering procession began to pass again, much in the same manner as before, only the Queen sat beside the King in the crystal and gold coach with the big crown on the top. As they passed through the Puerta del Sol they bowed and smiled to the people; their happy young faces were flushed with heat and excitement. When the coach had disappeared down the Calle Mayor I confessed my plan to the company.

"I am going to leave you, to slip round by the back streets to the Youngs' house, opposite the palace. From their windows I can see the procession turn from the Calle Mayor into the palace yard and drive up to the door."

"Do not let her go," I heard Don Jaime say emphatically in Spanish; he added something that I did not hear.

"It will be very hot," said Lucia.

"Ninety in the shade," Patsy agreed. "One of us will have to go with you."

"Luncheon is ready," said our hostess.

"Iced melon in the hand is worth a good deal in the bush," said J., "but of course I will take you if you really want to go."

"It's pretty jolly here," murmured Patsy.

"Champagne?" whispered the waiter.

"Take at least a biscuit, and you must drink the bride's health before you go," said the prince of hosts.

It seemed too bad to break up the party. They were evidently serious about not letting me go alone. I yielded and stayed.

The restaurant was filling up with men in uniform and ladies in court dress who had come from the wedding; most of the people staying at the hotel were of the diplomatic world. At a table near us sat Mrs. Cartwright, looking as handsome in her white court dress as when Villegas painted her when she was a bride. At another table the King's former tutor, Señor Merry del Val, a handsome, distinguished man (brother of the Cardinal), and his charming wife. It certainly was very jolly in that pleasant company, talking over the dresses, the coaches and the coming fêtes.

If I had not stayed at the Hotel Paris, if I had gone to the Calle Mayor, I should have seen the gay procession of coaches, with the attendant postilions and *palfreniers* walking on either side, turn into the palace yard one by one, till there was only left in the Calle Mayor for the crowd to gape at the *coche de respecto* and the King's coach. Then suddenly out of the heavens fall what at first looked like a great bouquet, not unlike those that had been showered down from window and balcony all along the route; then a blinding flash, a dreadful crash, a cloud of smoke; and when that cleared away the crystal coach shattered, the brave horses staggering on a pace or two, the King looking from the wrecked coach and crying:

"It is nothing; we are neither of us hurt."

"Nothing?" But that is what King Umberto said, when he fell mortally stabbed at Monza.

The wheel horses reeled and fell, done to death, their shining sides, their white plumes all dabbled with blood. The King jumped out—his coat torn from his back—and helped out the bride. They were neither of them hurt, as he had said. The Queen was pale but wonderfully calm and brave,—till she looked down and saw the hem of her wedding dress covered with blood! Then through the distracted crowd, a small phalanx of resolute men pushed their way to the front, tall men in uniform, who surrounded the Queen, walked with her through the awful carnage down the Calle Mayor, across the palace yard to the door of her new home.

Who were they? Where did they come from? Some said they were the staff of the British Embassy, who had seen the accident from the Youngs' windows; some that they were six tall life-guardsmen, who had played some part in the pageant. The important thing is, they were Englishmen; they and Sir Maurice de Bunsen, the English Ambassador, appeared, as if by magic, at the moment they were wanted.

No whisper of the tragedy reached the Paris. In the restaurant the gaily dressed people lingered at the tables, toasting the bride. Our party was one of the first to break up. A friend drove me to the Consulate, where finding the Consul had not returned, I waited to see him. He came in shortly, white as a ghost, and cried out for a glass of water. From Mr. Summers I heard the first account of the horror. He had seen the bodies of the innocent people killed by the bomb carried by. He had counted eight soldiers, seventeen civilians, all strangers to him. One he had known by sight, a little girl, the five-year-old daughter of a great house. He had seen her a few minutes before standing on a neighboring balcony with her parents. "Such a little body," he said; "where the face had been, there was a twist of child's curls, nothing more; the face was gone."

What awful sights I had been spared! I carried the news home to the Tower. Villegas had not yet come back, the others had heard nothing.

Lucia clapped her hands to her heart when she heard of the outrage. "God grant," she said with white lips, "that it was not an Italian who threw the bomb." She is a Roman; her first fear, her first hope were for Italy.

"What was that thing Don Jaime said to you at the Paris, when I proposed going to the Youngs' house?" I asked Patsy.

He said "Do not let her go; the police fear that a bomb will be thrown in the Calle Mayor."

If the police knew so much, why could they not have averted the horror?

This was never explained.

XVI

WEDDING GUESTS

"*LOS Reyes! los Reyes! Bueno, Bueno!*" Don Jaime waved his sombrero wildly over his head and ran across the wet grass, followed by Patsy, who had snatched off his Panama and was roaring as if this were a football game:

"Hip, hip, hurrah! The Queen, the Queen!"

It was the morning after the wedding; considering the hour—it was still early—there were a great many people sitting in the chairs or pacing slowly under the trees of the Recoletos. All Madrid was drawing its breath, trying to steady its nerve by a little air and exercise. Without warning, without escort, the King and Queen whirled by in an open automobile. The bride and groom had slipped out of the palace and had been driven to the hospital to see the eighty people who were wounded by the bomb that had been meant to kill them. They had flashed through the Puerta del Sol, through the most crowded quarter of the city, and were now returning to the palace, attended only by a chauffeur.

"*Bravo va!*" cried the seller of orgeat from his booth; then, yielding to enthusiasm, he vaulted over the counter, left the till unprotected, and joined in the chase.

"*Viva, viva!*" The crowd in the Recoletos lost its head; women waved parasols, men hats or handkerchiefs. The applause was fine, spontaneous, electrical.

"They're game!" cried Patsy. "He's a man, and I guess she's a good deal of a woman."

They looked so brave, the blonde bride so grave, so loyal, so fresh, that we were all moved; there was heart in the cries of *viva, bueno, bravo*, that followed them, applause of a very different calibre from the rather perfunctory toasting and hurrahing of yesterday.

There was but one dissentient voice. I heard the old gentleman who had been forty years in diplomacy say: "It is against all precedent! Without even an escort! It will be much criticised."

It may have been criticised at Court; the people liked it. Don Alfonzo is wise enough to know that the applause of the gallery is more important to the actor than the appreciation of the stalls.

The wedding fêtes lasted a week. The gala performance at the opera, the bull-fight, the battle of flowers, the balloon race, the ball at the palace and all the more private festivities such as dinners and luncheons, had been carefully planned, so that no hour should hang heavy on the wedding guests. Time had to be made for one more function, the funeral of the officers and soldiers killed by the bomb. It took place the very day after the disaster. I did not see that black pageant of death, I wish I had; but J. saw and told me about it.

At very nearly the same hour as that gorgeous marriage procession, there passed over the same ground, through the Puerta del Sol and down the Alcalá, a long string of black hearses. The first two, the coaches of honor, were splendid with sable trappings; on the top lay the arms of the dead officers. The King, the Prince of Wales, and most of the other royalties walked in the procession that followed.

In spite of the gloom cast by the dreadful disaster, the fêtes went on with slight modifications, as if nothing had happened. The ball at the palace was changed into a reception. Dancing when so many mourned their dead was out of the question. It was decided that the King and Queen must not appear at the battle of flowers. It was too dangerous; the deadly bouquet that masqued the bomb held a warning.

For perhaps a day there was a panicky feeling. The crowd was nervous, keyed up; it would take nothing to make a stampede. I was never allowed to go out alone lest "something should happen." Very soon, however, Madrid recovered its tone. Crowds of orderly, well-dressed people thronged the streets day and night, admiring the magnificent illuminations, the splendid decorations. Where other cities use bunting and cotton cloth, Madrid used satin, silk, damask, brocade. The fronts of the houses were brave with rich embroideries and priceless tapestries. The famous ruby velvet hangings covered the façade of the Duke Cestus' palace, the pattern of the silver blazonry outlined at night with electric light. During the whole week those priceless treasures hung exposed to the burning sun, or to the chance of rain, which fortunately never came.

Villegas was busier than ever, devising schemes for decoration, giving advice about a costume, receiving a distinguished visitor. He was continually summoned to the Prado to show the pictures to one or other of the wedding guests. Some days he hardly did more than look into the studio, where Cisera always had his brushes ready, and Angoscia, the model, waited, sometimes all day, to pose for one little half hour.

One morning we met the Maestro on the stairs—J. had the studio next door to his. "Just in time!" cried Villegas. "I was afraid I should not get you. They have telephoned from the palace that

VILLEGAS IN HIS STUDIO.

we must meet the Prince and Princess of Wales at the museum. They haven't given me time enough even to go home and put on a black coat."

Villegas had on his funny little blue studio jacket, buttoned up to the neck, a jacket not quite like any other; he designed it for himself when he was a student. I never saw him in any other coat, except when on Court duty.

It was so late that Villegas and J. jumped into a cab; Patsy and I followed them on foot.

"We are in time," said Patsy, as we drew near the Prado; "there are the red legs."

Each of the King's guests was provided with two carriages, a court carriage and a state-department carriage. The every-day carriages, in which they drove about in the morning and did their shopping or sight-seeing, were handsome but simple landaus with the royal coat-of-arms on the panels. The main distinction was the red stockings and blue velvet breeches of the servants. Patsy always kept a sharp lookout for the red legs.

There were more people than usual going into the museum, most of them country folk come to Madrid for the fêtes. Patsy and I stood in the crowd and watched the Prince and Princess get out of the carriage with Mr. Keppel, the equerry. Villegas met the Prince at the door and asked leave to present his English pupil (J.). Then they all disappeared together into the Prado, Villegas leading the way with the Princess. She is tall, slender, with pretty yellow hair and an air of great distinction; there is a strong family resemblance between her and the young Queen.

Villegas said that the Princess, like most of the royalties he escorts over the museum, was greatly interested in the royal portraits. When the pictures are artistically important like the Velasquez, the Moros, even the Goyas, he is able to tell all about the originals; but when they are of mediocre value, by unimportant painters, poor Villegas is harrassed with fear lest he may not always give the right name, date and title.

The Prince admired immensely, and seemed to enter into the spirit of the Velasquez "Siege of Breda." When the magnanimous attitude of the conqueror was pointed out—he cannot take the keys of the city because both hands are occupied, the Prince said:

"That was so nice of him!"

He paused a long time before Paul Veronese's picture of the Marriage of Cana. On the table before the Saviour is a dish of meat that, the Prince pointed out, resembled a roast sucking pig. "But," he said, "they were all Jews; they would never have eaten pork!"

J. said this showed that the Prince really looked

THE SPINNERS. *Velasquez*

at the pictures and thought about them; many of the people he has helped Villegas take through the museum walk through as if it were a duty to be got over as soon as possible. The Prince asked how much various of the pictures were worth. He studied carefully St. Paul and St. Gerome in the desert, by Velasquez (the dear one with the ravens flying to the hermitage carrying loaves of bread in their beaks to feed the unthrifty old saints).

"How much is that picture worth?" he asked. "Almost anything, isn't it?"

Villegas says royalties never know what things cost. They may have a sense of the value of money, but no sense of the value of things.

The Prince lingered longest in the portrait room. Well he might—it contains some of the consummate portraits of the world!

"That is very fine," said the Prince, pointing to Van Dyke's portrait of himself with his patron the Earl of Bristol; "and that Cardinal of Pavia by

Raphael, and this Holbein. Yet one hears more about John Sargent's portraits. I don't think them as good as these, do you?"

It was very hot in the Ribera room, where they had lagged a little behind the others. J. took off his hat to mop his brow, and for the sake of being cooler did not put it on again.

"Keep on your hat," said the Prince. Supposing this was merely politeness J. forgot all about it, and a few minutes after did the same thing again.

"*Please* put on your hat," said Mr. Keppel; "we don't want to attract attention to the party."

"Yes, yes," laughed the Prince lightly, "we don't want to attract attention!"

That, then, was the reason such short notice of the visit had been given—they did not wish to attract attention! The only person who showed the least nervousness was the detective from Scotland Yard, who followed with the Chief of the Madrid police. The detective, J. said, "was in a blue funk; he seemed to see a nihilist in everybody who came within bomb-shot of the Prince." While they were lingering in the Ribera room, the detective begged Mr. Keppel that the Prince should keep up with the Princess and Villegas; "they must all keep together; it was too dangerous, too difficult for the chief of police to watch them if they scattered."

We heard that the English police had informed the Spanish before the outrage that a man had been observed practising throwing various articles from a balcony, as if gauging the distance to the street.

The shadow of fear darkened every sunny hour of these festival days. It was with us when we started at eight o'clock one golden June morning to drive to the review, held on the Castilian plain eight miles from Madrid. We had tickets for the grand stand of the Senate. We were a little late; by the time we arrived the seats were all taken. We were turning sadly away when Patsy espied Don Luis.

"Here is the Key!" he cried. "He will get us in somewhere." Don Luis was called the Key because he contrived to open every door to us. How did he manage it? It was not with a silver key; Don Luis was very poor. He had an uncle who stood high in office; he was never caught without the uncle's card, the open sesame of many doors. This time it opened the military tribune, where we found admirable places. This tribune was less crowded than the others; most of the military were busy with the manœuvres. It was a morning of extraordinary emotions; there was a thrill of controlled excitement in the air; every face wore a smile, every heart held a fear. The royalties were all present; the young Queen, looking fresh and rosy, drove by with her mother-in-law. Don Alfonzo, in the uniform of an officer of halberdiers, rode at the wheel of her carriage. All through the fêtes the young lovers were the centre of interest; we saw them so often that we grew to feel quite intimate with them.

All the ambassadors extraordinary were there, and all the royalties. We saw the Prince and Princess of Wales, the Crown Prince of Sweden, the Russian Grand Duke Vladimir, the Duke of Genoa, Prince Albert of Prussia, and Prince Louis Philippe, the young Crown Prince of Portugal; a lovely looking lad, about whose future consort, young as he was, the court gossips were already busy.[4]

We trembled for these great people, come together from every part of the world to take part in the wedding celebration; our hearts were full of fear and pity for them.

"It seems," said Patsy, "as if the Reign of Terror had returned, only instead of being in France alone it is over the whole world. A list has been found of Anarchy's next victims, headed by——" he whispered three great names.

Meanwhile the infantry regiments, the backbone of the army, were marching by. The men were well dressed, well looking, full of dash and vigor; they marched worse than any troops I ever saw.

"When it comes to the drill, the steady hammer, hammer, hammer, of the drill sergeant, they haven't it in them," said Patsy. "They may get it, they haven't it now."

The music was very bad; the military bands lacked the same thing that the soldiers lacked,—training, the stiff, hard, daily grind, the thing that makes the difference between every man and his brother, between every nation and her sister. What remains, if marching and music are bad? The glory and insolence of youth in those squadrons of cavalry and artillery dashing by. The vast arid plain soon became like a battlefield as soldiers describe it and as painters of battles try to paint it. The bands of cavalry began to pass slowly, the officers in advance, picked men, with picked horses, as gallant a troop as I ever saw. The officers rode with the naked sword raised as if for a charge. Just after they passed our stand, the pace quickened from a trot to a canter, to a mad gallop, as each troop swung short round an imaginary curve and disappeared in a cloud of dust. The dust they raised gave the effect of dust and smoke combined. A real battle-field must look like a thing seen on the stage with transparencies of dust and smoke. Through the veil of gray haze, we caught glimpses of distant squadrons marching and countermarching, pack mules with mountain batteries, engineers with field telegraph apparatus and pontoon bridges, long boats made very squat and solid so they will not easily capsize, and longer planks to lay upon the boats.

"They can bridge a river in fifteen minutes," said Don Luis.

"The Guadalquiver or the Manzanares, perhaps," murmured Patsy, "hardly the Amazon or the Mississippi. These pontoons are metal, the latest thing. Ours are of wood; we shall soon have them of metal like these Spanish ones."

"Who told you so much?" I asked.

"I heard Lieutenant Grant say so," said Patsy. "Didn't you see him drive by with our Ambassador? I should like to ask him if this looks to him as it does to me, like a miniature Gettysburg."

We were thankful when the review was safely over and everybody gone home safe and sound. It seemed to us the most dangerous of all the fêtes. The distance covered was so great that to protect all these royal people must have been well-nigh impossible.

"Lightning never strikes twice in the same place," said Patsy. "The only thing to do is to assume that there is no danger."

The most original of all the fêtes was the balloon race. Engracia sent us invitations to the Park of the Society of Aeronauts to see the start. We found all Madrid in the large enclosure; what was more important, we found Engracia in the midst of that crowd of smartly dressed people.

"The race," Engracia told us, "has been arranged as a compliment to the Queen. She and the King will see it from their windows. All the balloons will pass over the palace."

"Wind and weather permitting," laughed Patsy. "Isn't this the latest word in the way of Sport? I never heard of such a thing in New York or Paris."

"*Claro!*" the *Madrileña* flashed out at him. "You think Spain is behind the rest of the world, yet you must come to Madrid to see a balloon race."

The centres of attraction were the thirteen balloons entered for the race. Each monster air ball swaying in the stay ropes was surrounded by a group of people. Engracia led the way to one where the crowd was thickest.

"It is a good thing to have a friend in every place, even in the inferno," she said. "I have a friend who is going up in that balloon. It must be terrible to go alone!"

Way was made for Engracia; Patsy and I followed, and took a good look at the balloon at close quarters. It was shaped like a globe with a stovepipe coming out of the bottom. The basket car was small and high, coming up to the armpits of Engracia's friend, a man of average size. The color of the balloon was like a modern warship's neutral gray, the tint most easily confounded with cloud or smoke. Patsy peeped inside the basket, hoping to see some interesting apparatus for steering or at least guiding the flight.

"Nothing inside," he reported, "except a few bags of sand just like those:" he pointed to the sand bags hanging from the outer edge of the basket. "That," he showed a small instrument shaped like a pedometer hanging in the shrouds, "is to measure the distance, and that to gauge the velocity of the wind."

"What, nothing more? No modern contrivance to help them navigate the air?"

"Nothing but sand," said Patsy. "It takes a lot of two kinds of sand."

It was such a breathless afternoon: it seemed as if there could not be wind enough to lift the great captive swaying awkwardly in its ropes. The breeze must have come up without our noticing it, for there was a sudden commotion in the crowd, and we were all ordered to stand back. Engracia waved a last adieu to her friend.

"*Abour!*" she cried, as the balloon shot up to a great height. "If he had only taken some one with him!" There was something terrible in the loneliness of that solitary figure in the balloon.

In a few seconds another balloon shot up; it was perhaps lighter than the first, for it seemed to overtake it immediately. The two great balloons drifted nearer and nearer to each other; when just above our heads they noiselessly collided.

"*Por Dios!*" cried Engracia, and hid her face.

There was a slight depression in each balloon, then they sprang apart, like two vast rubber balls, and sailed off, each in a slightly different direction, neither the worse for the collision.

Taking advantage of the light breeze, the remaining eleven balloons were loosed and shot up to a great height. Soon the whole fleet looked no larger than so many toy balloons. We watched them sail away over the palace of the King, where the young Queen was watching for them, forgetting perhaps for a moment her terror, as the balloons sailed over the palace, over the bare plains of Castile, towards the Guadarramas, and the grim Escorial, her last home.

In the Park of the Society of Aeronauts, there was a deal of jesting, as the toy balloons sent off by Engracia and a dozen other ladies, followed the real ones.

"They all behaved," said Patsy, as we drove home after the race, "as if there were no such things as bombs; courage, it seems, is still an aristocratic virtue."

The night of the reception at the palace was very dark. The sky looked like black velvet; the streets blazed with clusters, chains, pyramids of light. The Puerta del Sol was a sea of sparkling flames, that shone on triumphal arches, flags, flowers, and the entwined letters A and V.

The servants at the palace recognized Villegas. They did not even look at our invitation, but motioned us to pass with him through that door we knew so well from the outside. We found ourselves in a big shining hall at the foot of the *escalara principal*, a magnificent double staircase, guarded by fierce marble lions and fiercer halberdiers standing on each step, their halberds touching, making a line of flashing steel on either side, just as the Argentino described—a sight "well worth seeing indeed!" We lingered at the foot of the stair to watch some of the people pass up.

"Who is that?" I asked, as a lady of superb bearing walked slowly up the stair. "I think she is the most distinguished looking woman I have seen in Spain."

"That is the Duquesa San Carlos," said Engracia, who had just come in.

"And who is that?" A beautiful Saxon woman in white satin and rubies was passing.

"That is one of the English party, Lady Castlereagh."

As each Grandee or Ambassador passed, the halberdiers saluted by striking the marble stair with their halberds. It had a fine effect, like a peal of thunder or a salvo of artillery. When we had seen a few of the King's guests go up, we followed after them.

Bang, bang! the halberds came down again in another salute. I looked behind to see who was coming. Nobody, we were the only people on the stair.

"Can that be for you?" I cried.

"Oh, no!" laughed Villegas. "For this," touching the decoration he wore, "or possibly for the Director of the Prado."

We entered a room paved with marble, ceiled with porcelain, hung with ivory satin embroidered in gold. It was filled comfortably, not crowded. Many of the uniforms were very handsome; some of the ladies were sumptuously dressed, with beautiful jewels, others wore very simple evening gowns. In Spain you cannot judge people by what they wear; they dare to be poor here as nowhere else. The King and Queen were receiving the Ambassadors in the Salon de Embajadores. This we could not see at the time. Later in the evening we went in and admired the superb throne with its four steps guarded by big gilt lions, the rock crystal and silver chandeliers, the painted ceiling by Tiepolo, representing the "Majesty of Spain." Standing under this picture, the King said to one of the Ambassadors:

"Well, here I am, you see. I came very near not being with you to-night!"

A little later the King and Queen made the tour of the apartments leading from the throne rooms. The crowd here was so great that we could see nothing but two lines of people bowing and curtseying as the royal cortége passed down the middle.

"Come," said Villegas, "you can see nothing here." He led us through hall after hall. I caught glimpses of a marble room and a porcelain room, of cabinets filled with precious pictures, sculpture and bric-a-brac. We halted in a perfectly empty gallery hung with the most astonishing tapestries.

"Flemish," said Villegas, "but unlike any others ever made in Flanders. *Miré*, they are worked with silver and gold thread."

While we were looking at the wonderful tapestries, and puzzling out the subjects, Isabel and Larz Anderson came into the room. We were all studying the tapestry representing the "Conquest of Tunis" when we heard voices, and suddenly, without a moment's warning, the royal party entered the gallery. The King and Queen walked first. Don Alfonzo wore a white broadcloth uniform. The Queen looked charming; there was no trace of what she had endured in her radiant complexion or her calm blue eyes. She wore white satin brocaded with little pink and blue velvet flowers, and on her head the new diamond crown made especially for her, Engracia had told us about. It was small, of the real classic shape, like the crown of the queen in Walter Crane's picture book.

The King and Queen both bowed and smiled to the Andersons and ourselves. Then Don Alfonzo, recognizing the Maestro, waved his hand and cried out in a cheery genial voice:

"*Ai Villegas, com' esta V.?*"

Queen Maria Cristina, who was walking next, stopped, called Villegas, and gave him her hand. The Infanta Isabel, the Infanta Eulalia, and the Infanta Maria Teresa, all stopped and spoke to him. The tall Swedish Crown Prince followed suit, and the Russian Grand Duke Vladimir, who seemed overjoyed at seeing him, patted him on the shoulder.

When the royal cortége swept out of the room, I was breathless with surprise and excitement.

"They all seem to know you," I cried. "What is the bond between you and the Russian Grand Duke?"

"*Quien sabé?*" said Villegas, "He has been at my studio; and the Czar once bought a picture of mine."

That reminded me of the portrait of the King. I persuaded Villegas to take me to the room where it hangs—and holds its own—among the other royal portraits.

XVII

HASTA OTRA VISTA

"ARE you painting?" Don Luis, the Valencian, put his head into the studio. "Am I too early? The fandango is to-day, isn't it?"

"*Adelante!*" cried Villegas, "the ladies have come. Imperio will be here soon. I am only preparing my work for to-morrow." He stood before a new canvas making a charcoal drawing of Angoscia.

"He cannot waste five minutes!" sighed Lucia.

"It seems that we are either working, or getting ready to work, day and night. Where does life come in?" asked Don Luis.

"Turn the head this way," said Villegas to the model. "Hold the guitar better—so." Then to Don Luis: "To those accustomed to work, work is life."

"I have noticed," said the Argentino, who came in at that moment with Patsy, "that only working people know how to play. That's the reason artists play so much better than the rest of us."

"What did you see in Barcelona that made up for missing the fêtes?" I asked the Argentino.

"A woman clerk who sold me a railroad ticket. A butcher's shop where the meat was cut up and sold by women," he answered.

There were cries of protest from all the party. "That's going a little too far if you will," the Argentino acknowledged; "but it's a sign of progress—things will adjust themselves. I saw the cathedral too; that's a joy forever. I hardly knew the old city—expensive buildings are springing up everywhere in the *art nouveau* style, pandemonium in stone, an echo of the 'greenery-yallery Grosvenor Gallery' nonsense, the tag end of the 'æsthetic' movement. Big granite buildings with window frames, whole façades even, carved into flowers. Lilies, poppies, what you like. No more idea of architecture, of style, of subordinating parts to the whole, than—than——"

"That comes of progressive republican ideas," growled Don Luis; for once our cheerful Valencian was out of sorts.

"You have no sympathy with them?" I asked.

"Frankly, I have never had time to occupy myself with such matters," Don Luis confessed. "I don't know if a Republic is good for the arts or not.

The Republicans I know are all barbarians. They come to the Prado; I hear them say to the guides,

THE DOGARESSA. *Villegas*

'Are these dingy old pictures all you have to show?' I once took a Chilian to Rome. When he saw the Sistine Chapel he was furious. 'Why do the writers deceive us?' he said, 'we have better chapels in Valparaiso.' Suppose Don Alfonzo should order a hundred portraits of himself—people might laugh but nobody could stop him. If the President of the Argentine ordered twenty, or five, or even one portrait of himself, and paid for it out of the public money, would you reëlect him?"

"Art is a luxury," the Argentino began.

"Ah, there's your mistake, it's a prime necessity, it is the great civilizer!" Don Luis was roused. "North Americans are not so ignorant of art as South Americans," he added, remembering there were two present. "They are the great buyers now. Villegas' Baptisimo is in New York, and now his Dogaressa has gone to Washington."

Here Patsy plunged into the talk and reminded Don Luis of the Age of Phidias, the painters of the Dutch and Venetian Republics. The great periods of art had little to do with the form of government under which they flourished. Art was a rare and wonderful flowering of the human intelligence, the fairest flower on the tree of life. It depended on the development of the race, not the will of the ruler.

"That may be," said the Argentino, "but if we are ever again to have a great art, the artist must be protected, his trade must be taken as seriously as the baker's or the plumber's. If art is the fine flower of civilization, it must in its very nature be the costliest of products—so to most people it seems a luxury."

"Is religion a luxury, is poetry a luxury? Is anything that lifts the ideals, or stimulates the imagination a luxury?" cried Don Luis, passionately.

The old arguments were brought forward and threshed out, the discussion became heated; meanwhile Villegas worked on steadily. On the flat bare canvas a dim foreshadowing of what would be Angoscia's perfect face grew and grew under his hands. While the others talked about art he was at work upon his latest masterpiece, the portrait of Angoscia.[5]

This was our last visit to the dear studio in the Pasaje del Alhambra, where for six months J. had worked, where we had all been so happy together. Our stay in Madrid was drawing to a close; we counted the hours now as misers count gold.

"The picture the Czar bought is of the same subject as this," said J., pointing to The Death of the Matador.

The wounded matador lies on a litter in the chapel of the bull-ring. An old priest stands at his head, reading the prayers for the dying. A group of gorgeously dressed bull-fighters stand about him, their eyes fixed on their comrade's pale face. At the back of the picture an opening in the wall gives a glimpse of the crowded arena, where the spectators are watching the great game of death, unconscious that a few feet away one of the heroes of the *corrida* is dying, gored to death by the last bull.

While I was looking for the last time at the picture, Don Jaime came into the studio with a stranger, an immense man, deep in the chest, broad in the shoulders, small in the hips. His head was scarred, so were both his hands. He wore his hair brushed down on his forehead. At the first glance he looked like a priest, at the second like a prize fighter.

"Jaime has kept his word," whispered J., "that is—the most famous matador in the world."

"That is something I have seen more than once," said the matador, looking at the picture. "In my time there was a mass before every *corrida*, when the priests carried the oils of the extreme unction in procession. I stopped that; it took the heart out of a man."

The matador came nearer the picture, studied it carefully, taking now the attitude of one figure, now of another. "*Muy bien!*" he said, nodding his great head in approval.

"You cannot know," said the Argentino to me, "how good that picture is. No one who is not familiar with the ways of *torreros* can know. See the one who crosses himself, and bends his knee—it is exactly their manner. See the civil guard in the corner explaining to the other how the accident happened—look at his hand, it tells the story."

"How many bulls have you killed?" asked Patsy of the matador.

"In twenty-five years I killed three thousand five hundred bulls."

"Were you ever afraid?"

"I was afraid many, many times. On those occasions I never put my faith in the Virgin, but rather in my legs and ran as fast as I could. The bull, however, is the noblest of animals and the bravest. He never makes a cowardly attack from behind; he is so frank! He is terrible, though; a man needs nerve to face him when he comes into the ring pawing the earth and bellowing."

"Will you tell me about the bull that was the hardest of all to kill?" asked Patsy.

The matador's face changed: "He was a white bull," he said, slowly, "and he didn't want to fight. When he first came in, he put his muzzle in my hand. He followed me about like a little

THE DEATH OF THE MATADOR. *Villegas*

dog. I led him with the cloak wherever I wanted him to go. Yes, that was the hardest bull of all to kill."

J., who had been looking at the matador ever since he came into the studio, nodded his head as if satisfied.

"He's the man," he said. "I had forgotten the name; I remember the face. I saw you kill a bull in Cadiz once. I wonder if you remember it? The bull put his head down to charge, and you put your foot between his horns, stepped on his head, ran along his back and jumped down behind."

"Ah, that happened at Cadiz? No, I don't remember. The Cadiz audience is the best in Spain, the most intelligent, the most sympathetic; it has the best knowledge of the art. It is not like the Madrid audience, that must sit in judgment and criticise. The American audience is good, especially the Mexican. Yes, the Americans have a real understanding of the art."

"Have you ever been wounded?" asked Patsy.

"Often; twice badly. Once I spent three months in bed; that was not amusing, I can tell you. The bull's horn went through my thigh and wrenched the muscles apart. I recovered though. The wound of the bull's horn is a good wound; one either recovers from it, or dies quickly."

"Have you any scholars?" asked Patsy.

"No," sighed the matador. "My art is one that does not allow of disciples. A man cannot be trained to it if he has not the gift. It is an inspiration, like poetry." He sighed. "It is five years since I retired. It seems twenty-five."

He was silent a few minutes, looking down as if distressed; then he brushed back his hair with a spirited gesture and glanced again at the picture.

"Most of us end that way," he confessed. "I have escaped to become an alderman and interest myself in the hygiene of the city that once criticised me!" Then to Villegas: "It was kind of you to ask me to see Pastora Imperio; I have not seen her since she was a child. Her father used to make my professional clothes. They tell me she is a great dancer."

Villegas had arranged that Imperio should dance for us at the studio. The others had seen her often and were never tired of talking about her.

"Until I saw Imperio dance," said Patsy, "it was always a mystery to me why Herod had John the Baptist's head cut off to satisfy the whim of a dancing girl. Now I quite understand it."

While they were discussing her, Imperio walked into the studio with her mother, followed by her brother Dionisio and another youth, each carrying a guitar; behind them came attendant nymphs with sisters or mothers, the inevitable chorus that keeps time with hand clapping, foot patting, and encourages the performance with cries of *ollé, ollé*, and *andar*.

The two studios had been made miraculously neat and tidy. They smelled of turpentine and beeswax. Gil and Cisera had been at work half the day preparing for the fandango. They had spread two tables in the inner studio where J. worked; one with tea and cake for us, the other with sandwiches, sliced sausages, and manzanilla, a thin, white wine, for the performers.

First we had songs; the curious long-drawn chanted wailing songs of Andalusia that have more of the East than of the West in them. To our ears they were a trifle monotonous but to the Spaniards, to the Andalusians especially they were tremendously moving. Dionisio, a strange-looking youth of eighteen, with odd slate-colored eyes and a lovely smile, threw back his head and wailed out couplet after couplet.

"This I tell to you; to see my mother, I would give the finger from my hand—but the finger I need the most to use.

"My stepmother beat me because I prayed for my mother; my father turned me out of doors. Where can I go to be a little warm?"

There was a shadow walked behind me. It was the spirit of my mother. It said to me, "to give thee life, I gave my life."

"*Ay de mi!*" cried Imperio and shivered.

"I am in prison on account of a bad woman. Tell the jailer when I am dead not to unbar the door, for even dead, I would not see her."

"*Virgin!*" sighed Dionisio's mother.

Imperio repeated the words slowly to me, line by line. I can see her now! her burning green eyes fixed on mine, her face that made all the other faces seem expressionless in comparison. She was at once immortally young and immemorially old. Her face was young, the spirit that looked from those marvellous eyes was immemorially old. The grace of her wild chaste dance is world old and has come down from the ages. I despair of making any one imagine her! Small, lithe, graceful as a young tigress from the jungle, now laughing like a child, now brooding like the world spirit.

When I could not understand what she said she was furious;—I must have had a bad teacher, she herself would teach me Spanish. When she arrived with her mother she was demurely dressed in a pretty white frock like any other young Andaluz. Her short, thick black hair was curiously arranged in curls on either side of her face, held in place by tortoise-shell combs set with turquoises. I gave her a pair of crimson peonies I had bought from the old flower woman at the corner. These evidently decided the color of her dress. After a while she disappeared behind the vast canvas of the Death of the Matador, that takes up the whole end of the studio, and from this improvised dressing room she soon reappeared in a scarlet moreen skirt, and a manton de Manila draped gracefully *a la maya*, about her lithe figure. She had stuck the peonies in the curls on either side of her pale face.

Dionisio and the other lad began to play a strange droning, wailing chant; the chorus clapped hands keeping time. Imperio sat watching till she caught the right rhythm, then she sprang to the dance, the castanets on her fingers. What it all meant, I cannot begin to tell. It seemed the primitive expression of the joy, the pain, the mystery of life. As she made "the charm of woven passes," like Vivian—only Vivian was bad, this child was virginal and pure—the combs dropped out, the short, black hair clung about her face and neck, the color surged to her cheeks; she seemed as one filled with the divine fury of the dance; a pythoness, a Bacchic priestess, might have looked like this. We had seen in Granada, in the Gypsy King's cave, somewhat similar dances given by very old women and little girls of ten or eleven. These were as the past and the future. Imperio made the dance part of a glowing, splendid, breathless present. Life called to life, the life blood in our veins danced in time with those wonderful gestures of arms, of feet, of the whole perfect body of the creature. I believe she drew power from us, that it was all give and take. She gave us youth and the dance, the dance which is the natural expression of the lust of life; and we gave her the elixir of our sympathy. Suddenly she stopped and broke forth into song—singing a long panegyric of Seville:—

"Ay Sevillia, la poblacíon mas hermosa del mundo emtiero, la ciudad que yo amo mas que mi madre."

Ah Seville town the most delightful in the entire world, city that I love better than my mother.

The flexibility of her body was unbelievable. I can see now the little, little hands held over her wild head, the fingers snapping rhythmically, for the castanets were soon thrown away and her fingers themselves marked the measure to which she danced; the impatient tapping of the feet, the wild leaps in air when she seemed to grow taller, to tower above us and her own original self, and finally the abandon of her last pose, the final attitude; the head thrown back, the red lips parted, the gasping breath coming from between the small perfect teeth, the left arm down, the right arm thrown above her head, her whole body quivering with the ecstacy of the dance—it was worth coming to Spain—just to see one of Pastora Imperio's poses!

"I have never seen dance any gel as Imperio," Jaime exclaimed. "More gracious, great spirit in her *figure* (he meant face) always smiling!"

"There's something half dramatic, half religious about this," said Patsy—"like David's dancing before the Ark or like the Pyrric dance, don't you think?"

"Maybe," Don Jaime agreed, "I have not seen La Davide, nor the other dancer, La Pyrrique, you speak of. In Spain the dance is according to the region; in Madrid, the madrileña, in Seville the sevilliana, in La Mancha the manchego, and so on. The base of all our Spanish dances is oriental; this is rather correct, any lady may see it. Imperio dances with the entirety of the corpe. The French dance with toes, feet, and legs only."

"Who taught you to dance?" I asked Imperio, "your mother, was it not?"

"Nobody!" she exclaimed proudly. "I have danced since I was eight years old."

"She see her mother dance every day since she were born. She imitate her dancing as her walking, but do not know—each of them have their own manner."

"That dance is as old as Eve," said the Argentino, "Imperio adds the sum of her own personality to it, and it is new again."

"Will Imperio dance to-night?" I asked.

"Always at the Kürsaal after middlenight," said the Don. "How a pity you cannot go Missis. There are some French and English performers would not please ladies."

"Ask her to tell you about her doll," said Villegas; "her mother says that she still plays with it on rainy days when she has to stay at home."

"Don't you think Imperio dances better in the studio than in the Kürsaal?" Patsy asked.

"*Claro!*" the mother smiled and agreed with him.

"*Natural,*" said Villegas, "we are all *Sevilliani*, born in the same parish, baptised from the same font in the cathedral. When I first came to Madrid—to copy Velasquez—I was just sixteen years old then—Imperiou's mother was the first dancer in Spain. How is it? Have you forgotten the dance you gave before Queen Isabel at the palace?"

The grave, fat, middle-aged woman said she remembered something of the dance.

"Well, show us how it went."

"Yes, little mama," said Imperio kindly, "show us how you danced before the Queen."

The old dancer rose with a curious action springing with one step from her chair to the first position of the dance. Then with a noble solemnity she danced the same dances, only not with the same spirit as Imperio; that would have been incongruous. She danced with the most magnificent and splendid dignity as became the mother of a family. Patsy was right, so might David have danced before the Ark. Little saucy Imperio sat by and encouraged.

"*Viva tu madre, ollé ollé!*" she cried, clapping her little hands.

Dionisio nodded kindly to his mother, looking at her with eyes that were her very own. The gentle mother, so long relegated to the second place, danced and rejoiced in the tardy attention and applause of the company.

"Isn't it time for refreshments?" asked Patsy. "They all look as if they needed something to eat." We adjourned to the inner studio where the dancers and musicians fell upon the good things with the appetite of demigods and heros. Imperio seeing that I was not eating anything, came across the room holding between a small thumb and finger a thin slice of sausage which she offered me, which I made out to eat.

Don Jaime seemed in a dream, he had felt the dance deeply; Patsy tapped on the shoulder. "Wake up," he said, "have you forgotten where you are?"

"It is like the lotus," sighed the Don, "it make you forget all the world."

Imperio had changed her dress again; the fandango, the very best *fiesta* of all we saw in Spain, was over.

"Show us my portrait, Maestro," she said, pointing to a veiled picture on an easel.

Villegas threw back the curtain and showed us a second Imperio standing with one hand raised above her head, one held behind her back, a red matador hat upon her short curls, the emerald fire in her eyes. Patsy stared at the picture, then at Imperio, once more a demure child in a white frock as she was when she came into the studio, save for an added touch of color in her cheeks.

"To the life!" cried Patsy.

Villegas rubbed his fingers over the canvas; "It needs a little scraping down," he said, "a little repainting, the color is too thick. It is like her, yes? *Quien sabé!* She is different from the

IMPERIO. *Villegas*

rest. When she falls in love and marries she will be like the others. You have seen, I have tried to paint the first dancer of Spain in her flower." Then he went with the dancers to the door.

"Villegas says," Patsy quoted him, "'that an artist should leave behind him a true picture of his own time; that he should be like a phonograph, preserving the character of his own period to posterity. The matador and the dancing girl are two of the most characteristic figures of the Spain of his day; he has painted both supremely well: he seems to be doing the thing he set out to do!'"

All too soon after the *fiesta* came the day we had fixed to leave Madrid. Not till then did I realize the strength of the spell Spain had laid upon me. We were going to Rome—even that could not console me—for the spell of Spain, so dark, so noble, so tremendous, is not to be shaken off once you have yielded to it.

The promise the child made so lightly, "to see Spain, and tell the other children what it is like," has yet to be kept. I did not begin to see Spain, I have told but a halting story of what I did see. It was enough to make me love Spain, to love the Spaniards. They are more like us Anglo-Saxons than any people I have lived among. Villegas says, "In every one of us Spaniards there is a Sancho Panza, and a Don Quixote." That is as true of us as it is of them.

Several of our friends came to the station to see us off as is the pleasant custom of a land where people are rich, because they have time to be kind. Lucia, hospitable to the last, came followed by Gil carrying a great net basket with a roast capon, some *torrones*, and a bottle of Valdepeñas. Engracia, the lovely soft-eyed, willful beauty of Madrid, brought us chocolates from Paris, a characteristic gift, for she is a true Cosmopolitan: *mi paisano*, Robert Mason Winthrop, Secretary of the American Legation, who had been endlessly kind and added in a thousand ways to the interest of our life in Madrid, brought a bunch of wonderful Spanish carnations.

Don Jaime and Patsy were both more cast down at parting than either wished the other to realize.

"Come and see us in America, Don," said Patsy, "We will give you the time of your life."

"Though I would like to take another climate," said the Don, "I have not the *dinero fresco*, fresh money as you say. I have not the habitude to spend very mooch to voyage; I could not justificate the emprize at present."

"Where is Villegas?" asked J.

"There he comes," said little Don Luis, the Valencian, "bearing the flowers of San José."

Villegas was hurrying along the platform with a great sheaf of annunciation lilies in his arms.

"*Adios, adios,*" we cried from the window as the train began to move.

"No, no!" came a cordial chorus from the platform.

"*Hasta otra vista.*"

FOOTNOTES:

[1] James Freeman Clarke's "Seven Great Religions."

[2] The other day a Moroccan embassy to the German Emperor asked for his help against the too drastic rule of Morocco's new masters, the French, on the strength of that old kinship. Blood is thicker than water. The blue eyes of William of Hohenzollern may have looked with something akin to sympathy into the blue eyes of the Berber hillmen when he went hunting among them on his famous shooting trip to Morocco, the beginning of so much diplomatic palaver!

[3] (Mr. White's good offices eventually won a public expression of gratitude from the head of the German Government.)

[4] The Crown Prince of Portugal and his father, Don Carlos the King, were killed in the winter of 1908. The dreadful murder was curiously glossed over by the newspapers as a "political crime," and outside of Portugal at least has apparently been quickly forgotten. The boy was a sweet-faced youth with charming manners. I cannot think of him without remembering the superstition that "whom the gods love die young." As I look back at those fabulous fêtes in the light of the dreadful double regicide, there seems something curiously suggestive and characteristic in the representatives sent by the different monarchs to the King of Spain's wedding. It must be an openly accepted fact that there is great risk in attending such a celebration. The Kaiser thriftily sent his uncle, the Czar sent another uncle, Russia, Germany, Austria, Italy, all sent old men, uncles or cousins of the sovereign, whose lives were not particularly valuable. England (so like England) sent the King's only son; Sweden sent the heir to the throne, and Portugal, unsuspicious, trustful in the character of its solid, serious, law-abiding people, sent the heir to the throne. The countries that have suffered most from the assassins of Anarchy—Austria, Russia, and Italy—risked only a small counter on the dreadful hazard.

[5] The picture is owned by Miss Dorothy Whitney of New York.

www.ingramcontent.com/pod-product-compliance
Ingram Content Group UK Ltd.
Pitfield, Milton Keynes, MK11 3LW, UK.
UKHW042147281224
453045UK00004B/209

9 789364 734448